Interior Design Sourcebook

DiCara Law Office. Jung Brannen, Boston.
Photograph by Peter Vanderwarker.

Design Reference Series
VOLUME 3

Interior Design Sourcebook

*A Guide to Resources
on the History and Practice
of Interior Design*

By Susan A. Lewis

Omnigraphics, Inc.

Penobscot Building • Detroit, MI 48226

Susan A. Lewis, *Editor*

Lamia Doumato, *Series Editor*

Omnigraphics, Inc.

Matthew P. Barbour, *Production Manager*
Laurie Lanzen Harris, *Vice President, Editorial*
Peter E. Ruffner, *Vice President, Administration*
James A. Sellgren, *Vice President, Operations and Finance*
Jane J. Steele, *Research Consultant*

Fredrick G. Ruffner, Jr., *Publisher*

∞

This book is printed on acid-free paper meeting the ANSI Z39.48 Standard. The infinity symbol that appears above indicates that the paper in this book meets that standard.

Printed in the United States

Dedicated,

with affection and gratitude to my friends for their support
and patience during this project

and,

to all the Tanners, Davises, Lewises, and Printzes,
but most particularly to Eleanor and Tanner.

Contents

Series Preface

In the past decade a steadily growing interest in the areas of architecture, landscape architecture and interior design has resulted in a proliferation of publications (books, journals, CD-ROM's) as well as in expanded cirriculums and programs at colleges and universities in these fields. It is our intention to provide easy accessibility to the burgeoning information in these disciplines through a one-volume sourcebook.

Going beyond the usual scope of a bibliography or a directory, these Omnigraphics sourcebooks were compiled by information specialists who through years of practical work experience were able to identify the potential needs of college and university students and professors, librarians and information specialists, interested lay people, but more importantly practicing professionals in the field. This is a somewhat unique approach since handbooks and guides usually address either the academic community or the practicing professional. Omnigraphics editors have carefully weighed the material included to meet the needs of both entities. Architects, landscape architects and landscape designers, interior designers and decorators must integrate their art into the highly functional world of business. In this era of down-sizing, time becomes a more essential commodity, and readily available information a valuable resource.

The Omnigraphics sourcebooks endeavor to guide research by identifying, arranging, describing and indexing sources, programs, services and agencies. The editors of these guide books have carefully assessed the needs of researchers to include annotated core lists of books, journal and newsletters thus enabling a non-specialist to establish a working library. The volume on architecture provides basic materials on building types; landscape architecture includes timely information on organizations that would otherwise encompass hours of research; interior design includes timely lists of associations and services. Where appropriate, guides also include essays on the latest technologies in information retrieval through automated systems, especially visual systems.

The descriptive details provided in each of the guides on organizations, foundations, and research centers and agencies will prove invaluable to all researchers. The format of the Omnigraphics sourcebook will ensure quick and easy access for professionals and students alike.

Lamia Doumato,
Series Editor, *Design Reference Series*

Acknowledgements

All of the individuals I have met through this project have been uniformly helpful, enthusiastic, and supportive. The interior designers showed a thorough professionalism and desire to help me find answers even when answers were not readily available. It has been a pleasure to work with a profession which deserves such respect.

I particularly want to thank three interior designers, Faith Baum (AIA, IIDA) of the Boston Architectural Center, Christine Cavataio (NCIDQ) of the Interior Design program at Mt. Ida College, and Rachel Pike (IIDA, IDEC), of the Interior Design program at Wentworth Institute of Technology. They have acted as my mentors during this very long process, always willing to answer one more question or read one more revision.

I also want to thank the current and former staff members of the Boston Architectural Center Library for assisting me both actively and passively in a project for which I volunteered them. I could not possibly have produced this volume without Margaret Bartley, Matthew Burfeind, Sally Cogliano, Sarah Dickinson, and Glen Sherman.

My colleagues in the library profession have been tremendously supportive. The Art Library Society New England Chapter gave me a vote of confidence in awarding me the 1995 Wolfgang Freitag Professional Development Award. A Boston Architectural Center Education Committee Grant supported the illustrations for the volume.

My thanks go to Lamia Doumato, series editor, for giving me the opportunity to write *Interior Design Sourcebook*. Thanks also to Laurie Harris of Omnigraphics for her calm and intelligent support.

The CAD section of Visual Communication Methods, Chapter 8, was written by Henry Cugno, principal at Angeli Design, Inc., and Leo Murphy, a CAD specialist at Payette Associates. Chapter 11, Magazines, was written with me by Margaret Peterson Bartley of the Wellesley College Clapp Library. Chapter 12, Publishers and Bookstores, was compiled by Sarah W. Dickinson, Associate Librarian at the Boston Architectural Center and Chair of the New England Chapter of the Art Library Society.

Though there are many other individuals who have assisted me in producing this volume, I would particularly like to thank those whose names are included here: Jon Andersen, Saira Austin, Elizabeth Banks, Paula Baxter, Dana Berg, Richard Cheek, Henry Cugno, Hikmet Dogu, John Eade, Ann Elwell, Lew Epstein, Arnold Friedmann, John Gambell, Kathy Gips, Nick Goff, Jane Grabowski-Miller, James S. Hodgson, Robert Humenn, Jeanne Kopacz, Don Lonergan, Maryrose MacGowen, Drew MacIness, Henry MacLean, Greg Moore, Leo Murphy, Peter M. Nielsen, Lisa Petterson, John Powell, Jennifer Richmond, Thomas W. Robinson, Steve Rosenthal, Bernard P. Spring, John Ames Stefian, Jane Staley, Bill Thoene, Peter Vanderwarker, and Karen Vagts.

Introduction

This book, a selective annotated bibliography of sources of information, is written for interior design practitioners, educators, and students. It should also be useful to those interested in architecture and other adjacent areas of study as there are few, if any, other current titles which closely examine the literature of interior architecture or design.

Interior design is a complex and demanding profession. Yet, its practitioners would not hesitate to proclaim it one of the most rewarding. The layperson thinks of the designer as an artist, someone who has an eye for what looks right, someone with inherent talent. In truth, interior design is a combination of art and science, with success requiring talent, training, and diligence. There are a multitude of skills one must acquire to be a successful designer, and a great deal of information must be assimilated and molded, with talent, into a personal theory and knowledge of design. Architectural structures must be understood, as well as heating, ventilating, and air-conditioning systems; the subtleties of lighting and acoustics; the stringent application of life safety codes; and the necessity of rational business practices. At the same time, the designer endeavors to please clients with widely varying personalities and needs. This volume is a selective listing of sources of information to be used by the designer or student of design in all phases of a project: programming or strategic planning, schematic design, design development, construction documents, and contract administration.

Included are various types of sources, such as books, codes, magazines, magazine indexes, organizations, publishers, bookstores, competitions and awards, and product and conference expositions. Each item was selected and commented upon specifically for interior designers. Interior design is a relatively new profession, whose practitioners have been more intent upon tangible results than consciously creating a body of theory. Designers were forced to borrow from the theory of more established disciplines, such as fine, decorative, or one of the other applied arts. Designers have, by now, pretty well made the necessary theory their own, integrating and altering it to suit their own discipline, as can be seen by the substantial work represented in this volume.

The following definition of an interior designer, which has been approved by members of the National Council for Interior Design Qualification, provides an accurate picture of the knowledge and abilities that are essential to practice interior design.

> *"The professional interior designer is a person qualified by education, experience, and examination who*
>
> > *I. identifies, researches and creatively solves problems pertaining to the function and quality of the interior environment*
> >
> > *II. performs services relative to interior spaces, including programming, design analysis, space planning and aesthetics, using specialized knowledge of interior construction, building systems and components, building codes, equipment, materials and furnishings and*
> >
> > *III. prepares all drawings and documents relative to the design of interior spaces*
>
> *in order to enhance and protect the health, safety and welfare of the public."*
>
> (*NCIDQ Examination Guide*, 5th ed., White Plains, N.J.: National Council for Interior Design Qualification, 1989, title page)

This definition of interior design practice provides an overview, with minor differences, of the contents of *Interior Design Sourcebook.*

The profession has developed from many sources, from the wall paintings of Pompeii, to the brilliant holistic designs of Robert Adam in the eighteenth century and Frank Lloyd Wright in the twentieth century, whose designs encompassed buildings, interiors, and furnishings. The craft professions of drapers and upholsterers reached their zenith in the home decorating departments of Liberty of London and Tiffany and Affiliated Artists in New York City. These businesses ultimately led to the professionalization of interior decoration, personified in Elsie de Wolfe, who crowned herself the first professional interior decorator. In England, William Morris and others revolted against the machine-made furnishings produced by the Industrial Revolution. His disgust with the lack of character of these products spurred him to revive the idealism of handcrafts. The Arts and Crafts movement created many small workshops for woodworking, tile, pottery, and weaving. These workshops led, in England, Germany, and Vienna, to the creation of formal schools like the Bauhaus, the Glasgow School of Art, and the Royal School of Art Needlework in London.

The Arts and Crafts movement had a similar effect in the United States, creating small furniture, pottery, and weaving studios. This activity created a demand for formal programs. Schools of interior design in the United States developed from three different sources: one type grew from the art schools, another evolved from the great land grant colleges of the Midwest, and a third developed from academic architectural programs, which were based primarily on the East Coast. These three approaches to interior design have shaped the literature. The Midwestern schools began in strong home economics programs, becoming research-oriented programs that encouraged design theory which was based primarily in the client's program rather than the designer's concept. Most of the behavioral research is generated by the doctoral programs and research centers at these schools. The art schools evolved a more sculptural theory of design and the architectural schools emphasized the design concept and the designer over the client's program.

Interior design is often spoken of as a profession which has been established only relatively recently. Interior design has, of course, a long and glorious past. When Robert and James Adam worked in Great Britain in the eighteenth century, they designed entire complexes of buildings, individual buildings, interiors, decorative plaster motifs, and furniture—entire built environments. The literature of interior design is quite another matter. Some scholars feel that interior design was not addressed as an independent profession until Edith Wharton and Ogden Codman wrote *The Decoration of Houses* in 1897. They created the first volume of work that established interior design as it is now perceived, and they brought into discussion the difference between "architectural proportion" and "superficial application of ornament" (Edith Wharton and Ogden Codman, *The Decoration of Houses*,

New York: Charles Scribner, 1897, p. [3]). They defined two different directions in design: interior decoration as the world of surface treatments and interior design or architecture as design of interior spaces. Interior design as a profession is still and always will be a part of the broader continuum of the creation of the built environment—from urban planning to textile design—and, as such, books which address this continuum will always inform the profession.

The books referred to in this volume are in English and are particularly suited to the practice and study of interior design in the United States, Canada, and the United Kingdom. Most of the titles chosen have been published since 1980. Some older titles of particular significance and continuing relevance have been included. This book is a selected bibliography, its goal being to provide readers with practical reviews of current literature in a readily accessible format. The selections have been made by the author with valuable input from interior design educators and practitioners. Titles were evaluated by several criteria—an author's knowledge of his or her topic, the pertinence of the material, and the quality of the presentation itself. Interior design, as mentioned, is an interdisciplinary field. It is only recently that many books have been written that are devoted exclusively to the topic. I have favored these titles in an effort to provide a coherent base which is useful to both practitioners and educators.

Each chapter and section begins with an introduction which discusses the nature of the literature of that topic. These introductions, read in succession, give a comprehensive overview of the book. Throughout the volume, two notations are used to assist readers. The acronym "**NCIDQ**" appears in boldface to indicate titles which have been recommended by the National Council for Interior Design Qualification to study for its licensing exam. Most of the titles on the NCIDQ reading list are reviewed in this volume. An asterisk, "*", denotes works which are of exceptionally high quality or which are essential to the subject being reviewed. The library of a design school should probably have most of the titles in *Interior Design Sourcebook* in its collection. A design firm, or an individual, will, of course, be much more selective. In this case, the annotations provide guidance as to the value of various titles to each reader.

Chapter 1 contains basic and specialized reference materials. The general section contains basic resources such as contract forms, periodical indexes, dictionaries and encyclopedias of design, art, and architecture, bibliographies, and various graphic standards. The codes and standards section is divided into two components: Codes and Standards, which covers model codes, ASTM, and NFPA standards, etc.; and Accessibility Standards, such as the *Americans with Disabilities Act* and the *Architectural Barriers Act*. The final section gives references to specialized products, such as one would find in the *Old-House Journal Restoration Directory*. These are not reproductions of manufacturers' catalogs in the manner of *Sweet's Catalog File*.

Chapters 2 through 7 are self-explanatory reviews of theory, history, furniture, and project-type books.

Chapter 8 has three divisions, two of which, Drawing and Rendering—Manual and Model Building, follow the same format as previous chapters. The section on computer-aided design departs from this format. Long lists of annotated titles would be of little use because books on CAD are quickly out of date. Instead, a textual description of the application and handling of CAD in a design office is presented. There is a brief discussion of journals, books, and other sources of information at the end of the section.

Chapter 9 returns to the bibliographic format with books for professional practice.

Competitions, Awards, and Scholarships, Chapter 10, is a comprehensive listing of over 130 opportunities for interior design professionals and students of design. It follows the bibliographic format and is arranged by specialty.

The journals and magazines cited in Chapter 11 include material in languages other than English, although English summaries or parallel texts are common. International journals are absolutely necessary in providing designers with an up-to-date picture of the worldwide market in design and products.

Chapters 12 through 15, which cover publishers, professional and trade organizations, government agencies, additional research centers, and national product expositions and conferences, are in the annotated bibliographic format and are self-explanatory.

Despite relatively recent copyright dates, many of the books described will be out of print. To ascertain whether or not a book you wish to acquire is in print or may have been reissued in paperback, consult *Books in Print*, which is available in any bookstore or public library. If a book is out-of-print, it may still be available from a specialty bookdealer or from a design or public library. Even if your local library does not have the book you desire, the library can probably obtain the title for you through its interlibrary loan program. If you wish to purchase an out-of-print book, Chapter 12, Publishers and Bookstores, lists design bookstores which may maintain stocks of out-of-print titles and bookdealers who specialize in searching for used copies of out-of-print titles.

Boston Athenaeum, second floor reading room. Edward Clarke Cabot, 1847–1849. Enlarged and rebuilt by Henry Forbes Bigelow, 1913–1914. Photograph by Peter Vanderwarker.

Chapter 1

Reference

General References

The most productive strategy in pursuing any research problem is to proceed from the general to the specific. In that process, consulting a reference book, in whatever format, is usually the first step. A judicious selection of reference books will usually form the core of any library or office collection and will shape or define the library's greater holdings. The reference books and codes in Chapter 1 form an excellent foundation for libraries in schools of interior design. Design firms will want to make selections from this chapter, enhancing them with personal favorites and specialty titles.

Printed reference materials essentially consist of two types: general directories and handbooks of facts, formulas, or information; and subject-specific sourcebooks, bibliographies, and indexes which guide the user, step-by-step, to even more specialized works. Items as simple and ubiquitous as a dictionary, an almanac, or even the telephone yellow pages (nothing less than an efficient subject guide to regional goods and services), are examples of the first type of reference book. They are consulted for specific bits of information, usually as an end product, and frequently under pressure of time.

Bibliographic sourcebooks such as the volume in hand, periodical indexes such as the *Avery Index*, and even general histories and surveys of the type found in the Design Theory and History chapters following, represent a different kind of reference. After initial consultation, they provide a point of departure leading one to more specific, more discrete information and to the ultimate resolution or conclusion of the research.

The annotated entries for reference books in interior design which follow are divided into four sections beginning with works of general usefulness alphabetically arranged. No project in the professional office can proceed without reference to several of the many building codes and standards of acceptable practice, as well as guides and surveys as to their applicability and effective usage, cited in the second section. The *Americans with Disabilities Act of 1990*, and its antecedents and descendants, has affected the design professions so profoundly that many guides to interpretation and compliance have been published. A synopsis of the act and annotations for a selection of the best usage guides follows in a third section. The chapter concludes with a survey of references to product literature and sources, another type of printed matter unique to the professions.

Much of the information in reference books and indexes lends itself easily and obviously to digitization and electronic delivery. References to several sources currently available online, or available in both printed and electronic formats, are included in the entries following. Although the printed book will certainly always be with us, it is just as certain that many reference sources, spec books, product information, etc., currently available only in hard copy, will eventually become accessible through the personal computer as well. New sources will also emerge, commercially and on home-grown websites. As in all professions, it is important for students and practitioners in interior architecture and design to keep their education current and dynamic.

AIA*Online*. AIA*Online*, c/o Telebuild, 10550 Richmond Ave., Ste. 250, Houston, TX 77042. (800) 864-7753. Cost varies according to connect time, but is reasonable. AIA members have free access via the World Wide Web at http:\\www.aia.org.

> Services and databases offered include the following: *Commerce Business Daily*, the AIA Library catalog and bookstore, product catalogs, legislation information, forum and roundtable information, and directories of AIA member firms. Also available are MASTERSPEC Evaluations, ASTM Abstracts, ADA regulations and guidelines, building code information, and *CMD Early Planning Reports*, which identify construction projects for which contracts have not yet been let. The range of information available is impressive, but some of the information is out of date and searching can be frustratingly slow. Searches of the library and

AIA Journal
Full text Academic Search 20
July 1/97—

bookstore databases were unable to produce records for AIA publications known to have been published over a year ago. The system will need more work if it is to live up to its promise.

America Preserved: A Checklist of Historic Buildings, Structures, and Sites. Washington, D.C.: Prints & Photographs Division, Historic American Buildings Survey/Historic American Engineering Record, 1995.

The Historic American Building Survey was founded in 1933 as a WPA (Works Progress Administration) project to record and to make accessible documentation of historic structures and sites. This current edition notes over 14,000 structures and is arranged geographically by state, with city indexes. Location and format of documentation is included.

*American Society of Interior Designers. *Contract Forms.* ASID Service Corp., P.O. Box 1437, Merrifield, VA 22116-1437.

Standardized contract forms for client, designer, and owner, contractor agreements, and compensation agreements protect both designers and clients. ASID and the American Institute of Architects copyright ASID documents jointly. ASID standard forms are customized to suit interiors projects. The standardized documents are widely accepted by interior designers for all types of projects. The forms were updated and reissued in 1996.

Architectural Index. P.O. Box 1168, Boulder, CO 80306. $24/one issue.

Architectural Index is inexpensive and quite thorough within its limited coverage: nine primary U.S. professional magazines (such as *Interiors* and *Architectural Record*) for architecture, interior design, building, and landscape are cross-indexed by designer, location, and project type. It is essential for any design office. The index for the previous year is published in March of the year following. It is available only in hard copy.

Artbibliographies Modern. ABC-Clio, P.O. Box 1911, Santa Barbara, CA 93116-1911, and Oxford, England.

ABM indexes and abstracts journals and selected books. The value to interior designers lies in its international coverage of furniture and textiles. The bias is decidedly theoretical, academic, and historical—as evidenced by the fact that neither *Domus, Interior Design*, nor *Interiors* is indexed, but the *Journal of Design History* is.

Art Index. H. W. Wilson Co., 950 University Ave., Bronx, NY 10452. Service basis; price varies/four issues with annual cumulation.

Indexes national and international journals by author and subject in the areas of art, architecture, and interior design. Emphasis is on professional and academic research and design education. *Art Index* provides excellent access for U.S., European, and Japanese design journals and associated topics such as textiles and decorative arts. It is also available through online services and on CD-ROM, where abstracts (or summaries) of articles are included with the index beginning with journals published in 1994.

Auer, Michael, Charles Fisher, Thomas Jester, and Marilyn Kaplan, eds. *Interiors Handbook for Historic Buildings, Vol. II.* Washington, D.C.: U.S. Department of the Interior, National Park Service/Historic Preservation Education Foundation, 1993.

This reference provides guidance for the restoration of furnishings; ceilings, walls, and floors; wall and floor coverings; and textiles. An annotated bibliography and a directory of services and products are included.

Avery Index to Architectural Periodicals. Columbia University, Avery Library, G. K. Hall & Co., Macmillan Publishing Co., 866 Third Ave., 17th floor, New York, NY 10022. Annual/$395 for print copy; CD-ROM with annual update/$995 first year, $495 subsequent years; online through RLIN-CitaDel service/price varies.

The *Avery Index to Architectural Periodicals* has been produced by the Avery Library of Columbia University since 1934, with supplements appearing in 1963, 1973, and annually thereafter. One of the oldest and most comprehensive indexes of design serials and journals, it is now published in collaboration with the Getty Art History Information Program. Avery provides thorough coverage of over 300 major American and international periodicals in architecture, interior design, decorative arts, and urban planning. Publications covered include academic journals, professional and trade periodicals, well-done popular magazines, and important foreign language journals. The indexing terminology offers access by style and period, geographic location, building type, and designer and firm names, as well as numerous topic headings. Given its scope, depth, and comprehensive treatment of publications indexed, *Avery Index* is essential for libraries supporting interior and architectural design education.

Ballast, David Kent. *Architect's Handbook of Formulas, Tables, & Mathematical Calculations.* Englewood Cliffs, N.J.: Prentice Hall, 1988.

> Ballast's handbook is one of the most useful desk references for the design professional's office. It provides handy preliminary planning data for space planning, metal finishes, wood species, finish materials, acoustics, etc.

*Ballast, David Kent. *Interior Design Reference Manual: A Guide to the NCIDQ Exam.* Belmont, Calif.: Professional Publications, 1992.

> The *Manual* has been endorsed by NCIDQ and is an essential study guide for students preparing for the Council's exam. It provides a clear overview of the subject areas encompassed by the profession, although some interior designers may well be displeased with Ballast's references to their "lesser" role in design. Sample questions, practicum problems, line drawings, and tables are useful additions. Professionals may find it useful as a quick desk reference.

Baxter, Paula. "Thirty Years of Growth in the Literature of Interior Design." *Journal of Design History* 4, no. 4 (1991): 241-50.

> Baxter, who is the curator of the Art and Architecture Collection at the New York Public Library, continues the significant work of the NYPL in interior design with this bibliographic essay. Baxter's essay picks up where *Interior Design and Decoration*, the bibliography written by Gertrud Lackschewitz and published by the NYPL in 1961, ends. Baxter cites both scholarly and popular literature and discusses the nature of this division in the literature. Both the essay and the attendant notes will be of interest to scholars of interior design.

Bayley, Stephen, ed. *The Conran Directory of Design.* New York: Villard Books, 1985.

> This dictionary-style guide to consumer products, designers, manufacturers, and movements from 1885 to 1985 reflects the taste of Sir Terence Conran. Most entries are three to four paragraphs in length, include an interesting illustration, significant dates, and a smattering of bibliographic references. In short, each entry provides enough information to satisfy a quick inquiry or to direct the user to more detailed sources.

Boger, Louise Ade, and H. Batterson Boger. *The Dictionary of Antiques and the Decorative Arts: A Book of Reference for Glass, Furniture, Ceramics, Silver, Periods, Styles, Technical Terms, etc.* New York: Charles Scribner's Sons, 1967.

> The authors, who consider themselves "semi-professional connoisseurs," worked on this and other books over many years and many continents as they collected pieces of decorative art. Entries in this thorough and well-organized volume vary from single paragraphs to several columns, as needed. The bibliography is divided by subjects and includes works written primarily before 1950. Illustrated with line drawings and black-and-white and color photos.

*Boyce, Charles. *Dictionary of Furniture*. 2nd ed. New York: Henry Holt, 1988.

> The coverage of designers, woods, construction details, and terminology is excellent, with the concise descriptions of styles being particularly useful. Relationships between illustrations (line drawings) and text are coherent, and there are many useful cross-references. Boyce and Gloag (see below) together provide very thorough coverage of furniture in the dictionary format.

Humber ∗ Fanshaw has 2001 ed. on order

Butler, Joseph T. *Field Guide to American Furniture*. New York: Henry Holt, 1986.

> See **Chapter 5, Furniture, Finishes, and Textiles,** under **Furniture** section.

*Byars, Mel. *The Design Encyclopedia*. New York: John Wiley & Sons, 1994.

> The *Encyclopedia* provides very good coverage of individuals and firms involved with the applied and decorative arts in Eastern and Western Europe, Australia, Japan, and North and South America during the past 125 years. Entries include biographical information, professional accomplishments and exhibitions, and selected bibliographies. The black-and-white photo illustrations are grouped in four sections and are limited to single objects; no interiors are included. International and specialized exhibitions and fairs are listed. The volume is well organized and well made, and, with a price of $60, is a must for academic libraries.

*Calloway, Stephen, gen. ed.; Elizabeth Cromley, consultant ed. *The Elements of Style: A Practical Encyclopedia of Interior Architectural*

Details from 1485 to the 1996. Rev. ed. New York: Simon and Schuster, 1991.

NA
2850
.44
.96

copy
1991

This carefully compiled and produced encyclopedia devotes approximately 30 pages to each stylistic period of British and U.S. interior architecture with no bias toward either country. Each section begins with a three- to four-page introduction peppered with names and dates. Well-illustrated and annotated coverage of the elements of interior architecture, i.e., woodwork, lighting, services, follows. Elements are color-coded to tab keys so that they may be traced through all periods. The dense, clear visual shorthand is complemented by a good glossary and bibliography, and by directories of British and U.S. suppliers of restoration services and materials. Particularly useful for residential interior details. Other works by Calloway on specific topics are found in the design literature and may be appropriate for some designers' needs.

X Carpet and Rug Institute. *Carpet Specifier's Handbook*. Dalton, Ga.: Carpet and Rug Institute, 5th ed., 1992.

The CRI *Handbook* provides an understanding of the factors that constitute a basis for selecting carpet and a guide to writing carpet specifications. Composition, manufacturing techniques, and maintenance of carpeting are covered.

X Carpet and Rug Institute. *Standard for Installation of Commercial Textile Floorcovering Materials, CRI 104*. Dalton, Ga.: Carpet and Rug Institute, most recent ed.

CRI 104 and *CRI 105*, for residential installation, are the definitive industry minimum installation standards. The thorough descriptions and diagrams assist in specification writing, layout, and planning. Standard floor preparation, tools, and materials are enumerated.

X *Construction Index*. Construction Index, c/o ARCHITEXT, 410 S. Michigan Ave., Ste. 1008, Chicago, IL 60605-1402. (312) 939-3202. Annual/ $75. Hard copy; available online through STN International (800) 848-6533 and Orbit (800) 421-7229.

Construction Index is one of few indexes to have a true construction, as opposed to design, focus. It indexes *and* abstracts 42 journals, such as *Design Solutions* published by the Architectural Woodwork Institute, *Facilities Design & Management, Tile and Decorative Surfaces*, and titles on painting, lighting, and commercial renovation, as well as the standard magazines of architecture and interior design. The editors seek to fill the niche that falls between the design-oriented *Architectural Index* and the technical *Engineering Index*. References are indexed according to Construction Specification Institute Masterformat numbers, which are familiar to designers. Custom database searches by keyword, with abstracts of cited articles, are available between annual issues. *Construction Index* may soon be available through AIA*Online* (see above), c/o Telebuild, 10550 Richmond Ave., Ste. 250, Houston, TX 77042. (800) 864-7753. $300. + $.10 per minute.

DeChiara, Joseph, Julius Panero, and Martin Zelnik. *Time-Saver Standards for Interior Design and Space Planning.* New York: McGraw-Hill, 1991.

Ref
NK
2110
.D33
1991

> This standards manual for the interior design profession—the interiors version of *Architectural Graphic Standards*—is more useful to students than to professionals. Be aware that some of the details are dated in terms of current technology; for example, little cabinetry is now made with a face frame. Recent changes in handicapped accessibility laws are not addressed. **NCIDQ**

X *Design and Applied Arts Index.* Design Documentation, Old Manor Lodge, Bodiam, Robertsbridge, E. Sussex TN32 5UJ, England. Two/year print version (print + CD-ROM $1,300); four/year CD-ROM $1,200.

> *DAAI* is an international index to periodical literature in architecture, interior design, and allied fields, including photography, couture, antiques, marketing, design education, and design management. Most of the 250 journals indexed are British-based. Research value and current interest are the criteria for inclusion of materials; *DAAI* is thus attempting to bridge the needs of both academics and practicing professionals. Brief annotations are usually given for each citation along with basic biographical and historical data for designers, firms, and consultancies when they are sighted. The indexing language provides access by designer or firm name and by application, project, or problem type, with the latter subdivided geographically. In addition, the practice of giving detailed information on the illustrations in articles, e.g., whether they are suitable for slides or not reproduced elsewhere, is a real boon for librarians and design faculties. *DAAI* is an excellent resource for collections strong in contemporary European design literature or endeavoring to become so.

X Doumato, Lamia. *Architecture and Women: A Bibliography Documenting Women Architects, Landscape Architects, Designers, Architectural Critics and Writers and Women in Related Fields Working in the United States.* New York: Garland, 1988.

> Although few interior designers are specifically cited, the scarcity of information regarding women in design makes this work a valuable addition to a design school library. Manuscript material, special collections, monographs, and citations to books and journal articles are included.

Duncan, Alastair, ed. *The Encyclopedia of Art Deco.* New York: E. P. Dutton, 1988.

> This book has value despite an awkward layout which places long essays, brief biographies, and illustrations relating to both on the same page. The illustrations, both in color and black-and-white, are numerous and very good, while the one-paragraph biographies provide introductions to designers in all media who worked in the Deco style.

Ref
N6494
.A7
E54
1988
Humber
ref.

**Ehresmann, Donald L. *Applied and Decorative Arts: A Bibliographic Guide.* 2nd ed. Englewood, Colo.: Libraries Unlimited, 1993.*

> One of a series of bibliographies on the documentation of the history of art, this volume, as well as the other titles in the series, is essential for a design school library. *Fine Arts* and *Architecture* have already been published, while bibliographies on sculpture, painting, and graphic arts are planned. In this volume, books published in English and Western European languages between 1875 and 1990 have been reviewed. The thorough subdivision of topics in the table of contents and the author-title and subject indexes allow easy access to an enormous quantity of information. Museum and exhibition catalogs and price guides are included. Annotations are brief, analytical, and include tables of contents from outstanding titles. Furniture, textiles, metalwork, porcelain, and wallpaper are topics which will be of special interest to designers.

Encyclopedia of Associations: An Associations Unlimited Reference: National Organizations of the U.S. Sandra Jaszczak, ed. 32nd ed. Detroit: Gale Research, 1997.

> While not an essential purchase for the small firm, the *Encyclopedia* is a valuable resource which is available in public and university libraries. Published in three volumes, covering U.S., international, and U.S. regional associations, the *Encyclopedia* provides the following information for each entry: address, phone, and fax numbers; mission statement;

personnel; publications; and convention dates. Access is provided through name and keyword indexes.

Fisher, Charles E., III, Michael Auer, and Anne Grimmer, eds. *The Interiors Handbook for Historic Buildings*. Washington, D.C.: Historic Preservation Education Foundation, 1988.

> A three-ring binder format encourages users to make this volume their own with notes and updates. Included are papers given at the 1988 Interiors Conference for Historic Buildings, an annotated bibliography, a special issue of *Old-House Journal* devoted to interior restoration, and interpretations of the Secretary of the Interior's Standards for Rehabilitation. The National Park Service and several architectural conservation programs collaborated with Historic Preservation Education Foundation on the publication, creating a "who's who" list of interior preservation professionals.

*Fleming, John, and Hugh Honour. *The Penguin Dictionary of Decorative Arts*. New ed. London: Viking, 1989.

> This desk reference book contains generally short but well-researched definitions of terms and biographies of influential designers. The entries are enhanced by having their meanings placed in social and historical context. Illustrations include crisp black-and-white and color photographs as well as reproductions of period illustrations. Brief bibliographies are provided for longer entries.

*Gloag, John. *A Complete Dictionary of Furniture*. Revised and expanded by Clive Edwards. Woodstock, N.Y.: Overlook Press, 1991.

> Gloag's is a thorough dictionary of well-deserved high repute. The introductory chapters on the "description" and "design" of furniture are excellent contextual introductions to the topic, as well as bibliographical essays on the history of publishing in the field. The definitions are clear and illustrated with a superb selection of line drawings and reproductions from pertinent periods, some taken from manuscripts. Brief biographies of cabinet makers and a bibliography of books and journals complete the volume. Designers and furniture from the Modern Movement are virtually ignored.

Grimmer, Anne E. *Historic Building Interiors: An Annotated Bibliography*. 2 vols. Washington, D.C.: U.S. Department of the Interior, National Park Service, Preservation Assistance Division, 1994.

Volume 1 was compiled as part of the 1988 Interiors Conference listed above under the author's name, "Fisher"; volume 2 was prepared in 1993 as an update. The combined bibliography cites about 350 references to books and periodical essays, limited primarily to readily accessible American publications. Entries are classified topically: Finishes and Materials, Systems and Fixtures, Rehabilitation Case Studies, Inspection, Safety, Codes, and Planning. There are no author, keyword, or subject indexes. Of particular value are the case studies, codes, and accessibility sections, as they are not particularly easy to find elsewhere.

Harling, Robert, ed. *Studio Dictionary of Design & Decoration*. New York: Viking Press, A Studio Book, 1973.

With beautiful, seldom-seen black-and-white photos and brief, intelligent entries, this volume covers architecture, furniture, interiors, and decoration. Individual designers and historic and modern periods are included. Some of the articles were originally published in such Conde Nast magazines as *Vogue* and *House and Garden*. No bibliography.

Henley, Pamela E. B. *Interior Design Practicum Exam Workbook.* Belmont, Calif.: Professional Publications, 1995.

Half of the NCIDQ exam consists of tests of practical applications of design skills and knowledge. The "practicum" includes design problems in programming, three-dimensional design, and visual interpretations of written programs. This brief, forthright guide will certainly be valuable as a preparatory tool. However, some designers will be surprised at the second-year-design-level approach in the chapter on design presentation and the inclusion of shade and shadow techniques when there is no time for their use when actually taking the exam.

Hiesinger, Kathyrn B., and George H. Marcus. *Landmarks of Twentieth-Century Design: An Illustrated Handbook*. New York: Abbeville Press, 1993.

Four hundred objects are depicted in color and black-and-white. Arranged by decades, the book provides brief biographical and bibliographical information about the designers of the objects. There is also a general bibliography for the period.

X *IFI International Handbook: Interior Design Practice*. Amsterdam:
International Federation of Interior Architects/Interior Designers, 1991.

> This basic guide to professional organizations, professional practice,
> educational requirements, and contract administration in 15 member
> countries is not comprehensive, but is essential for any designer inter-
> ested in international work. For example, the entry for Italy provides not
> only the name and address of the Italian architecture and interior design
> association, but also that of a related organization, the European Bureau
> of Designers. In contrast, there is no entry whatsoever for France. In such
> instances, the designer may contact IFI directly.

X *IFI Lexicon: Interior Design Glossary*. Amsterdam: International Federation of Interior Architects/Interior Designers, n.d.

> The *Lexicon* defines and translates terms associated with interior design
> into English, Spanish, French, and German. The definitions are uncom-
> plicated but a user may not find all the words he or she needs. However,
> this small volume provides a real service.

X *IFI World Directory of Schools*. Rev. ed. Amsterdam: International Federation of Interior Architects/Interior Designers, 1993.

> The directory provides a thorough description of the programs and
> requirements of schools worldwide. It is available on disk or in hard
> copy.

X *IIDA (International Interior Design Association). *Forms and Documents
Manual*. Chicago: International Interior Design Association, 1997.

> This volume is the successor to the IBD (Institute of Business Designers)
> *Forms and Documents Manual* which was last published in 1995, prior to
> the formation of IIDA. The IBD volume was considered by many
> designers to be the "Bible" for professional guidelines and numerous
> forms, such as those for accounting; project programming, specifying,
> purchasing, and contracting; administration; and correspondence.
> Designers can choose between the contract forms provided by IIDA and
> those published by ASID (American Society of Interior Designers, cited
> above).

International Hospitality and Tourism Database. John Wiley & Sons, 605
Third Ave., New York, NY 10157-0228.

> The database is produced by the Consortium of Hospitality Research
> Information Services, of which the American Hotel & Motel Association

is a member, and provides an index to approximately 65 industry journals. Coverage begins in 1988 and includes abstracts of articles in addition to the index. Published in CD-ROM format, the database is updated quarterly and costs $450 annually.

Jagger, Janette, and Roger Towe. *Designers International Index.* 3 vols. London: Bowker-Saur, 1991.

An index to periodicals and books which retrieves information on the work of designers in 31 categories including furniture, textiles, set design, retail spaces, CAD, etc. The major objective of the compilers (librarians at the Leicester Polytechnic) was to provide at least one citation for *any* recognized designer and that is the single, essential value of this expensive set. Volumes one and two cite references to individual designers in alphabetic sequence; volume three offers geographical and typological indexes. Formerly issued somewhat regularly (on microfiche only) as *Design International*, the *Index* shows no internal evidence or promise of supplements or updates.

Jervis, Simon. *The Facts on File Dictionary of Design and Designers.* New York: Facts on File, 1984; published in Britain as *The Penguin Dictionary of Design and Designers*, London: Allen Lane, 1984.

Jervis' introductory essay on design history and development is valuable in its own right. The dictionary itself is historical, covering European and North American design, including furniture and interior decoration, beginning in 1450. Other dictionaries, of which there are many, provide more thorough coverage of twentieth-century design. Significant peripheral figures who were not actually designers are also included, providing valuable information which is not readily obtained elsewhere.

Julier, Guy. *The Thames and Hudson Encyclopedia of 20th-Century Design and Designers.* London: Thames and Hudson, 1993.

The *Encyclopedia*, part of the *World of Art* series, features brief (one to six paragraphs) entries, small but good black-and-white photographs, a chronology of significant events in the design world, and a bibliography. Graphic and industrial design receive the most attention, though furniture designers and design movements are included.

X *Kemp, Wayne. *Design for Aging: An Annotated Bibliography, 1980-1992*. Washington, D.C.: Aging Design Research Program (ADRP) of the AIA/ACSA Council on Architectural Research, 1993.

> This concise bibliography annotates books that were purchased by the AIA Library through a grant from the ADRP. The titles are carefully selected, clearly described, and publishers' addresses and telephone numbers are included for easy purchasing. AIA members may borrow the books from the AIA Library.

X Lackschewitz, Gertrud. *Interior Design and Decoration: A Bibliography*. New York: New York Public Library, 1961.

> Lackschewitz's work was sponsored by the American Institute of Decorators, the predecessor of the American Society of Interior Designers, a group which had shown its interest in the scholarship of interior design by its publication of an earlier bibliography in 1938. Lackschewitz's work is a carefully selected and arranged listing of titles found in the New York Public Library's own collection. Of particular interest to scholars are the titles under the heading "Theory and Practice of Interior Design and Decoration," which reflect the sophisticated thinking of the time.

X Lauzzana, Raymond, ed.-in-chief. *International Directory of Design*. 4th ed. San Francisco: Penrose, 1997.

> The directory is published annually, with indexes in Arabic, Chinese, English, French, Japanese, German, Italian, Russian, and Spanish. It provides the names, addresses, telephone numbers, and names of contact persons for schools of architecture, building, interior design, textile design, decoration, ornament, ceramics, and many other design fields. The entries are arranged geographically, with subject indexes. There are 144 entries for interior design. Penrose also publishes a CD-ROM, *International Design Review*, which provides images of student work from these schools and descriptions of school activities.

X Lewis, Philippa, and Gillian Darley. *Dictionary of Ornament*. London: Macmillan, 1986.

> The *Dictionary* is a selective glossary with small black-and-white photo illustrations of "ornament, pattern and motifs in the applied arts and architecture."It addresses European and North American motifs from the Renaissance to the twentieth century. Greek, Roman, Egyptian, and Oriental antecedents are included. There is no bibliography.

X *Lopez, Michael J. *Retail Store Planning & Design Manual.* 2ⁿᵈ ed.
National Retail Federation Series. New York: John Wiley & Sons, 1995.

> This is an excellent "retail graphic standards," which should be in the
> libraries of schools of design and retail design firm offices. It is particu-
> larly useful when dealing with clients who don't have enough experience
> to really know what they need or for young or inexperienced designers.

MASTERSPEC. Washington, D.C.: American Institute of Architects,
subscription. Order from ARCOM Master Systems, (800) 424-5080.

> "Comprehensive, yet cumbersome in the view of some users. Offered in
> broad and narrow form and simplified for smaller projects. Compatible
> with numerous word-processing programs." Despite these rather negative
> comments in *Architectural Record* (December 1994, p. 26), many
> architects and designers use this master guide specification form. Using a
> "delete-and-edit" format, *MASTERSPEC* can be adjusted for extent of
> detail offered, so that it can be used in outline form for schematic design
> and full detail for construction documents. It is sold on a subscription
> basis and specific sections may be ordered. Interior designers could order
> the "Interiors" or "FF&E" sections, rather than the entire document.
> Since both product literature and such standards as ANSI and ASTM are
> referenced in the document, it also serves to point out new products or
> standards to users.

X McGowan, Maryrose. *Specifying Interiors: A Guide to Construction and
FF&E for Commercial Interior Projects.* New York: John Wiley & Sons,
1996.

> This is one of a few new, welcome publications that focuses specifically
> on "hard" issues of interior design. It is frequently difficult for a contract
> design specifier to understand the differences in similar products and
> McGowan's book assists in making that process objective. It will be
> useful as a supplementary text for materials classes and as an office
> reference. It is thorough in its references and provides page references to
> specific ASTM and ANSI standards. A bibliography and a glossary are
> included, but an introduction that defines the goals of the book is lacking.
> ("FF&E" is the accepted phrase for furniture, furnishings, and equip-
> ment.)

*Myers, Bernard S., ed. *McGraw-Hill Dictionary of Art.* 5 vols. New York:
McGraw-Hill, 1969.

> Coverage includes art, architecture, and artists from all geographical
> locations and cultures throughout history. Though termed a "dictionary,"

this work has many entries befitting an encyclopedia. The entries are signed, cross-referenced where appropriate, and include bibliographies. The reproductions and illustrations, many of which are color, are of uniformly high quality. Included are cogent entries on major design schools, designers, craftsmen, and furniture styles. The *Dictionary* is out of print, but it may be available through such out-of-print and search services as are mentioned in **Chapter 12, Publishers and Bookstores.** The set is appropriate for academic libraries.

Naeve, Milo M. *Identifying American Furniture: A Pictorial Guide to Styles and Terms, Colonial to Contemporary.* 2nd ed. Nashville, Tenn.: American Association for State and Local History, 1989.

> There is a plethora of guides to furniture styles, but very few are small enough or lightweight enough to travel as is Naeve—a true "pocket book." Black-and-white photos, with numbered references to specific elements of each piece, are combined with a brief text for each style. A bibliography and an index are included in this convenient guide written by a curator of American Arts at the Art Institute of Chicago.

O'Dwyer, Barry. *Profile/European Designers.* Bookham, Surrey, England: Elfande Art Publishing, 1991.

> The designers included have been invited by the editors to submit illustrations for this directory. Business interiors, exhibit design, retail design, and graphic design, which is emphasized, are illustrated with good color photos. The languages spoken by the members of the firms represented are cited. Approximately one and one-half pages are devoted to each firm.

Organising International Design Competitions & Award Schemes: Regulations and Guidelines. Amsterdam: International Federation of Interior Architects/Interior Designers, 1989.

> This 17-page pamphlet offers concise standards and directions for the sponsors of design competitions as agreed upon by three major international design associations: International Council of Graphic Design Associations (Icograda), International Council of Societies of Industrial Design (ICSID), and International Federation of Interior Designers (IFI). The regulations set high, but rational, standards of organization and conduct and have been developed to be applicable in any country.

Osborne, Harold, ed. *The Oxford Companion to the Decorative Arts.* Oxford: Oxford University Press, 1991, reprint of corrected 1985 ed.

> A comprehensive international historical survey of the decorative arts. Included are brief biographies of key artisans; longer essays on periods, cultures, and movements; and essays on materials and techniques. Black-and-white line drawings and photographs and a 940-item bibliography supplement the well-written text.

Pellam, John L., ed. *Who's Who in Interior Design: 1994-1995.* Laguna Beach, Calif.: Baron's Who's Who, 1994.

> The editorial board consists of esteemed professionals in the field. Among the criteria for inclusion are a BA or advanced degree, experience, honors and awards, publication, membership and activity in professional organizations, and community service. Coverage is international and includes both contract and residential designers. Approximately one-half of the designers included practice in the United States. Only the most well-known designers are included. Other, perhaps more significant, measures of professional success are inclusion in ASID's "Hall of Fame" and Fellow status in IIDA.

*Pendergast, Sarah, ed. *Contemporary Designers.* 3rd ed. Detroit: St. James Press, 1996.

> The excellent *Contemporary Arts Series* published by St. James Press includes books on artists, architects, photographers, and contemporary arts. *Contemporary Designers* presents over 800 20th-century designers from all fields of design. Biographical information, chronology of projects, a bibliography of books and magazine articles by and about the designers, an analysis of the work, and an illustration are included for each designer. Authoritative.

Phillips, Steven J. *Old-House Dictionary: An Illustrated Guide to American Domestic Architecture (1600-1940).* Lakewood, Colo.: American Source Books, 1989.

> A dictionary that includes an index is unusual, but the index and its companion listing of terms arranged by subject make sense for the user who knows what he or she is looking for but not the precise term. Pleasing line drawings complement the textual definitions. The book has a clearly defined purpose which is well executed.

Pile, John. *Dictionary of 20ᵗʰ-Century Design*. New York: Facts on File, 1990.

> A valuable, well-written reference work. "Design" is clearly defined and coverage is excellent. Design professionals, schools, products, manufacturers, technical terms, writers, and philosophies are addressed. Of particular value is the inclusion of significant, but less-well-known designers about whom information is difficult to obtain. Illustrated with black-and-white photos.

Placzek, Adolph K., ed.-in-chief. *Macmillan Encyclopedia of Architects*. 4 vols. New York: Macmillan, Free Press, 1982.

> Although the coverage here is almost exclusively limited to architects and designers of structures, it is impossible to compile a sourcebook intended for the design professions without recommending this superb, authoritative biographical dictionary. A few of the most distinguished interior designers (such as Eames or Morris) are awarded entries and, from Adam to Wright, pure architects have often attended closely to the design of interiors. Individual entries have each been written by recognized scholars; bibliographies are attached; and many are illustrated with at least one halftone.

*Ramsey, Charles George, and Harold Reeve Sleeper, eds. *Architectural Graphic Standards*. Edited by John Ray Hoke, Jr. [for] The American Institute of Architects. 9ᵗʰ ed. New York: John Wiley & Sons, 1994.

> The "bible" for both interior designers and architects has been updated to address developments in ADA requirements and the environmental impact of building materials. The 9ᵗʰ edition has more to offer interior designers than previous editions, with an expanded woodworking section and new information on space planning. Included are bibliographies, lists of organizations, and the hundreds of line drawings and charts that provide a uniform graphic vocabulary for the design professions. Both annual paperback updates (estimated at $75) and a CD-ROM version (approximately $300) are planned. The CD-ROM version, which includes hypertext and images that can be enlarged onscreen, is based on the 9ᵗʰ edition and was published in June 1996. **NCIDQ**

*Reznikoff, S. C. *Interior Graphic and Design Standards*. New York: Whitney Library of Design, 1986.

> This volume is similar to its architectural counterpart, *Architectural Graphic Standards*. It provides measurements of standard interiors

components, dimensioned drawings of a variety of residential and commercial interiors layouts, and cites applicable codes and standards for products. Construction Specifications Institute Masterformat numbers have been expanded to include interior design applications and all chapters begin with a complete listing of the chapter's contents, the appropriate CSI numbers, and the page numbers. The quality of the organization and production of the volume makes it a pleasure to use; however, *Graphic Standards* is more thorough and more widely used. **NCIDQ**

Russell, Beverly. *Women of Design: Contemporary American Interiors.* New York: Rizzoli, 1992.

Biographical information for contemporary designers can be scarce, so Russell's lushly illustrated, well-written volume about 33 successful American female designers is very welcome. It is enhanced by Andree Putman's foreword, an excellent synopsis of the history of women in the profession. Office addresses, a brief bibliography, and an index add value to the title.

Schomer, Victoria. *Interior Concerns Resource Guide: A Guide to Sustainable and Healthy Products and Educational Information for Designing and Building.* Mill Valley, Calif.: Interior Concerns Environmental Resources, 1993.

This unpretentious and inexpensive guide does as the title says, listing products and providing a concise introduction to the concept of friendly design and construction. Essays on specific aspects of design, techniques, processes, and classes of products enhance the product listings. Citations for periodicals and consultants which deal with ecological interiors, case study examples, and sources of more information on the topic make this a significant publication in its field. Product information is presented in CSI format and is annually updated.

SEARCH. SEARCH Publishing Inc., 102 Brighton Circle, Devon, PA 19333. Four/year $110 library edition in hard copy (indexes 33 titles); two/year $95 for small office edition (indexes 12 titles); also available on computer disks.

SEARCH is a particularly useful information management tool for small- to medium-sized firms. It provides good coverage of important design magazines ranging from the essential *Interior Design* and *Interiors* to good shelter magazines, and such foreign titles as *Abitare* and *Architectural Review*.

X *Showcase of Interior Design: International Commercial Edition*. Grand
Rapids, Mich.: Vitae Publishing, 1992.

> Presentation of high-quality color photographs of recently completed
> commercial installations by respected firms. Photos are accompanied
> with very brief texts written by the firms, all self-selected. Both designers
> and photographers are credited. The candid introduction was written by
> *Interior Design* magazine's editor-in-chief, Stanley Abercrombie.
> Directories such as this and *Who's Who* are especially useful to students
> and professionals who are conducting job searches.

SPECTEXT. Washington, D.C.: National Institute of Building Sciences,
subscription.

> *SPECTEXT* contains over 450 specification sections and is suitable for
> large, complex projects. *SPECTEXT II* is appropriate for smaller projects,
> consisting of 100 spec sections. The system is updated quarterly to
> reflect changes in codes, standards, and construction practices. The
> organization and numbering system coordinate with the CSI *Manual of
> Practice* and AIA's contract format. *SPECTEXT* uses the "edit-and-delete
> format," while also permitting some fill-in-the-blank areas to customize
> the specification. The four specifying methods—reference standards,
> descriptive, performance, and proprietary—can all be accommodated. It
> is available for both WordPerfect and Microsoft Word processing
> programs. *SPECTEXT* was created by Construction Sciences Research
> Foundation, which was founded by Construction Specifications Institute.

X Treanor, Betty McKee, comp. and ed. *IDEC Comprehensive Bibliography
for Interior Design*. 2nd ed. Richmond, Va.: Interior Design Educators
Council, 1987.

> This bibliography provides an overview of the history of publishing for
> interior design in the twentieth century, but is really too comprehensive
> to be useful in any specific research.

X Turner, Jane, ed. *The Dictionary of Art*. New York: Grove, 1996.

> The Grove *Dictionary of Art* is a monumental publication (34 volumes)
> in the field of art history, unmatched in scope and ambition. It contains
> 45,000 signed entries on countries, cities, sites, movements, groups,
> building types, materials, and techniques. Almost half of the entries are
> biographical. Coverage of non-Western cultures and civilizations is
> particularly strong. Interior design topics are covered in the *Dictionary*,
> although they are often tangential and covered within the scope of other

broader subjects. For instance, there is no single section on "furniture" or "interior decoration"; both subjects are found within essays on specific countries or cultures. Specific furniture types (e.g., "chair," "screen," or "bed") are given good coverage in individual essays, as are such topics as "upholstery," "furniture," and "lighting." Appropriate topics are illustrated in color.

U.S. Department of the Interior, National Park Service. *Historic Preservation Act of 1966*. Washington, D.C.: U.S. Department of the Interior, 1966, as amended 1993.

The *Historic Preservation Act* was enacted in 1966 largely in response to the concern and criticism of several years of indiscriminate takings, land clearing, and destruction of individual buildings spawned by earlier urban renewal legislation of the "Great Society." The act established the *National Register of Historic Places* as well as *The Secretary of the Interior's Standards for the Treatment of Historic Properties*. The *Standards* affect all government-owned historic buildings and privately-owned historic buildings whose owners wish to receive preservation tax credits through the National Park Service's Outreach Tax act office in Philadelphia. The original act was amended in 1993 to include historic landscapes and historic boats and ships. There is a desire by some members of the Park Service to add historic furnishings to the legislation.

Waters, Nancy H. "Draft Standards for the Treatment of a Distinct Cultural Resource." *CRM: Cultural Resource Management: Information for Parks, Federal Agencies, Indian Tribes, States, Local Governments, and the Private Sector* 18, no. 10 (1995): 10-13.

Forty museum professionals wrote and are continuing to develop draft standards for the evaluation and preservation of furnished historic interiors based on the quality and format of the *Secretary of the Interior's Standards for the Treatment of Historic Properties*. The four treatment options—preservation, restoration, reconstruction, and rehabilitation—available in the Secretary's *Standards* are adapted for furnished historic interiors.

White, Antony, and Bruce Robertson. *Furniture & Furnishings: A Visual Guide*. New York: Design Press, 1990.

This unique guide provides detailed line drawings of many versions of the same object arranged on the same page. There is a glossary/index of terms and an enlightening "Style Timechart" from 200 B.C. to 2000 A.D. which places periods and styles in graphic context with social and political events. The volume is not intimidating and should be very helpful to students who are just developing a knowledge of styles.

Codes and Standards

Building codes are known to have existed since the Babylonian *Code of Hammurabi*, always with the view of promoting the safety of the populace. "Codes and standards" is a frequently used phrase in the design and construction industry, but the two words have different meanings. Codes are law and are enforced in the geographic jurisdiction that legislated them. Standards represent practices that have been accepted as reasonable guidelines by those professionals with expert knowledge of the specific field. Standards are developed by many responsible organizations, such as the American National Standards Institute (ANSI) or the National Fire Protection Association (NFPA). Individual standards can be referenced in the codes, like NFPA 101, the *Life Safety Code*, thus making them law within the specified jurisdiction. There are three "model codes" for building in the United States, each of which also refers to mechanical, plumbing, fire prevention, and existing structures codes. (Annotations of the model codes complete this section.) They have been written to simplify and clarify building construction requirements across jurisdictional boundaries. Most jurisdictions have adopted, or adopted with amendments, one of these codes. "The only regulations that are consistent in every jurisdiction are the federal regulations that are made mandatory by law" (Sharon Koomen Harmon, *The Codes Guidebook for Interiors*, John Wiley & Sons, 1994, p. 5). The most well-known example of such a federal regulation is the *Americans with Disabilities Act*. When two codes conflict, the strictest code usually prevails. However, the local code official makes the final decision.

Code research is part of the programming or pre-design process. The earlier in the process codes are taken into account, the more likely it is that the designer will make them a part of the design, rather than adapting the design to the codes after the design has gained form. The more a designer understands the codes, the more in control of the design he or she can be. It is always good practice to work with a code expert in the locale.

American Institute of Architects, Building Performance and Regulation Committee. *An Architect's Guide to Building Codes & Standards*. 4rd ed. Washington, D.C.: American Institute of Architects, 1997.

This concise volume is a useful handbook for offices and an excellent reference for a class in codes. It outlines the development of codes and standards, describes the goals and programs of the 18 regulating bodies with which the BP & R Committee deals, provides the addresses of those groups, and explains how to use the model codes.

American Society of Heating, Refrigerating, and Air-Conditioning Engineers, Inc. *ASHRAE Standard 62-1989, Ventilation for Acceptable Indoor Air Quality*. Atlanta, Ga.: American Society of Heating, Refrigerating, and Air-Conditioning Engineers, 1989.

This standard is of particular interest to designers. A revised version is now in public review draft. The revision, comments, and purpose and scope description may be viewed at the ASHRAE web site, ftp: www.ashrae.org.

American Society for Testing Materials. *Standards in Building Codes*. Philadelphia: American Society for Testing Materials, 1996.

The 600 ASTM standard specifications, practices, test methods, and definitions are sold in three volumes or as individual, and much less expensive, standards. The three-volume set is issued annually.

Architectural Woodwork Institute. *Architectural Casework General Detail and Specification Guide*. Centreville, Va.: Architectural Woodwork Institute, 1984.

This brief pamphlet (17 pages) offers reliable guide specifications, detail nomenclature, and convenient graphic standards for casework (interior cabinetry and furniture).

*Architectural Woodwork Institute. *Architectural Woodwork Quality Standards*. 6th ed., version 1.1. Centreville, Va.: Architectural Woodwork Institute, 1994.

This is *the* standard for architectural woodwork. The layout and text are comprehensive and clear, and are further elucidated by explicit line drawings. It follows suggested CSI format, defines the grades of woodwork, construction, finishing, and finishing systems. The language can be integrated directly into specifications.

Council of American Building Officials. *CABO/ANSI A117.1-1992, American National Standard—Accessible and Usable Buildings and Facilities*. Falls Church, Va.: Council of American Building Officials, 1992.

> These standards are as strict as the *ADA Accessibility Guidelines* (*ADAAG*) and in some instances more strict. *ANSI 117.1* has been accepted by all three model codes.

Council of American Building Officials. *One and Two Family Dwelling Code*. Falls Church, Va.: Council of American Building Officials, 1995.

> Having been written by CABO, this code is accepted by all three model codes. It is the primary building code for single and duplex housing.

Directory of Building Codes & Regulations. Herndon, Va.: National Conference of States on Building Codes and Standards, 1989.

> Five sections cover the following topics: history and description of codes, state residential codes, city residential codes, state commercial codes, and city commercial codes. This overview of U.S. codes is useful for both classes in codes and designers who work in many different states.

Graf, Don. *Basic Building Data*. Revised by S. Blackwell Duncan. 3rd ed. New York: Van Nostrand Reinhold, 1985.

> An amazing little book (4 1/2" x 7 1/4") with more information between its covers than can be imagined. It ranges from "abbreviations, lumber" to "Z ceiling runners," with "furniture styles" as an unexpected bonus. There are line drawings or charts on every page. An index provides access. **NCIDQ**

Guidelines for Construction and Equipment of Hospital and Medical Facilities. Washington, D.C.: American Institute of Architects Press and U.S. Department of Health and Human Services, 1996.

> This title was first published by the U.S. Department of Health and Human Services. However, the Department's authority extended only to medical facilities owned by the federal government or facilities that received federal funding. Some state Departments of Public Health wished to adopt the document and came to an agreement with the American Institute of Architects for its Academy of Architects for Health to write and publish the standards. The title is updated every four years and has been adopted by approximately 20 states as constituting the

[handwritten marginalia: "Can equivalent?", "RA 983 .A1 C385 1983", "standards for accreditation of Canadian health care facilities)"]

42

requirements that must be met in order to obtain licensure for a medical facility. The states that have not adopted this title write their own requirements, which are based on this document in the manner of a model code. It should always be noted which edition of this title a state has adopted.

*Harmon, Sharon Koomen. *The Codes Guidebook for Interiors*. New York: John Wiley & Sons, 1994.

> Harmon has written *the* interiors code textbook and professional reference. The codes and their interactions are detailed. The lucid writing, organization, and layout of the book simplify this sometimes confusing subject. Bibliographies, a glossary, a list of abbreviations, a model building codes cross-reference chart, and a list of bookstores complete this tour de force.

Illuminating Engineering Society of North America. *IES Lighting Handbook: Reference & Application.* 8th ed. New York: Illuminating Engineering Society, 1993.

> This is an essential source for lighting standards. As IES says, the volume includes "...concepts, techniques, applications, procedures, systems, definitions, tasks, charts, and diagrams." Software for use in lighting calculations is included. The glossary alone makes the title valuable.

Kira, Alexander. *The Bathroom*. New and exp. ed. New York: Viking Press, 1976.

> Kira provides a detailed explanation of the function and design of one of the most important spaces in our environment. He presents exacting detail of all clearance requirements and all human experiences necessary to design the bath space. Despite being over 15 years old, the book retains its value.

Klein, Burton R., ed. *Health Care Facilities Handbook*. 4th ed. Quincy, Mass.: National Fire Protection Association, 1993.

> This volume includes not only the full text of *NFPA 99*, listed below, but also explains the application of the standards. The standards and the explication are clearly differentiated by different colors of print. This hardcover volume is considerably more expensive than the slimmer softcover *Standards*. Illustrated.

National Fire Protection Association. *NFPA 101, Life Safety Code*. Quincy, Mass.: National Fire Protection Association, 1994. (1997, 2000)

TH 9445 .P8 L54 1981

> *NFPA 101* has been adopted by the American Hospital Association and the Federal Department of Public Health as a requirement for hospitals, nursing homes, medical centers that are used by the public, and any other medical facility that is specified in the document. When a state or local code is more strict than *NFPA 101* in a specific regulation, the state or local code is applicable in that specific regulation. The code is updated every three years.

National Fire Protection Association. *Standards for Health Care Facilities, NFPA 99*. Quincy, Mass.: National Fire Protection Association, 1993.

> *ANSI/NFPA 99* is an update and compilation of 12 different NFPA documents relating to health facilities. Lists of referenced and pertinent publications, such as ANSI, ASTM, UL, and other NFPA documents, are included. Essential reference when specifying for health care interiors. Includes line drawings and charts.

o|o Nov|o1

*Panero, Julius. *Anatomy for Interior Designers*. Illustrated by Nino Repetto. 3rd ed. New York: Whitney Library of Design, 1962.

> This is an important standards manual for human-scale (anthropometric) design. It is a graphically entertaining volume which presents all the standards one needs to deal with spatial design. No index. **NCIDQ**

Panero, Julius, and Martin Zelnick. *Human Dimension and Interior Space*. New York: Whitney Library of Design/Watson Guptill, 1979.

Ref NA 2542.4 P356 1979

> This information is included in *Time Saver Standards for Interior Design* by the same authors DeChiara, Panero and Zelnick in this chapter under the General References section. **NCIDQ**

Przetak, Louis. *Standard Details for Fire-resistive Building Construction*. New York: McGraw-Hill, 1977.

> This volume is a valuable source of details for wall and partition construction. Some of this information is included in *Graphic Standards*, but Przetak provides greater coverage. Wall and partition information is based on the 1973 and 1976 *Uniform Building Code*. For updates on this data consult the *U.S. Gypsum Construction Handbook* cited below.

Reznikoff, S. C. *Specifications for Commercial Interiors: Professional Liabilities, Regulations, and Performance Criteria*. Rev. ed. New York: Whitney Library of Design, 1989.

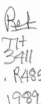

This is a useful reference tool which brings together regulations and standards, 1989 specification data from the Construction Specification Institute, information about interior systems and materials, and recommendations for managing drawings, schedules, and specification documents. It highlights the professional responsibilities of interior designers in regard to public safety and the attendant liability. The book contains many charts, drawings, and definitions, and is well organized and well made. **NCIDQ**

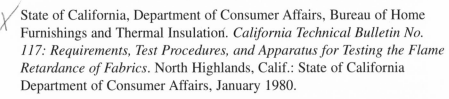

State of California, Department of Consumer Affairs, Bureau of Home Furnishings and Thermal Insulation. *California Technical Bulletin No. 117: Requirements, Test Procedures, and Apparatus for Testing the Flame Retardance of Fabrics*. North Highlands, Calif.: State of California Department of Consumer Affairs, January 1980.

This is the strictest flame retardance standard for residential furniture and has been adopted as code by other jurisdictions.

State of California, Department of Consumer Affairs, Bureau of Home Furnishings and Thermal Insulation. *California Technical Bulletin No. 133: Flammability Test Procedure for Seating Furniture for Use in Public Occupancies*. Rev. North Highlands, Calif.: State of California Department of Consumer Affairs, January 1991.

CAL 133 is a composite open-flame burn test required by the state for furniture that may be used in public live-in occupancy buildings. It differs from currently existing ASTM tests in that it tests an entire piece of furniture rather than individual components. This law became effective in California on March 1, 1992, and has influenced manufacturers on a national and international level. Compliance cannot yet be predicted for a piece of furniture prior to testing, but research is being conducted to establish a range of compliance criteria. *Technical Bulletin 133* is sponsored by BIFMA for adoption by ANSI.

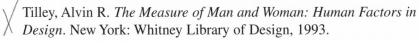

Tilley, Alvin R. *The Measure of Man and Woman: Human Factors in Design*. New York: Whitney Library of Design, 1993.

The author, the anthropometrics specialist at Henry Dreyfuss Associates for 20 years, addresses the technical aspects of human movement as it applies to environmental and product design. The book is well organized and graphically pleasing, is ADA compatible, and includes a glossary.

U.S. Department of Commerce. *Uniform Commercial Code, 1978.* Rev. Washington, D.C.: U.S. Department of Commerce, 1978.

Originally passed in 1958 in all states except Louisiana, this federal code governs interstate commerce. Article II controls sales and is therefore pertinent to designers who purchase *for* clients and then resell items *to* those clients. This form of sales is more prevalent in residential than in commercial design. Each state may differ in which parts of the code are valid in that state; some states and local jurisdictions have codes that supersede the UCC.

U.S. Department of the Interior, National Park Service, Cultural Resources, Preservation Assistance Division. *The Secretary of the Interior's Standards for the Treatment of Historic Properties with Illustrated Guidelines for Preserving, Rehabilitating, Restoring, and Reconstructing Historic Buildings.* Edited by Kay D. Weeks and Anne E. Grimmer. Washington, D.C.: U.S. Department of the Interior, 1995.

The *Standards* are unchanged, but the *Guidelines* have been updated in this most recent edition. First written in 1979, this brief document has been used to evaluate projects for buildings on the National Register of Historic Places, by the Secretary of the Interior to evaluate proposed work on properties owned by agencies of the federal government, and, though not required by federal law, by state or local agencies to evaluate proposed projects. There are only 10 standards and they are quite straightforward. The *Guidelines* interpret the *Standards* and recommend specific practices, all of which emphasize preservation of the historic character and fabric of a building. Interior concerns relate to the structural system, mechanical systems, and interior spaces, features, and finishes. There is a project underway to expand the Secretary's *Standards* to include historic furnishings.

U.S. Environmental Protection Agency. *Clean Air Act Amendment of 1990,* Washington, D.C.: U.S. Environmental Protection Agency, 1990.

The *Amendment* set standards which took effect January 1, 1994, for ozone-depleting substances (ODSs) that affect furniture manufacturing (some voc's [volatile organic compounds] found in adhesives and foam). Furniture made with these substances will have to be so labeled. Manufacturers are striving to make "label-free" products. Steelcase, for one, has achieved this status with some products.

*U.S. Gypsum. *Gypsum Construction Handbook.* 4th ed. Chicago: U.S. Gypsum, 1992.

> This conveniently sized, inexpensive handbook provides essential data for drywall construction, application, finishes, standards, and specifications. It includes hundreds of line drawings, black-and-white photos, charts, and a glossary.

Woodson, Wesley E., Barry Tillman, and Peggy Tillman. *Human Factors Design Handbook: Information and Guidelines for the Design of Systems, Facilities, Equipment, and Products for Human Use.* 2nd ed. New York: McGraw-Hill, 1992.

> As the subtitle indicates, this is a comprehensive volume. Sections that are applicable for designers include explanations of design criteria for all aspects of bodily functions and movement. All the senses are addressed. Accessibility information pre-dates current (ADA) standards.

There are three national model building codes:

BOCA Building Officials and Code Administrators International
(*BOCA National Building Code*)
4051 W. Flossmoor Rd.
Country Club Hills, IL 60478-5795
(708) 799-2300; (800) 323-1103

> This code is used primarily in the Eastern and Mid-Eastern regions.

ICBO International Conference of Building Officials
(*Uniform Building Code*)
5360 S. Workman Mill Rd.
Whittier, CA 90601
(310) 699-0541

> The *UBC* is used not only in the Midwest and Western states, but also as the basis for the codes of other countries and the design portion of the *Tri-Services Manual* of the U.S. Navy, Army, and Air Force.

SBCCI Southern Building Code Congress International
(*Standard Code*)
900 Montclair Rd.
Birmingham, AL 35213-1853
(205) 591-1853; (800) 877-2224

> The *Standard Code* is used in the Southern states and the SBCCI has
> developed its own standards for subjects that are not already covered in
> *ANSI* or *ASTM* standards.

Council of American Building Officials (CABO),
Board for the Coordination of Model Codes (BCMC)
5203 Leesburg Pike, Ste. 708
Falls Church, VA 22041
(703) 931-4533; fax (703) 379-1546

> The three model code groups formed the council in an effort to create
> uniformity in code requirements. The council publishes a supplement to
> the three codes in an attempt to reduce discrepancies among the three. In
> addition to codes noted above, it also publishes the *Model Energy Code*,
> 1995.

Two additional organizations which provide guidance in understanding
and applying codes are noted below.

National Fire Protection Association
Batterymarch Park
P.O. Box 9101
Quincy, MA 02269-9101
(617) 770-3000

> The NFPA is one of the largest standards organizations. In addition to
> the standards it publishes on fire safety, it produces the *Life Safety Code*
> and the *National Electrical Code*.

Fire Code and Building Code of Canada

National Research Council of Canada. Associate Committee on the
National Fire Code. *National Fire Code of Canada*. 5ᵗʰ ed. Ottawa: National Research Council of Canada, 1985.

National Research Council of Canada. Associate Committee. *National Building Code of Canada.* 6th ed., 2nd rev. printing. Ottawa: National Research Council of Canada, 1985.

Subsequent revisions have been bound with this edition.

Codes and Standards: Accessibility Standards—ADA, UFAs, etc.

Interior design professionals must be cognizant of the implications of the *Americans with Disabilities Act of 1990* (ADA) which took effect on January 26, 1992, and understand the special requirements that affect design. Clearance in layouts, aisle width, signage, and ergonomics (the physical relationship between workers and their environments) represent just a few of the areas of standards that must be incorporated into designs. The existing *Americans with Disabilities Act Architectural Guidelines* (ADAAG) have been enacted and are enforceable, and additional guidelines will be written, as allowed in the act. Legal judgements that result from lawsuits brought under the ADA may affect designers and should be followed in the trade journals. An understanding of what the ADA is, how it impacts a project, and which projects are subject to its guidelines are essential to all designers.

There are instances in which the ADA does not correspond with state building codes. In fact, the state of Washington has the only code that the U.S. Attorney General has certified as compliant. Because of this lack of clarity, in conjunction with the fact that relatively few court cases have been adjudicated under the ADA, many designs are vulnerable to lawsuits. Not only should all the pertinent state and local building codes and the ADA be consulted, but a briefing from the firm's insurance agent is in order.

As more state and local code jurisdictions voluntarily seek certification by the Department of Justice of meeting or exceeding ADA requirements, these difficulties will lessen. The building owner and other responsible parties will then have evidence of compliance with the ADA in the face of potential future legal challenges regarding accessibility.

The *Americans with Disabilities Act* deals not only with new construction, but with renovations and existing facilities. The act is in five parts, each dealing with a different area of concern. The act extends civil rights protection to all people who have disabilities. To be considered disabled under the ADA, a person must have a condition that substantially impairs a major life activity. There are five sections in the *Americans with Disabilities Act of 1990*, 42 U.S.C., defined as follows. Of the five Titles, Titles II and III are pertinent for designers and are addressed in the books annotated below. Citations of the laws themselves are in the prior section of this chapter, Codes and Standards. Additional sources of information are included in **Chapter 13, Professional and Trade Organizations and Government Agencies.**

Title I: Employment—prohibits employers with 15 or more employees from discriminating against qualified job applicants and workers who are disabled.

Title II: Public Services and Transportation—prohibits state and local governments from discriminating against people with disabilities in their programs and activities. The law requires bus and rail transportation to be accessible.

Title III: Public Accommodations and Services Operated by Private Entities—prohibits privately operated public accommodations from denying goods, programs, and services to people based on their disabilities. New and renovated commercial buildings must be accessible. Existing public accommodations must remove architectural barriers where removal is "readily achievable."

Title IV: Telecommunications—requires telephone companies to provide continuous voice transmission relay services that allow hearing and speech impaired people to communicate over the phone through telecommunications devices for the deaf.

Title V: Miscellaneous Provisions—miscellaneous provisions in Title V require state Access Boards to bring their standards, at a minimum, into compliance with the federal standards. It also allows for future standards to be added to the act.

Achieving Physical and Communication Accessibility. Washington, D.C.: National Center for Access Unlimited, 1991.

Provides information about four major disabilities—physical, hearing and speech, visual, and cognitive. Though this book was written as the ADA standards were being developed, it provides useful insight and information. Valuable lists of pertinent organizations and books are included.

*ADA Compliance Guidebook: A Checklist for Your Building, Meeting the Title III Provisions of the Americans with Disabilities Act: Public Accommodations and Commercial Facilities. New York: Building Owners and Managers Association International, 1991.

> This guidebook for accessibility in buildings under Title III of the ADA offers an explanation of the act and an evaluative checklist which applies to most commercial buildings. It is also available in software format.

Architectural Barriers Act (ABA) USC (code) Title 42, Section 4151, et seq. August 12, 1968, 82 stat. 718. Public Law 90-480. Washington, DC: U.S. Government Printing Office, 1968.

> The code states that "...nearly all buildings...designed, constructed, altered, or leased with certain federal funds since 1969 must be accessible and usable by persons with disabilities" (American Institute of Architects, Building Performance and Regulation Committee, *An Architect's Guide to Building Codes & Standards*, 3rd ed., Washington, D.C.: American Institute of Architects, 1991, p. 52). The Architectural and Transportation Barriers Compliance Board (ATBCB), which now also oversees ADA compliance, was established to ensure compliance with the ABA. The current revised code is U.S. Code 1988, Title 42, sections 4151 et seq.

Arditi, Aries, and Kenneth Knoblauch. *Color Contrast and Partial Sight.* New York: Lighthouse, 1995.

> Arditi, director of vision research at this well-known vision rehabilitation organization, has written a technical guide to selecting colors that enhance the ability of people with low vision to see. This brief brochure is available from the Lighthouse.

*Barker, Peter, Jon Barrick, and Rod Wilson. *Building Sight: A Handbook of Building and Interior Design Solutions to Include the Needs of Visually Impaired People.* London: Royal National Institute for the Blind, 1995.

> Universal design is emphasized in this excellent volume. The nature of visual loss and its implications for both interior and exterior design are clearly explained and enhanced with drawings and photographs. The titles in the extensive bibliography are primarily British in origin.

Barrier Free Environments, Inc. *UFAS Retrofit Guide: Accessibility Modifications for Existing Buildings, Designed to be Used in Conjunction with the Uniform Federal Accessibility Standards for Compliance with Title II of the Americans with Disabilities Act, Section 504 of the Rehabilitation Act of 1973, and The Architectural Barriers Act of 1968.* New York: Van Nostrand Reinhold, 1993.

> The UFAS has been in effect since 1984 for any building whose owner receives federal funds. This volume analyzes the modifications necessary to retrofit specific building types, such as restaurants, health care facilities, and mercantile buildings. Clear graphic representation of the standards. Discusses model codes and ANSI A117.1 of 1980.

Evan Terry Associates. *Americans with Disabilities Act Facilities Compliance: A Practical Guide.* New York: John Wiley & Sons, 1993.

> This volume is the same as the title below, but is in paperback format and does not include supplements.

*Evan Terry Associates. *Americans with Disabilities Act Facilities Compliance Workbook.* New York: John Wiley & Sons, 1993.

> This workbook provides survey instructions for facilities that are governed by Titles II and III. The clarity and thoroughness of coverage makes this volume an industry standard. The three-ring binder is updated by subscription.

Evan Terry Associates. *Pocket Guide to the ADA.* New York: John Wiley & Sons, 1993.

> This is an edited version of the *ADA Accessibility Guidelines for Buildings and Facilities.* It is a pocket-sized summation which offers good definitions and highlights of the act in quick reference format.

*Goldman, Charles, Barbara Anderson, Robert Lloyd, and Robert Ardinger, contributing eds. *ADA Compliance Guide.* 2 vols. Washington, D.C.: Thompson Publishing Group, 1990.

> The information in these large three-ring binders provides the text of the entire act, history, overview, and employment requirements of all aspects of the federal regulations, statutes, and standards. Coverage of court cases and monthly supplements are included. Glossary.

X *Kearney, Deborah S. *The ADA in Practice.* Rev. ed. of *The New ADA: Compliance and Costs.* Kingston, Mass.: R. S. Means, 1995.

> This is an excellent general reference manual for ADA Titles I-IV. It offers a good checklist with cost parameters and includes legal precedents, a product selection guide, and samples of compliance solutions. The presentation is clear, complete, and well organized.

X *Readily Achievable Checklist: A Survey for Accessibility.* Washington, D.C.: National Center for Access Unlimited, 1991.

> This volume provides a checklist for evaluating building accessibility and teaches the designer how to create an access plan and a cost summary.

X *Rehabilitation Act of 1973.* U.S.C. Title 29, Section 701 et seq., September 26, 1973, PL 93-112, 87 stat. 355. Washington, DC: U.S. Government Printing Office, 1973.

> The act is an outgrowth of the *Architectural Barriers Act* of 1968 and prohibits discrimination against individuals with disabilities by federal agencies and their contractors. Title V of the *Rehabilitation Act*, 29 U.S.C. et. seq., influenced concepts found in the ADA. Sections 502, 503, and 504 of the act are particularly pertinent to designers.

X *Uniform Federal Accessibility Standards.* Washington, D.C.: U.S. General Services Administration/U.S. Department of Defense/U.S. Department of Housing and Urban Development/U.S. Postal Service, 1985.

> *UFAS* was originally published in the *Federal Register* on August 7, 1984 (49 FR 31528). This publication includes corrections made subsequent to its printing in the *Register*. The *Standards* are "...enforceable minimum standards for the design, construction, and alteration of facilities required to be accessible under the ABA" (American Institute of Architects, Building Performance and Regulation Committee, *An Architect's Guide to Building Codes & Standards*, 3rd ed., Washington, D.C.: American Institute of Architects, 1991, p. 52). These standards also relate to compliance with Section 504 of the *Rehabilitation Act of 1973*.

U.S. Department of Justice. Civil Rights Division. "The Americans with Disabilities Act Questions and Answers." Washington, D.C.: U.S. Department of Justice, 1992.

> A simple question-and-answer pamphlet which deals clearly with issues of employment and public accommodations.

U.S. Department of Justice. Office of the Attorney General. 28 CFR, Part 36, *Nondiscrimination on the Basis of Disability by Public Accommodations and in Commercial Facilities, Final Rule*, Part III. Washington, D.C.: Federal Register, July 26, 1991.

"This rule implements Title III of the Americans with Disabilities Act, Public Law 101-336, which prohibits discrimination on the basis of disability by private entities in places of public accommodation, requires that all new places of public accommodations and commercial facilities be designed and constructed so as to be readily accessible to and usable by persons with disabilities, and requires that examinations or courses related to licensing or certification for professional and trade purposes be accessible to persons with disabilities." Effective January 26, 1992. Includes diagrams. ("CFR" refers to the Code of Federal Regulations)

U.S. Postal Service. *Standards for Facility Accessibility by the Physically Handicapped: Handbook RE-4*. Washington, D.C.: U.S. Postal Service, 1985.

This handbook outlines standards used by the Postal Service, the Department of Defense, H.U.D., and Special Services Administration for leased space. The ADA is derived from these guidelines. Indexed, good graphics. It is a good guide for disability standards for general use and sets very clear standards for the design professional.

Wilkoff, Wm. L., and Laura Abed. *Practicing Universal Design: An Interpretation of the ADA*. New York: Van Nostrand Reinhold, 1994.

Thoughtful design problems and solutions follow a lucid history of the confusing succession of accessible design regulations promulgated over the past three decades. Included are excellent bibliographies for each chapter and the full text of the ADA as it relates to design. The author is a fellow of the Institute of Business Designers and has written extensively about the application of accessibility laws to interior design. **NCIDQ**

Product Sources

Information sources on products and product availability are an essential part of a professional library. Manufacturers and suppliers are understandably helpful in providing specifications, illustrations, and samples of their products to designers. Sources included here may be either those which analytically present products and sources or information which is provided by the manufacturer or source and, although accurate, is more promotional in nature. The literature itself can take many forms: style surveys and sourcebooks, buyers' guides and directories, trade catalogs, manufacturers' spec sheets and promotional matter, and actual sample books. One should remember, however, that many of the style and/or typology survey books cited in the General References section of this chapter, or in later chapters of this book, will often cite product sources in appendices—the various Conran books are good examples.

Interior design magazines are essential sources of the most current products. Not only do they provide annual resource guides, but also the ubiquitous and convenient reader service cards in each issue. Each product is identified with a numerical code which is then listed on a tear-out postcard. The designer has only to circle the numbers of items of interest to receive further documentation for the product. As in all published literature, the shorter time required for magazine publication renders the information in magazines more timely than that in books.

The listings in this section of the Reference chapter may be used in conjunction with the **National Product Expositions and Conferences** listing in **Chapter 15.**

Bangert, Albrecht, and Karl Michael Armer. *80s Style: Designs of the Decade.* New York: Abbeville Press, 1990.

> Representing the avant-garde of 1980s designs in furniture, lighting, tableware, and textiles in full-color illustrations. Includes Memphis, Post-Modern, and individual visions of designers of note (for example, Philipe Stark) and students. Professional biographies are valuable, but do not include addresses.

Bullivant, Lucy. *International Interior Design.* New York: Abbeville Press, 1991.

> Installations by interior designers and architects for commercial and cultural uses are presented in large color photographs with plans and brief texts. As in the Abbeville International Contract Design and International Design Yearbook series, this series provides students with access to the current work of the best designers as well as information on

materials and finishes, addresses of suppliers, etc. Biographies of designers are cited. This series is also known as *International Interiors.*

NA2850 Calloway, Stephen, gen. ed., and Elizabeth Cromley, consultant ed. *The*
.E44 *Elements of Style: A Practical Encyclopedia of Interior Architectural*
1996 *Details from 1485 to 1996.* Rev. ed. New York: Simon and Schuster, 1991.

> The volume includes approximately six pages of resources in the United States for purchase of items, including architectural salvage houses. See full entry in this chapter under **General References.**

NK2117 Conran, Terence. *Terence Conran's Kitchen Book: A Comprehensive*
.K5 *Source Book and Guide to Planning, Fitting, and Equipping Your Kitchen.*
C66 Edited by Elizabeth Wilhide and Deborah Smith-Morant. Woodstock,
1993 N.Y.: Overlook Press, 1993.

> See **Chapter 7, Project Types,** under **Residential** section.

Emery, Marc. *Furniture by Architects: International Masterpieces of Twentieth-Century Design and Where to Buy Them.* Exp. ed. New York: Harry N. Abrams, 1988.

TT196 An authoritative, well-organized, one-volume reference which includes
.E48 excellent black-and-white photographs of 600 chairs and items for home
1983 furnishing designed by 100 international designers. This lush collection
provides brief biographical information about the designers, the current
(as of 1988) manufacturers of the pieces, and the manufacturers' addresses.

not same edition but older book by the author

Grow, Lawrence, and Dina Von Zweck. *American Victorian: A Style and Source Book.* New York: Harper & Row, 1984.

NK2003.5 Grow has written several specialized publications such as this which
.G76 present accurate information about different historic periods in residential
1984 styles and sources for appropriate services and goods for restoring those
structures. His publications are written for the informed homeowner, but
can be useful for professionals. This volume covers glass, hardware, wall
coverings, lighting, furniture, paint, fabric, and accessories. The sources
may be updated by consulting the most recent edition of *The Old-House
Journal Restoration Directory* (below), which is a source guide for all
historic periods of houses in the United States. Photographic illustrations
and line drawings.

X *The Guild: The Designer's Source of Artists and Artisans.* Madison, Wisc.: Kraus Sikes, annual.

> This annual publication lists approximately 250 artists and artisans who work in North America. Each artist is represented by several color photos; his or her name, address, and phone number; a brief description of his or her work; and the price range of the work. Indexes provide multiple access points. A selection of galleries is included.

X Habegger, Jeryll, and Joseph H. Osman. *Sourcebook of Modern Furniture.* 2nd. ed. New York: W.W. Norton & Company, 1997.

> Very similar to Emery's *Furniture by Architects.* 800 black-and-white photos represent the furniture and luminaires of 300 designers. Manufacturer's information, size of item, and supplier's name and address are provided. No biographies of designers.

Interior Design Magazine. *Interior Design Buyers Guide.* New York: Cahners Publishing, annual.

NK 1705. 158
2001
Ref.

> One issue per year, usually January, is devoted to sources of products, a list of trade marts and associations, and a calendar of events for contract and residential design. Some other interior design magazines provide this up-to-date information as well. This issue alone is worth the price of the subscription.

√ *Interiors* Magazine. New York: BPI Communications.

> Four to five "Preferred Resource Guides" are published each year in addition to the regular monthly issues of the magazine. Each monthly issue includes information about new products and provides reader service cards which may be sent in to request additional information. The "Resource Guides" are advertising supplements, each of which concentrates on a specific product, such as carpet, fabrics, or furniture. The information in these guides has not been selected by the magazine editors.

X *Interiors & Sources Directory & Source Guide.* North Palm Beach, Fla.: L. C. Clark Publishing, annual.

> The goals of this issue of *I & S* are similar to those of *Interior Design,* above. Both are cross-referenced to provide better access to information. Not all entries are found in both guides.

The International Design Yearbook. New York: Abbeville Press, annual.

NK 1510
- 158
1999
v 14
Ref

Stimulating collection of the year's most exciting designs in everything from furniture, lighting, and textiles to consumer products. Superb illustrations, thoughtful introductory essays, biographies, lists of suppliers. Each year items are chosen by a different, well-known guest editor. Inspiring!

International Interior Design Association (IIDA). Internet Website: http://www.iida.com.

Manufacturers' information is readily accessible, with the most current specifications, products, and color images, at the IIDA website. The user may search for specific items and then compare what different manufacturers offer that fulfill his or her requirements. Orders may not be placed through this site, but contacts are provided. Images and specifications can be downloaded and printed to show to clients or to add to the designer's own file.

Katoh, Amy Sylvester. *Japan, the Art of Living: A Sourcebook of Japanese Style for the Western Home.* Photographs by Shin Kimura. Rutland, Vt.: Charles E. Tuttle Company, 1990.

An idea and source book integrating Japanese and Western residential interior design. Of most use is the listing of sources. Most shops and museums are in Tokyo, but those in New York, San Francisco, Seattle, Texas, and Washington, D.C., are included. Glossy color photos. Reliable publishers on Japanese design are Tuttle, Kodansha in San Francisco, and Weatherhill in New York.

Miller, Judith, and Martin Miller. *Period Design and Furnishing: A Sourcebook for Home Restoration and Decoration.* New York: Crown, 1989.

Though written primarily for the layperson, the beautiful color photographs and intelligent text give this book value for the professional as well. It includes an index; a glossary; lists of interior designers, antique dealers, and auction houses; sources of fabric, fixtures, woodwork, and services; associations which may provide information; and historic houses and museums.

Nylander, Jane C. *Fabrics for Historic Buildings: A Guide to Selecting Reproduction Fabrics*. Rev. ed. Washington, D.C.: Preservation Press, 1990.

> See **Chapter 5, Furniture, Finishes, and Textiles,** under **Finishes and Textiles** section.

Nylander, Richard C. *Wallpapers for Historic Buildings: A Guide to Selecting Reproduction Wallpapers*. 2nd ed. Washington, D.C.: Preservation Press, 1992.

> See **Chapter 5, Furniture, Finishes, and Textiles,** under **Finishes and Textiles** section.

The Old-House Journal Restoration Directory: The National Catalog of Suppliers. Gloucester, Mass.: Dovetale Publishers, 1996.

> This is the standard source for original and authentic reproduction items for old houses, including building materials, fixtures, furnishings, fabrics, and for attendant services. The arrangement is informal, rather like the yellow pages of the telephone book, and includes photographic illustrations and line drawings.

*Sweet's General Building & Renovation Catalog File. New York: McGraw-Hill, annual.

> There is a *Sweet's Interior Design Catalog File*, but too much information has been edited. Designers use the more complete *General Building File*. *Sweet's* is the first stop for most designers when specifying a product they have not used before. It provides basic information about a product, specifications, and an 800 telephone number to a manufacturer's representative. The manufacturer's rep can then supply a technical information sheet of one or two pages describing the tests the product has passed and complete specifications. The representative can also discuss the best application of the product with the designer. It is arranged in the 16 divisions of the CSI format, so the "spec" number is consistent throughout the selection and contract process.

Capital, Rogers Building, Massachusetts Institute of Technology.
Welles Bosworth, 1937. Photograph by Peter Vanderwarker.

Chapter 2

Design Theory/Philosophy

The theory or philosophy of design that one develops motivates and infuses all of one's work. It is the "how" and "why" of practice. Comprehending the philosophy of other designers lays a foundation on which young designers gradually establish their own framework for design. Books included in this chapter are limited specifically to those on the theory of interior design. Regrettably, the literature of the field is not a large one and the selections are relatively few. The literature of general design theory, however, is quite large and from that extensive list one might recommend such Modernist works as, among others, the profound and far-reaching works of Gyorgy Kepes (*Language of Vision*, or his incredible *Vision + Value* series), Laszlo Moholy-Nagy (*The New Vision* and *Vision in Motion*, especially), Rudolph Arnheim, Suzanne Langer, Christopher Alexander, etc. These substantial works are mostly out-of-print now and hard to find outside of a good library or antiquarian bookstore. These and other excellent titles are found in the bibliographies of the books listed below.

*Abercrombie, Stanley. *A Philosophy of Interior Design*. New York: Harper & Row, 1990.

K

13

24

90

> This volume is thoroughly delightful and thought-provoking. Allusions and quotations from literature of all periods are woven through Abercrombie's own aesthetic. The chapters draw the reader from the outside to the inside and through every aspect of interior space. The

eclectic bibliography ranges from Heidegger to Emily Post to Edgar Allan Poe!

X *Alexander, Mary Jean. *Designing Interior Environments*. New York: Harcourt Brace Jovanovich, 1972.

> This is a thoughtful and comprehensive introduction for students to the process of design. Valuable illustrations; excellent annotated bibliography of books published prior to 1972.

NK
2110
.B33
1982

*Ball, Victoria Kloss. *The Art of Interior Design*. 2nd ed. New York: John Wiley & Sons, A Wiley-Interscience Publication, 1982.

> Though Ball's book is basic, it could not be called simple. Concepts, not just principles, are explored. High levels of practical and technical skills are given to the service of art. The author does, in addition, elucidate the basic principles and elements of design—the relationship of building structure to interior design, planning, organization, space, light, color, texture, and materials. Questions and projects for each chapter assist in developing analytic skills and design thought processes. Essential reading.

NA
2760
.C46

*Ching, Francis D. K. *Architecture: Form, Space, & Order*. New York: Van Nostrand Reinhold, 1979.

> Ching's third book, hand-lettered as are the first two, is a well-illustrated tool to teach beginning interior design students the processes an architect goes through in the creation of a building and the fundamentals of organization of spaces within. Design elements, form and space, organization, circulation, proportion and scale, and principles are the chapter headings which, taken in conjunction with the amazing illustrations, fully describe the book. Basic bibliography of classic design titles. **NCIDQ**

X Kilmer, Rosemary, and W. Otie Kilmer. *Designing Interiors*. New York: Harcourt Brace Jovanovich College Publishers, 1992.

> This 642-page paperback textbook is reasonably priced ($43.00) and covers the full range of pertinent topics, emphasizing both "creativity and skill." Included are black-and-white and color photos, detail drawings, plans, and charts; good bibliographies; and a glossary. Kilmer, Nielson, and Pile all strive to be comprehensive texts, but in so doing are forced to cover in one chapter topics that require entire volumes.

Kurtich, John, and Garret Eakin. *Interior Architecture*. New York: Van Nostrand Reinhold, 1993. 7.

The authors, both architects and design educators, express their view of interior architecture as fully integrating the design of the entire interior environment. They apply the case study method to a well-chosen group of buildings from all periods and give the reader a good feel for individual designers by quoting extensively from original writings. The plans and photographs are well chosen. Unfortunately, the quality of the photographs is uneven. Though the writing is sometimes awkward, the book is thought-provoking and is an addition to the literature.

*Malnar, Joy Monice, and Frank Vodvarka. *The Interior Dimension: A Theoretical Approach to Enclosed Space*. New York: Van Nostrand Reinhold, 1992.

This exceptional book is both accessible and scholarly. The coverage of the history, theory, technical, aesthetic, and ethical aspects of spatial design are clearly laid out. The format, illustrations, and allusions to a wide range of references are pertinent and pleasing. The authors consider both the art and science of interior design. For advanced students and professionals.

Nielson, Karla J., and David A. Taylor. *Interiors: An Introduction*. 2nd ed. Madison, Wisc.: Brown & Benchmark, 1994.

Nielson's book is a broad-based text for interior design students in the same vein as John Pile's 1995 volume and the Kilmer book from 1992, both noted in this section. Chapter headings indicate that all the usual topics are touched upon, from universal design to elements and principles of design and the ubiquitous history of design. A glossary, bibliography, numerous photographs, line drawings, and charts are well integrated into the text.

*Pile, John F. *Interior Design*. 2nd ed. New York: Harry N. Abrams, 1995.

Pile's book touches on seemingly all areas of interior design and will be widely used as a foundation text for students. It includes chapters on business, design history, residential and contract design, color, lighting, furniture, textiles, planning, and aesthetic evaluation. Appendices which support the text (symbols, perspective drawing guidelines, etc.) and a glossary and bibliography strive to make the book self-sufficient. The book is based on an earlier edition and not all areas have been updated.
NCIDQ

X Rossbach, Sarah. *Interior Design with Feng Shui*. Foreword and calligraphy by Professor Lin Yun. New York: E. P. Dutton, 1987.

> In her second book on feng shui, the author reveals the ancient Chinese "art of placement" to designers. As designers know, a person's surroundings affect one's sense of well-being; feng shui holds that they also affect one's destiny. By arranging those surroundings in a more balanced and harmonious manner, one's destiny may be improved. Whether or not a designer agrees with this philosophy, it will become more well known in the United States and designers should understand its principles.

X Smith, C. Ray. *Interior Design in 20ᵗʰ-Century America: A History*. New York: Harper & Row, 1987.

> This volume is comprised of the history, glossary, pronunciation guide, and indexes from the book by Tate and Smith listed below. **NCIDQ**

X Tate, Allen. *The Making of Interiors: An Introduction*. Drawings and illustrations by Amy Samelson-Moore. New York: Harper & Row, 1987.

> Explicit guide for beginning students of interior design. Includes an explanation of studio criticism, requirements of different types of visual and verbal design presentations, even which foods students should eat to sustain themselves through charrettes! It also outlines building elements and concepts of design elements from both historic and current perspectives. Excellent. **NCIDQ**

X *Tate, Allen, and C. Ray Smith. *Interior Design in the 20ᵗʰ Century*. New York: Harper & Row, 1986.

> Well-written, comprehensive introduction to the topic. *The Making of Interiors* by Tate and *Interior Design in 20ᵗʰ-Century America* by Smith were created by splitting this book in two. This volume includes interviews with designers, which are not included in either of the other volumes and which illuminate techniques outlined in the book. Good bibliographies, useful pronunciation guide. **NCIDQ**

*Whiton, Sherrill. *Interior Design and Decoration*. 4ᵗʰ ed. Philadelphia: J. B. Lippincott, 1974.

> Whiton provides an invaluable history of interior design and decoration from primitive societies into the twentieth century. It is written from an interior design, rather than an architectural, point of view, an asset that is recognized by the NCIDQ, which relies upon it for many exam questions. The book details the development and construction of design

materials such as floor and wall coverings, ceramics, cabinetwork, and hardware. Numerous black-and-white and color illustrations, excellent line drawings, extensive glossaries. The fifth edition is in preparation and should be published in 1997. **NCIDQ**

*Zevi, Bruno. *Architecture as Space: How to Look at Architecture*. Rev. ed. Edited by Joseph A. Barry and translated by Milton Gendel. New York: Horizon Press, 1974; reissued by Da Capo Press, 1993.

The elegant clarity with which Zevi describes and analyzes that "protagonist" of architecture—space—will make a permanent impression on any design student and cannot be introduced too soon in the educational process. One must be able to see space before one can create it and Zevi gives eyes to those who would see. In the process, he also introduces the student to significant works of architecture from Greece to those created in the twentieth century.

Stair hall at Berkeley Villa, Newport. Ogden Codman, 1910.
Photograph by Richard Cheek.

Chapter 3

History

The titles selected here are narrowly defined and follow the general guidelines for all titles included in this volume. Monographs on individual designers are excluded. These may be easily identified in the bibliographies of books that are included. Very broad histories, such as histories of architecture or art that also include interior design, are also excluded. The books that are cited are broad period histories within the specific field of interior design. Certainly monographs, such as Philippe Garner's excellent volume on Eileen Gray or Billcliffe's volumes on Charles Rennie Mackintosh, are very valuable, but they are also very personal choices. Additional titles that have an historic orientation are found in **Chapter 5, Furniture, Finishes, and Textiles.**

*Anscombe, Isabelle. *A Woman's Touch: Women in Design from 1860 to the Present Day*. New York: Penguin Books, Elisabeth Sifton Books, 1984.

> The title should not be misconstrued; this is not a "women's" book, but a wonderful history of design, which includes the professionalization of interior decoration and design. The text is well written and well documented with illustrations, footnotes, and bibliographies.

*Ball, Victoria Kloss. *Architecture and Interior Design.* Vol. 1, *A Basic History through the Seventeenth Century.* Vol. 2, *Europe and America from the Colonial Era to Today.* New York: John Wiley & Sons, A Wiley-Interscience Publication, 1980.

Scholarly, sophisticated, lucid history of architecture and interior design. Though architecture receives more attention in number of pages, the two topics are treated in their appropriately close relationship. The two volumes together are an excellent historical base for students, offering a stimulating overview. The chapter on the twentieth century should not be missed. Illustrations include black-and-white photos, line drawings, and some color plates. Extensive bibliography arranged by subject.

X Bayer, Patricia. *Art Deco Interiors: Decoration and Design Classics of the 1920s and 1930s.* Boston: Little, Brown and Company, 1990.

Good presentation of Art Deco and Streamline Moderne in France, Great Britain, and the United States. Private and public spaces are represented in contemporary and current illustrations. A bibliography and a list of museums that house collections are included.

Christensen, Erwin C. *The Index of American Design.* New York: Macmillan, 1950.

This title and Clarence Hornung's *Treasury of American Design* (New York: Harry N. Abrams, n.d.) reproduce 400 images from the watercolors of American applied and decorative arts created through the WPA (Works Progress Administration). These volumes include an index to the over 17,000 images in the collection. See below, Tinkham, Sandra Shaffer, ed., *The Index of American Design.*

X Eidelberg, Martin, ed. *Design 1935-1965: What Modern Was, Selections from the Liliane and David M. Stewart Collection.* New York: Harry N. Abrams, 1991.

Beautiful, scholarly presentation of 200 objects from one of the best collections of the period. The contributors' essays promote a true understanding of design development. Studying cohesive collections speeds the student along the path of understanding this period of design history. Good biographies, with footnotes, and company histories provide access to more information. Superb color and black-and-white illustrations.

Fehrman, Cherie, and Kenneth Fehrman. *Postwar Interior Design 1945-1960.* New York: Van Nostrand Reinhold, 1987.

Though readers will have seen the photos in other publications, the text is good and more thorough than that found in many chronologies. The explanations of methods and materials are good.

Gere, Charlotte. *Nineteenth-Century Decoration: The Art of the Interior.* New York: Harry N. Abrams, 1989.

This is a scholarly volume with lavishly reproduced period illustrations of European and American houses. Brief biographies of designers and architects and an annotated bibliography of a working library of a nineteenth-century designer are included.

Gere, Charlotte. *Nineteenth-Century Interiors: An Album of Watercolors.* New York: Thames and Hudson, 1992.

Beautifully reproduced watercolors of interiors are complemented by an authoritative text. Period illustrations provide a comprehensive picture of decoration, architecture, and furniture of the nineteenth century.

Gere, Charlotte, and Michael Whiteway. *Nineteenth-Century Design: From Pugin to Mackintosh.* New York: Harry N. Abrams, 1993.

Gere, a scholar of nineteenth-century decorative arts, and Whiteway, a dealer who specializes in nineteenth-century design, have collaborated to produce an authoritative volume with exquisite photographs of well-chosen designs. This book, as opposed to the two listed above, is devoted to objects, not entire interiors. The objects are placed in context through discussions of individual designers and movements. Profiles of designers and firms and an excellent bibliography are included.

Gore, Alan and Ann. *English Interiors: An Illustrated History.* Principal photographs by Peter Aprahamian. New York: Thames and Hudson, 1991.

Provides a strong background for the period 1066 to 1966, with emphasis on recurrent themes and decorative details. The illustrations are a highlight—most were made for this book and are therefore not repetitions of illustrations seen elsewhere. Not all illustrations are of opulent interiors and the contemporary paintings and drawings are well chosen. A chronology, bibliography, and list of houses illustrated enhance the book's value. Reprinted in paperback by Phaidon Press, Ltd. In 1995.

Jennings, Jan, and Herbert Gottfried. *American Vernacular Interior Architecture, 1870-1940*. New York: Van Nostrand Reinhold, 1988.

> The authors have provided a real service for designers working with the "everyday" styles of this period, rather than the lush interiors of the wealthy which are usually found in histories. Text and line drawings combine to clearly illustrate the elements (trim, hardware, mantels), service systems (heating, plumbing, lighting), ornament, and building styles. Primarily residential, but includes small-scale business and ecclesiastic interiors. Plan and isometric drawings are uniformly scaled.

NK
1980
.H37
1990

Massey, Anne. *Interior Design of the 20ᵗʰ Century*. London: Thames and Hudson, 1990.

> As with other books in the Thames and Hudson *World of Art* series, this is a reliable, small-scale, inexpensive paperback. The text is accessible, and the black-and-white and color illustrations are good. Selective bibliography, index.

NK
2002
.M39

Mayhew, Edgar, deN., and Minor Myers, Jr. *A Documentary History of American Interiors from the Colonial Era to 1915*. New York: Charles Scribner's Sons, 1980.

> The authors provide a substantial reference to the period, with fair and objective comments. The reader may choose to take advantage of the volume as a quick and easy reference, or gain deeper insights by pursuing the substantive notes and references to original documents. The bulk of the black-and-white period illustrations and facsimiles represent dwellings of common citizens.

McCorquodale, Charles. *History of the Interior*. New York: Vendome Press, 1983; published in Great Britain as *The History of Interior Decoration*, Phaidon, 1983.

> This history is listed in many bibliographies and covers the standard time period from Greece and Rome to the twentieth century. The text is very readable, with an art historical approach. It contains good, not great, black-and-white and color illustrations, including some period illustrations.

Parissien, Steven. *Adam Style*. Washington, D.C.: Preservation Press, 1992.

The title refers to Robert Adam, who, with his brother James, created buildings, interiors, and furnishings. Their designs and their practice of treating the built environment as a whole rather than distinct parts had a profound effect on subsequent design. The Adam brothers' influence reigned from the mid-1750s to the mid-1780s. The Federal style in the United States uses many of the same design elements.

Parissien, Steven. *Palladian Style*. London: Phaidon Press, 1994.

The Palladian style was embraced in Britain from 1715 until 1755. Parissien traces the style through both mansions and average homes. The materials, colors, fixtures and fittings, and textiles are discussed in context and presented in vivid illustrations.

Parissien, Steven. *Regency Style*. Washington, D.C.: Preservation Press, National Trust for Historic Preservation and London: Phaidon Press, 1992.

These three titles by Parissien comprise his series on Georgian residential design in England. The large format volumes are scholarly, accessible, and beautifully illustrated with both contemporary and current images. Each includes a glossary, biographies of designers, and bibliographies of contemporary and modern sources. The Regency volume covers the time period 1780-1840.

Praz, Mario. *An Illustrated History of Interior Decoration: From Pompeii to Art Nouveau*. New York: Thames and Hudson, 1982.

Praz is passionate about interiors, their lives and histories. His personal, philosophical, yet scholarly work amazes in the extent of its detail. The illustrations are all contemporary drawings and paintings of interiors occupied by the upper and middle classes. This volume presents historic interiors in their proper contexts.

Sparke, Penny. *Design in Context*. London: Bloomsbury Publishing, 1987.

One of the best histories of design, it includes coverage of furniture, architecture, graphic design, and product design from 1750 to 1985. Perceptively discusses the relationship of culture, industry, and mass consumerism to design and the designer. Numerous, well-chosen color and black-and-white illustrations.

X *Thornton, Peter. *Authentic Decor: The Domestic Interior 1620-1920*. New York: Viking, 1984.

> The outstanding illustrations, including period paintings, photographs, and plans; intelligent text; and overall superb scholarship make this volume essential for any history collection. A thorough bibliography is contained in the footnotes. Coverage includes Europe and America.

X Thornton, Peter. *The Italian Renaissance Interior: 1400 to 1600*. New York: Harry N. Abrams, 1991.

> This authoritative, detailed volume has exquisite period illustrations and a lucid text. The captions interpret the illustrations in such a manner that the significance of the interiors to present-day design is apparent. Superb coverage of the period.

X Tinkham, Sandra Shaffer, ed. *The Index of American Design*. Teaneck, N.J.: Somerset House, 1980.

> This is a color microfiche reproduction of over 15,000 of the original 17,000 watercolors held at the National Gallery of Art. There is a printed index to the images. The documentation of American applied and decorative arts took place in the 1930s under the WPA (Works Progress Administration), with the purpose of compiling an authoritative graphic survey of American decorative arts and crafts from colonial times to 1900. There are ten parts to the catalog, part six being "Furniture and Decorative Accessories." Textiles, ceramics, and metalwork are included in other sections. Four hundred of these items were reproduced in a 1950 book by Christensen; see entry above.

X Wharton, Edith, and Ogden Codman. *The Decoration of Houses*. New York: Charles Scribner, 1897.

> Reading Wharton's book is both a pleasant and necessary reading for anyone interested in the development of the profession of interior design in the United States. Although Wharton praised elegant simplicity in design, her definition of simplicity was based upon seventeenth- and eighteenth-century models which were beyond the financial reach of most of her readers. However, even middle-class homeowners found something to which they could relate in her philosophy and the book is still in print.

Wolfe, Elsie de. *The House in Good Taste*. New York: Century Co., 1913.

Both Edith Wharton and Elsie de Wolfe came from privileged backgrounds and De Wolfe designed only for her wealthy friends. She did a great deal to make interior decoration a profession in the United States, however, and a profession not only available to women, but also one through which women could achieve independence.

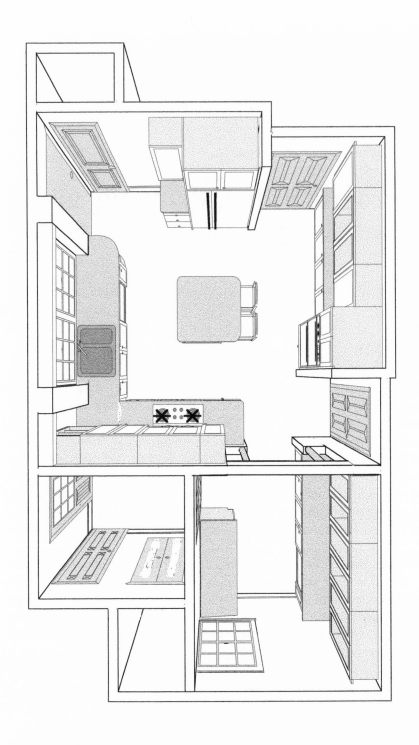

Bird's eye view, kitchen renovation. Robert E. Davis, Boston. CAD drawing with PlanitPro software.

Chapter 4

Programming, Planning, and Pre-Design

Programming or pre-design forms the foundation for all subsequent design and construction. During this phase, the designer defines the problem by examining the site and interviewing the client to ascertain needs. Research follows, in *Graphic Standards* for example, to determine basic dimensions, ergonomics, and spatial relationships and to prevent simple errors from becoming part of the larger plan. Equally important is to determine the client's active needs (how many desks, how many computers, etc.) and to gain insight into the client's perceived spirit of the project. Planning becomes geometrically more complex with the size of the job. In a commercial project, for example, surveying equipment requirements and incorporating that information into the early design is crucial.

Square-foot cost estimating, when one might use one of the *Means* guides, is a rough kind of estimating, used to establish an initial and reasonably realistic budget with the client. Costs are examined at each level of design. As one advances in the project, the numbers are firmer, with final figures when exact and/or bid prices from contractors, manufacturers, and distributors are obtained.

The titles included here aid in both theoretical (such as Pena or Norman) and practical (like Karlen or Sampson) programming and cost estimating, as in the Means guide.

Ching, Francis D. K. *Architecture: Form, Space, & Order*. New York: Van Nostrand Reinhold, 1979.

NA 2760 -C46 1979

See **Chapter 2, Design Theory/Philosophy.**

*Ching, Francis D. K. *Interior Design Illustrated*. New York: Van Nostrand Reinhold, 1987.

NA 285 0 .C45 1987 textbook

In this excellent introductory text Ching graphically touches on all aspects of design—theory, components of design, and building systems. It is particularly helpful for the early stages of the design process. His coverage of lighting is particularly good. The books in his brief bibliography should be required reading for students of interior design. **NCIDQ**

Deasy, C. M., in collaboration with Thomas E. Lasswell. *Designing Places for People: A Handbook on Human Behavior for Architects, Designers, and Facility Managers*. New York: Whitney Library of Design, 1985.

NA 2542.4 .D4 1985

Behavioral research enriches the programming, or predesign, phase of a project and thus the end product. Deasy states that the training designers receive alters their perceptions to such a degree that their intuition about client needs is skewed. This excellent volume translates scientific research into a language familiar to designers, allowing them to analyze client needs accurately. **NCIDQ**

Hall, Edward T. *The Hidden Dimension*. Garden City, N.Y.: Doubleday/ Anchor, 1969.

BF 469.H3 1966 ed.

How the social sciences might contribute to more human-focused design has been a longstanding issueSocial science information is often highly theoretical or in a format not immediately usable by designers. The work of anthropologist Edward Hall has been considered a major exception, however, and his studies of the "hidden rules" of culture at work in the perception and use of space are frequently recommended to designers. Hall's central thesis is that people from different cultural groups live in different perceptual worlds and thus do not share spatial or sensory norms. Although this premise may be controversial, Hall's work nevertheless provides thought-provoking reading for designers concerned with the relation of space and culture. **NCIDQ**

Harrigan, John E. *Human Factors Research: Methods and Applications for Architects and Interior Designers*. Amsterdam: Elsevier, 1987.

NA 2542.4 -H37 1987

Recommends specific scientific methodology for the study of human needs for the development of design criteria. Lists questions that should

76

be asked of occupants and details other research methods that enhance the value of the design for the end user. Methods are readily adapted to computer application and software programs are discussed by name. **NCIDQ**

*Karlen, Mark. *Space Planning Basics*. New York: Van Nostrand Reinhold, 1993.

This well-organized textbook has been written for classroom use by an experienced workshop leader in the ASID/STEP program which helps prepare young designers for the NCIDQ exam. It is designed for second- or third-year students and deals with spaces up to 4,000 square feet. Students will want to purchase most of the books in the bibliography.

Laseau, Paul. *Graphic Thinking for Architects & Designers*. 2nd ed. New York: Van Nostrand Reinhold, 1988.

Laseau's description of spatial relationships and bubble diagrams will be particularly useful in working out solutions to design problems in terms of non-representational graphic diagrams. An understanding of methods of diagramming a project in two dimensions in terms of spatial, program-matic, and environmental relationships in the early stages of planning is crucial to the quality of the final design and the efficiency with which it is achieved. **NCIDQ**

Means Interior Cost Data: Partitions/Ceilings/Finishes/Floors/ Furnishings. Kingston, Mass.: R. S. Means, 1994.

Interior Cost Data is a reliable source of square foot costs for both assemblies and unit prices for interiors. The most recent edition should always be consulted.

*Norman, Donald A. *The Design of Everyday Things*. New York: Doubleday/Currency, 1988.

Originally published as *The Psychology of Everyday Things*. Norman is an industrial designer, but the design process he propounds applies equally to all areas of design. The writing and logic are clear and persuasive. This book should be required reading for all design students. The bibliography is excellent.

X Pena, William, with Steven Parshall and Kevin Kelly. *Problem Seeking: An Architectural Programming Primer*. 3rd ed. Washington, D.C.: American Institute of Architects Press, 1987.

> The programming process gathers information about the needs of the client, allowing the programmer to formally define the problem that the design will address. The method outlined here is the one used by the architectural firm Caudill Rowlett Scott (now CRSS) for more than 20 years. This volume, with its simple, direct presentation, is frequently used to teach programming. Specific examples are included. **NCIDQ**

X Sampson, Carol. *Estimating for Interior Designers*. New York: Whitney Library of Design, 1991.

> This volume provides an accessible introduction to estimating costs for material and labor for carpeting, painting, wallcoverings, draperies, and upholstery. Line drawings and charts illustrate styles, measurement techniques, and work orders. More useful for residential work.

Sommer, Robert. *Personal Space: The Behavioral Basis of Design*. Englewood Cliffs, N.J:. Prentice Hall, 1969.

BF 469
. S 64

> Psychologist Robert Sommer has written extensively on the potential contribution of social science research to user-sensitive environmental design. This book focuses on status, dominance, and privacy in interior spaces. The first part reviews what is known about human spatial behaviors. In the second part, Sommer discusses applications of this research to particular settings such as hospitals, schools, taverns, and dormitories. A concluding section considers the advantages and pitfalls of various social science methodologies for post-occupancy evaluations. Even though the volume of environment-behavior research has grown considerably since 1969, this work remains a good general introduction to the study of the effects of environmental programming on behavior and attitudes.

X White, Edward T. *Space Adjacency Analysis: Diagramming Information for Architectural Design*. Tucson, Ariz.: Architectural Media, 1986.

> White is a prolific writer on this subject, and his other titles, particularly *Ordering Systems*, are worth studying. This volume offers a good source of procedures and graphic conventions used early in a job for the analysis of the relationships of spaces within a project. It is valuable for both students and professionals and is filled with usable examples of diagrams.

Hooked rug, "Beauport," Sleeper-McCann House, Gloucester,
Massachusetts. Courtesy of the Society for the Preservation of New
England Antiquities. Photograph by Richard Cheek.

Chapter 5

Furniture, Finishes, and Textiles

Furniture

Furniture design, one of the "useful and decorative arts," has long been examined and appreciated in the manner of the "fine arts" such as painting or sculpture. Any specific piece of furniture can be studied for its style, form, provenance, and precedents; its historical, social and cultural setting; and most significantly perhaps, as an example of an individual artist's or craftsman's *oeuvre*. To extend the comparison, furniture, like the various visual arts, has also been and continues to be collected with vigor and enthusiasm, both privately and publicly; most museums of stature maintain furniture collections with full curatorial and conservation support.

As a logical consequence of the serious approach to the study and collecting of furniture, the body of supporting literature and visual documentation is extensive. Publication trends follow, to a great extent, collecting trends. For example, European and American eighteenth-century furniture, which dominates most Western museum collections, also dominates the literature of the field.

Annotated below are basic sources for library collections. Furniture books tend to fall into three categories: general and historical surveys, museum and collection catalogs, and in-depth studies of the works of individual designers. This last category is not addressed in this listing; bibliographies found in the survey books will lead the reader to such titles as, for example, Thomas Heinz' *Frank Lloyd Wright: Interiors and Furniture*. Color illustrations should be looked for in period studies (the seventeenth- and eighteenth-centuries, for example) where rare woods, inlays, and elaborate upholstery are key features. For works on modern furniture, where line, form, and plain woods or metals take precedence, black-and-white reproductions often provide superior visual information (much as they do for sculpture).

As with any of the visual arts, the most desirable way to study furniture is the most direct: to experience the object in person. The aesthetic qualities of fine furniture defy reproduction in or reduction to pictures and words. Many of the books included here represent the holdings of significant museums or private collections. Therefore, these titles are recommended with an important caveat: students, craftsmen, and interior designers studying or working with furniture must use the books as guides or as inspiration to further their education and experience through visits to general museums, house museums, and auction galleries.

Aronson, Joseph. *The Encyclopedia of Furniture.* 3rd. ed. New York: Crown, 1967.

Aronson is comprehensive while remaining very readable. Coverage is biased toward European work between 1500 and 1800, but the book includes some coverage from Egypt to the twentieth century. This design-oriented guide is thoroughly illustrated with photographs and figures. The bibliography is arranged by subject.

Austin, Ken. *Contract Joinery.* Rev. ed. Fresno, Calif.: Linden Publishing, 1986.

Contract Joinery was written for the British Cabinetmakers Guild as an examination for students in trade schools and apprentice programs. It provides excellent text and line drawings about hand and power tools, materials, techniques, and specific applications. The high standards represented and the useful question-and-answer sections make this book an asset as a desk reference and when studying for the NCIDQ exam.

Boger, Louise Ade. *The Complete Guide to Furniture Styles.* Enl. ed. New York: Charles Scribner's Sons, 1969.

This guide is notable for the thoroughness of its scope and its scholarly coverage of its subject. Illustrations consist of separate black- and-white photographic plates. It does include coverage of Chinese furniture, but

80

not of twentieth-century design. The bibliography is extensive and is subdivided by subject.

Butler, Joseph T., in collaboration with Kathleen Eagen Johnson. *Field Guide to American Furniture: A Unique Visual System for Identifying the Style of Virtually Any Piece of American Antique Furniture.* Illustrations by Ray Skibinski. New York: Henry Holt, 1986.

> Graphic line drawings of furniture and details of furniture explicated by concise text make this volume a handy reference. The 1986 edition is a paperback and although it is too large for a pocket (7" x 10"), it is lightweight. A selected bibliography, glossary, and list of furniture collections in the United States enhance the value of this well-organized volume. **NCIDQ**

Cathers, David M. *Furniture of the American Arts and Crafts Movement: Stickley and Roycroft Mission Oak.* Photography by Peter Curran. New York: New American Library, 1981.

> Brief history of Arts and Crafts movement and development of Stickley and Roycroft shops. Illustrations of shopmarks, extensive photos with detailed information for identification and dating of pieces are included.

Cescinsky, Herbert. *English Furniture from Gothic to Sheraton.* 2nd ed. 1937. Reprint, New York: Dover Publications, 1968.

> Valuable, inexpensive reprint which describes clearly the development of styles in interior woodwork and furniture. Includes over 900 black-and-white illustrations with excellent descriptions pointing out key features. Approximately five pages of text on a specific style are followed by 30-50 illustrations of that style.

Chair: The Current State of the Art, with the Who, the Why, and the What of It. Produced by Peter Bradford and edited by Barbara Prete. New York: Thomas Y. Crowell, 1978.

> This book is based on the lecture series "The Evolving Chair," which was presented by the Cooper-Hewitt Museum, New York, in 1976. Eight designers and critics, including Ralph Caplan, Ward Bennett, Joe D'Urso, and Niels Diffrient, discuss the functioning chair and its evolution, and illustrate their views with modern examples. Appended to the main text are thumbnail illustrations of the complete submissions to the AIA International Chair Design Competition in 1977. The book is

imaginatively and provocatively designed with illustrations printed in very high contrast, a style typical in the 1970s.

Cheneviere, Antoine. *Russian Furniture: The Golden Age 1780-1840.* New York: Vendome Press, 1988.

> Exquisite photographs, primarily in color, of furniture and entire rooms provide excellent coverage of this period. The text describes the development of fine furniture making and provides biographical information for the cabinetmakers. The bibliography includes books, periodicals, and catalogs.

Cooke, Edward S., Jr. *New American Furniture: The Second Generation of Studio Furnituremakers.* Boston: Museum of Fine Arts, 1989.

> Published to support a unique exhibition at the Museum of Fine Arts, Boston, this catalog offers an especially fine survey of contemporary furnituremaking in America. Following a symposium at the museum in late 1987, 26 leading designers were invited to craft original pieces of furniture in response to a specific historical or traditional object of their choosing in the museum's existing collection. The results are described herein and illustrated with superb color reproductions.

Cooke, Edward S., Jr., ed. *Upholstery in America & Europe from the Seventeenth Century to World War I.* New York: W. W. Norton, 1987.

> Scholarly presentation by acknowledged authorities on period furniture and draperies. Sixteen color plates, many black-and-white illustrations— photos, line drawings, and reproductions of paintings of interiors. Step-by-step descriptions and illustrations of construction of chair upholstery and draperies.

Dormer, Peter. *The New Furniture: Trends + Traditions.* London: Thames and Hudson, 1987.

> Dormer's insightful, witty, and poetic history of modern furniture is beautifully produced. It has clear textual references to the color and black-and-white photos and provides a chronology of contract, residential, and art furniture; biographies of designers; a selective list of showrooms; bibliographies; and a list of galleries and museums.

Downs, Joseph. *American Furniture: Queen Anne and Chippendale Periods in the Henry Francis du Pont Winterthur Museum.* New York: Macmillan, 1952.

The Winterthur Museum has one of the best collections of American furniture. In this catalog, Downs provides a concise 20-odd page introduction to the origin of these styles in America, the terminology needed to understand the notes, and an explanation of variations in style in different regions of the country. There are color plates of entire rooms and excellent large black-and-white photos of individual pieces. All the original Viking Winterthur collection books were reprinted in a less expensive format by Bonanza Books. Both versions are out of print, but may be found in antiquarian bookstores.

Eames, Penelope. *Furniture in England, France, and the Netherlands from the 12ᵗʰ to the 15ᵗʰ Centuries*. London: Furniture History Society, 1977.

In this scholarly study of medieval furniture, Eames directly describes specific objects in public and private collections with a close analysis of correlated primary source documents. The author's intention is to illuminate the influence of medieval social concepts, especially courtly conventions, on furniture design. This is very dry reading but authoritative and well illustrated; recommended as the essential treatise on this early period and as an example of the fine, scholarly work fostered by the Furniture History Society. (Also issued in softcover as *Furniture History Society Journal*, vol. XIII, 1977.)

Fairbanks, Jonathan L., and Elizabeth Bidwell Bates. *American Furniture: 1620 to the Present*. New York: Richard Marek Publishers, 1981.

One of the best and most complete books on American furniture, Fairbanks' volume provides both good illustrations and text. Exploded drawings, line drawings, a glossary, and a comprehensive bibliography enhance the work's value.

Fales, Dean A., Jr. *American Painted Furniture, 1660-1880*. New York: E. P. Dutton, 1972.

A chronological survey of the type, including every manner of objects, from seventeenth-century New England to the American Victorian period. As with many surveys, the pace is brisk and the style vivid and readable. The author stresses regional trends and the historical evolution of style and technique, giving equal coverage to the established cabinetmakers of Windsor, Salem, Charleston, and Newport, etc., as well as the folk crafts of early New England and the unique designs of nineteenth-century Shaker and Pennsylvania Dutch communities. The book has become a classic, largely because of the enormous number of pieces illustrated and described.

✗ *Fiell, Charlotte, and Peter Fiell. *Modern Furniture Classics Since 1945.* London: Thames and Hudson, 1991.

> The authors, who own a decorative arts gallery in London, provide a thorough, beautifully illustrated look at postwar design, an area that is usually slighted in survey books. Detailed notes on individual pieces, notes to the text, and a bibliography provide scholarly support. Particularly valuable for designers are selective lists of international specialist dealers and galleries and museums with exceptional collections.

✗ Forman, Benno M. *American Seating Furniture, 1630-1730: An Interpretative Catalogue.* New York: W. W. Norton, 1988.

> This scholarly history introduces a catalog of the exceptional collection at the Winterthur Museum. The author, who studied and then worked at Winterthur, utilizes his understanding of both the physical attributes and cultural significance of the furniture. Black-and-white photographs, extensive notes, and a bibliography complete the volume.

✗ Gandy, Charles D., and Susan Zimmermann-Stidham. *Contemporary Classics: Furniture of the Masters.* New York: McGraw-Hill, 1981.

> Concise, authoritative coverage of seven designers from Breuer through Eero Saarinen, with black-and-white photos and uniformly scaled line drawings of their works, forms the bulk of the volume. Included is an intelligent discussion of design antecedents from the nineteenth century with lists of significant furniture designers from the nineteenth century through the 1970s and the movements with which they are allied.

✗ Gloag, John. *A Social History of Furniture Design from* B.C. *1300 to* A.D. *1960.* New York: Crown, 1966.

> Well-chosen black-and-white photos, reproductions of contemporary engravings and paintings, and line drawings illustrate Gloag's readable text. Furniture designs are shown in their social and physical contexts, not just as unrelated objects. Gloag has written numerous books on architecture and design, including the furniture dictionary found in **Chapter 1, Reference,** under the **General References** section.

*Hayward, Helena, ed. *World Furniture: An Illustrated History.* Secaucus, N.J.: Chartwell Books, 1965.

> Articles by highly respected curators, 1,000 black-and-white photos, 52 color photos, an index, a glossary, and a bibliography make this an

84

exceptional history of furniture. Numerous illustrations are clustered on a page.

✕ *Jackson, Albert, David Day, and Simon Jennings. *The Complete Manual of Woodworking*. New York: Knopf, 1989.

> Woodworkers will find this volume more valuable than designers, but designers involved in chair design or selection will appreciate it. It is user-friendly, with many (sometimes too many) illustrations. Its strength lies in illustrations of wood joints, with matrices relating the different types of joints to specific applications. It is a favorite with woodworkers, as attested by its recent fourth printing. Good glossary.

✕ Jobe, Brock, and Myrna Kaye. *New England Furniture: The Colonial Era: Selections from the Society for the Preservation of New England Antiquities*. Boston: Houghton Mifflin, 1984.

> This is a catalog of a significant, albeit limited, collection. The entries are detailed yet readable; the photographic reproductions are superb; and the appended bibliography is substantial.

Joyce, Ernest. *Encyclopedia of Furniture Making*. Revised and expanded by Alan Peters. New York: Sterling Publishing, 1987.

5 88o
J68
Ref

> Though written for the craftsman furnituremaker, much of this book is invaluable for the designer or student who has some familiarity with construction techniques. Clear photos and line drawings enhanced by textual description delineate different styles of furniture and construction, fittings and fasteners; how pieces of furniture and details are represented in drawings; and characteristics of different types of wood. The volume is valuable for any designer who is creating custom furniture.

✕ Kirk, John T. *The Impecunious Collector's Guide to American Antiques*. New York: Knopf, 1975.

> Kirk's unique method of teaching the eye to discern among fakes, furniture of poor design, and works of true aesthetic value will be a boon to any designer. Using a select group of objects to illustrate historical and stylistic trends, aesthetic merits, and telltale indications of authenticity, Kirk aims to train the budding collector to perceive an object truly and to trust his or her own knowledge, taste, and instincts—the essential facets of connoisseurship. The author is an authority on early American furniture and a prolific writer; any of his books, especially *American*

NK 2406
.K55
1982

Furniture & the British Tradition to 1830 (Knopf, 1982), are recommended.

Lucie-Smith, Edward. *Furniture: A Concise History*. London: Thames and Hudson, 1979.

NK 2270
.L82
1979

This is a readable, sometimes opinionated introduction for students to the history and significance of furniture from Egypt to the late 1970s. With the exception of Egyptian furniture, only Western styles are considered. The bibliography aids in detailed study of individual styles and periods. This title is frequently used as a class text as it is an inexpensive paperback. However, there is little original material and the content is too condensed for the book to stand alone as a text. Twentieth-century coverage is biased toward British design.

Metropolitan Museum of Art, New York. *19th-century America: Furniture and Other Decorative Arts*. New York: Metropolitan Museum of Art, 1970; distributed by New York Graphic Society.

This is a catalog of the Metropolitan's excellent collection, in the nature of that by Warren, listed below. However, the photos in this volume are not so fine as those in the Bayou Bend catalog. Furniture texts are by Marilynn Johnson.

Molesworth, H. D., and John Kenworthy-Browne. *Three Centuries of Furniture in Color*. New York: Viking Press, A Studio Book, 1969.

Superb all-color photographs illustrate this history of European domestic furniture from the sixteenth century to the nineteenth century. Each period includes a three-page introduction followed by annotated illustrations. Bibliography.

*Montgomery, Charles F. *American Furniture: The Federal Period in the Henry Francis du Pont Winterthur Museum*. New York: Viking Press, 1962. Reprint, Bonanza Books, 1978.

This volume is patterned after the excellent series documenting the museum's collection written by Joseph Downs (see entry above), the first curator. This volume also includes a bibliography and biographies of cabinetmakers.

Oates, Phyllis Bennett. *The Story of Western Furniture*. New York: Harper & Row, 1981.

Well-written and knowledgeable coverage of furniture from Egypt, Greece and Rome, Europe, and the United States. Includes detailed line drawings of furniture and interiors and a reliable selected bibliography.

Ostergard, Derek E., ed. *Bent Wood and Metal Furniture: 1850-1946*. New York: American Federation of Arts, 1987.

This substantial exhibition catalog (366 pages) comprehensively documents the evolution of modern furniture and is the best single source for the subject. The photographs are black-and-white, there is a glossary of terms, and the fine bibliography refers to primary and secondary sources.

*Pile, John. *Furniture: Modern + Postmodern, Design + Technology*. 2nd ed. New York: John Wiley & Sons, A Wiley-Interscience Publication, 1990.

Written by a designer with many years of practical experience, this volume is one of the first books to consult before designing or specifying furniture. The scope of the book is broad, including reference materials needed; the philosophy and process of design; pertinent engineering principles; the materials of design (metal, plastic, and wood) and their properties; and many photographs and line drawings illustrating good modern design, working drawings, joints, fasteners, and models. A dense, well-written, beautifully produced book.

Praz, Mario. *An Illustrated History of Furnishing: From the Renaissance to the 20th Century*. Translated by Wm. Weaver. New York: Braziller, 1964. Reprint, 1982.

Mario Praz was an important critic and historian of the applied and decorative arts. This title is a classic and, although not a textbook, is a delightful "must read" for anyone involved in these areas. The evocative illustrations are drawn from period paintings and drawings. Illustrations are color and black-and-white.

Richter, Gisela. *The Furniture of the Greeks, Etruscans, and Romans*. London: Phaidon Press, 1966.

Richter's is the standard title on the topic. It is thorough and scholarly, albeit rather pedantic. Included are numerous black-and-white reproductions.

Russell, Frank, ed. *A Century of Chair Design*. Drawings by John Read. New York: Rizzoli, 1980.

> Concise, intelligent introduction to styles of chair design from 1850 to 1950, with biographical information about primary designers. Color and black-and-white photographs.

Sack, Albert. *The New Fine Points of Furniture: Early American—Good, Better, Best, Superior, Masterpiece*. New York: Crown, 1993.

> Albert Sack is one of the sons of Israel Sack, a dealer in and authority on early American furniture. In addition to the thousands of pieces of fine American furniture that were sold through the firm Israel Sack, Inc., the files of Christie's and Sotheby's auction houses have been examined, resulting in the superb coverage of the subject seen in this volume. The first edition (1950) was reprinted more than 20 times. The author gives the designer the benefit of his trained eye, making functional comparisons which are based on aesthetic success, not just rarity or provenance. Side-by-side photos of similar items of differing quality with brief explanations as to why each piece is "good," "better," "best," etc. provide excellent training for the eye. Most illustrations are black-and-white. There is an excellent bibliography, which includes publications of collections and catalogs.

Shixiang, Wang. *Classic Chinese Furniture: Ming and Early Qing Dynasties*. Translated by Sarah Handler and the Author. San Francisco: China Books & Periodicals, 1986.

> This is a scholarly, beautifully produced, oversized volume with exquisite color photos and line drawings, which covers domestic furniture from the period 1368 to 1735, the "golden age of classic Chinese furniture." Included are descriptions of woods used, forms, joinery, and ornamentation. Glossaries and bibliography.

Spence, William P., and L. Duane Griffiths. *Furnituremaking: Design and Construction*. Englewood Cliffs, N.J.: Prentice Hall, 1991.

> The detailed, well-organized table of contents reflects the quality of the entire volume. Though the book is written for woodworkers, the line drawings and black-and-white photos clarify construction methods for interior designers and aid in specification writing. An illustrated history of furniture design introduces sections covering materials, construction, tools, and finishes.

X Stem, Seth. *Designing Furniture from Concept to Shop Drawing: A Practical Guide*. Edited by Laura Tringali. Newtown, Conn.: Taunton Press, 1989.

> Stem, who teaches furniture design at the Rhode Island School of Design, writes from the viewpoint of the artist-craftsman working primarily in wood whose work is destined for collectors. He emphasizes the process of design, with good discussions of the elements of design, composition, and proportion. He includes standard proportional systems such as the golden rectangle, Fibonacci series, and harmonic progression, and basic drawing and perspective techniques and modelmaking.

X Todd, Dorothy, and Raymond Mortimer. *The New Interior Decoration: An Introduction to Its Principles, and International Survey of Its Methods.* New York: Scribner, 1929. Reprint, Da Capo Press, 1977.

> Excellent black-and-white illustrations of furniture and interiors by Modernist masters, with a well-written enthusiastic text that expresses a contemporaneous viewpoint. It is an asset in understanding the Modernist aesthetic.

X *Verlet, Pierre. *French Furniture of the Eighteenth Century*. Translated by Penelope Hunter-Stiebel. Charlottesville, Va.: University Press of Virginia, 1991.

> Verlet, the late curator of furniture at the Musee du Louvre, wrote from an extensive and direct knowledge of French furniture and its context. His writings and connoisseurship are considered to have revolutionized the study of French furniture. This volume covers techniques, principle types, distinctive characteristics, and stylistic evolution of furniture of the period. Included are lists of furniture makers and illustrations of their marks.

X Walkling, Gillian. *Upholstery Styles*. New York: Van Nostrand Reinhold, 1989.

> The book is clearly focused on upholstery, separating it from the numerous furniture history books. It includes detail drawings which highlight design characteristics of each period, "how to" guidance to create specific upholstery elements, and the requisite color photos. Works and styles from the seventeenth century to the present are represented. Glossary.

Wanscher, Ole. *The Art of Furniture: 5000 Years of Furniture and Interiors*. Translated from the Danish by David Hohnen. New York: Reinhold Publishing, 1966.

NK
2270
W313

> Authoritative, well-written and documented history of furniture. Topics within the text are made more accessible by running headings in the margins. The illustrations, which are primarily black-and-white, are excellent and include photographs of individual pieces of furniture from different perspectives, drawings, scale drawings, and reproductions of paintings. Though the book purports to include twentieth-century furniture, that coverage is negligible.

X Ward, Gerald W. R. *American Case Furniture in the Mabel Brady Garvan and Other Collections at Yale University*. Photographs by Charles Uht. New Haven, Conn.: Yale University Art Gallery, 1988.

> *American Case Furniture* is a publication representing almost the entire collection of excellent American furniture at Yale. This volume is particularly notable for its inclusion of twentieth-century work. It is a scholarly publication with a brief introduction, bibliography, notes, black-and-white photography, and a limited number of line drawings.

X Warren, David B. *Bayou Bend: American Furniture, Paintings, and Silver from the Bayou Bend Collection*. Foreword by Ima Hogg. Houston: Museum of Fine Arts, 1975; distributed by New York Graphic Society, Boston.

> This is a catalog of one of the finest collections assembled privately. Owned and administered by the Museum of Fine Arts, the collection is housed at Ima Hogg's Bayou Bend. Although painting and silver are mentioned in the title, 90 percent of the catalog, which presents superb photographic reproductions, is devoted to furniture. The publication is somewhat typical of collection catalogs that have appeared in the past 20 years. Those of the Metropolitan Museum and the Society for the Preservation of New England Antiquities in Boston are noted briefly in this section.

X Watson, Sir Francis. *The History of Furniture*. Introduction by Sir Francis Watson. New York: William Morrow, 1976.

> This standard by Watson provides primarily color representations of elegant residential furniture from Egypt, the Classical world, Europe, and the United States. Limited coverage of twentieth-century and pre-Renaissance design is typical of most surveys of furniture design. Many

pieces are shown "in situ." Coverage is biased toward Great Britain. A well-defined, illustrated glossary and a good bibliography are assets.

X White, Antony, and Bruce Robertson. *Furniture and Furnishings: A Visual Guide*. New York: Design Press, 1990.

> A small, handy reference volume whose line drawings quickly differentiate an egg-and-dart motif from an egg-and-tongue design. The book consists of three sections: plates of line drawings of furniture, details of construction, and decorative motifs; an illustrated glossary of terms with references to the plates; and a time line of the progression of styles in Europe and the United States. No color.

Finishes and Textiles

Finishes and textiles can be examined through technical applications and accomplishments; evaluation of aesthetic success of the specific item or finish, as in a fine arts evaluation; or the success of the finish in the designed environment as a whole. This subject is usually taught in two parts, the technical specification of finishes, including testing such as that outlined by the American Standards for Testing Materials, and the application itself, how one uses the material or finish in relation to other materials and how this relationship is detailed. There are no really comprehensive books on interiors finishes. Certainly the standard texts like Riggs and Yeager are important for students. However, they need to be supplemented by texts on individual materials such as *J. J. Pizzuto's Fabric Science* and standards published by respected organizations such as the Architectural Woodwork Institute.

X Cohen, Allen C. *Beyond Basic Textiles*. New York: Fairchild Publications, 1982.

> Fairchild Publications specializes in fashion, making textiles an essential factor in its work. This three-ring binder is a textbook and workbook for advanced students, though a technical knowledge of fabrics is not necessary for comprehension. Chapters that are pertinent to designers include descriptions of testing procedures for textile performance; the nature of color, colormatching, colorfastness, and perception of color; and the construction and testing of carpeting. There is a good basic introduction to textiles, a list of trade and professional organizations, and a bibliography.

TS
1449
E42

Emery, Irene. *The Primary Structure of Fabrics: An Illustrated Classification*. Washington, D.C.: Textile Museum, 1980. Reprint, New York: Watson-Guptill/Whitney Library of Design and Washington, D.C.: Textile Museum, 1995.

> Emery is the "grandmother" of terminology for textile structure and technology, making this volume essential for anyone doing research in these areas. The bibliography and photos date from the first edition in 1966.

X Gordon-Clark, Jane. *Paper Magic*. New York: Pantheon, 1991.

> Although this book, part of a series which includes *Paint Magic* and *Fabric Magic*, is written for the layperson, it is one of the best of its kind and may be useful for discussions with clients. Includes a list of suppliers, a history of wallpaper, and papering techniques.

X Gray, Linda, with Jocasta Innes. *The Complete Book of Decorating Techniques*. Boston: Little, Brown and Company, 1986.

> Like the earlier book by Innes, *Paint Magic: The Complete Book* (updated in 1992 as *The New Paint Magic*), this title will be purchased by many amateurs. With clarity and detail, both books provide quick introductions to the mechanics of many decorative techniques utilizing paint and wallcoverings.

X *Hall, William R. *Contract Interior Finishes: A Handbook of Materials, Products, and Applications*. New York: Whitney Library of Design, 1993.

> Hall begins with a discussion of substructures, then takes the reader through the materials selection process required for any new or renovated building. Included are the properties of and manufacturing techniques for most current interiors finishes. Hall's realistic approach puts materials into a scheduling format which is used in contract documents. Students will find this book very useful.

X Haslam, Malcolm. *Arts & Crafts Carpets*. New York: Rizzoli, 1991.

> Authoritative and accessible history and analysis of the design theory and principal actors in British Arts and Crafts carpet production. Descriptive, exquisite illustrations, some double-page. Written by an Arts and Crafts scholar and a respected London carpet dealer. Bibliography drawn from both current and contemporary sources.

Innes, Jocasta. *The New Paint Magic*. New York: Pantheon, 1992.

This is a new edition of the classic monograph first published in 1987. It is written for the layperson, but can be used with clients or as a refresher for designers. It is well illustrated, contains a bibliography, and provides specific directions for applying the finishes described.

Jackman, Dianne R., and Mary K. Dixon. *The Guide to Textiles for Interior Designers*. 2nd ed. Winnipeg, Manitoba: Peguis Publishers, 1990.

Clearly written and organized, this comprehensive volume is both a student text and a professional reference. The book is a fascinating history of the development of textile production as an industry, linking fabrics to political, social, and labor developments across countries and centuries. Natural and synthetic fibers, fabric construction, finishes, and fabric selection and application criteria are presented in coherent charts and tables. Textiles as cloth, carpets, and rugs are examined. Valuable glossary. **NCIDQ**

Jerde, Judith. *Encyclopedia of Textiles*. New York: Facts on File, 1992.

Brief entries in encyclopedic format describing fabric types and production procedures, historic figures associated with fabric production and design. Primarily black-and-white illustrations.

*Larsen, Jack Lenor, and Jeanne Weeks. *Fabrics for Interiors: A Guide for Architects, Designers, and Consumers*. New York: Van Nostrand Reinhold, 1975.

Clear, concise coverage of the aesthetic and practical considerations required when using fabrics for upholstery, draperies, and ceiling and wall coverings. Professional approach to fabrics, including construction (with line drawings), characteristics, and specifications. Black-and-white and some color illustrations of fabrics and their application in interiors. Essential glossary.

Lynn, Catherine. *Wallpaper in America: From the Seventeenth Century to World War I*. New York: W. W. Norton, A Barra Foundation/Cooper-Hewitt Museum Book, 1980.

A scholarly and authoritative work which, in addition to thoroughly covering American styles, discusses developments in England, France, and the Orient. Hand and machine production techniques, preferences of specific patterns for particular rooms, hanging techniques, reference collections of wallpapers, and sources for wallpaper are all included. Color and black-and-white illustrations.

X Murphy, Dennis Grant. *The Materials of Interior Design*. Burbank, Calif.: Stratford House Publishing, 1978.

Murphy discusses the construction and manufacture of furniture, textiles and wall, floor and window coverings. Terms are particularly well defined and are further explicated with drawings, photos, and historical background.

X Neff, Ivan C., and Carol V. Maggs. *Dictionary of Oriental Rugs: With a Monograph on Identification by Weave*. New York: Van Nostrand Reinhold, 1979.

This is one of many reliable guides to Oriental rugs. Excellent detail color photos, explanations of weaving techniques and materials, and a bibliography make this volume particularly useful for designers.

X Nielson, Karla J. *Understanding Fabrics: A Definitive Guidebook to Fabrics for Interior Design and Decoration*. North Palm Beach, Fla.: L. C. Clark Publishing, 1989.

This is a succinct guide (88 pages) to the characteristics of fabrics and physical structure of fibers and yarns, fabric maintenance, design and professional practice. The illustrations are primarily black-and-white and a glossary and bibliography are included.

X *Nielson, Karla J. *Window Treatments*. New York: Van Nostrand Reinhold, 1990.

Nielson's well-organized book is *the* text for advanced students and professionals concerning all aspects of window treatments. Included are hard (i.e., shutters) and soft (i.e., curtains) design, specification, and installation guidance; period styles; energy efficiency; characteristics of fabrics and fibers; sources for fabrics, glass, hardware, and fabricating equipment; specification forms; advice on business practice; and glossaries of terms, the use of which are essential to good working relationships with tradespeople. The illustrations are primarily line drawings, with a few business forms and color plates for historic representations.

X   *Nylander, Jane C. *Fabrics for Historic Buildings: A Guide to Selecting Reproduction Fabrics.* Rev. ed. Washington, D.C.: Preservation Press, 1990.

> Nylander, an authority in this field, not only provides guidance in selecting and commissioning fabrics, but also characterizes the styles and uses of fabrics from 1700 into the twentieth century. The catalog is arranged by period, referring to documentary fabrics, and type, which lists nondocumentary fabrics. The volume includes a valuable glossary defining different types of fabric, manufacturer information, a good bibliography, and black-and-white illustrations.

X   *Nylander, Richard C. *Wallpapers for Historic Buildings: A Guide to Selecting Reproduction Wallpapers.* 2nd ed. Washington, D.C.: Preservation Press, 1992.

> Whether you agree with Andrew Jackson Downing, "We confess a strong partiality for the use of paper-hangings for covering the walls..." (Andrew Jackson Downing, *The Architecture of Country Houses*, 1850, reprint, New York: Dover Publications, 1969, p. 369) or Edith Wharton, who despised wallpaper, this catalog of reproduction wallpapers is valuable when restoring historic houses. Each period between 1700 and 1910 is introduced with an overview of trends in style and manufacturing techniques. Illustrations (both black-and-white and color), the glossary, bibliography, and list of suppliers provide excellent additional information.

X   Oman, Charles C., and Jean Hamilton. *Wallpapers: An International History and Illustrated Survey from the Victoria and Albert Museum.* Bibliography by E. A. Entwisle. New York: Harry N. Abrams in association with the Victoria and Albert Museum, London, 1982.

> This authoritative volume provides a history of papers from England, the United States, Japan, Europe, and China from 1509 to 1978. Wallpapers by both known and anonymous designers are shown and described, with biographical information for designers included. It is an oversized, beautifully produced volume with over 900 illustrations, multiple indexes, and an excellent bibliography.

*Price, Arthur, and Allen C. Cohen. *J. J. Pizzuto's Fabric Science.* 6th ed. New York: Fairchild Publications, 1994.

> This is a standard text for beginning students of textile and fabric design. In addition to thorough information regarding the construction and use of

Ref. TS 1445 P87 1999

individual textiles, the book includes lists of trade and professional organizations, a bibliography, and small black-and-white illustrations. A swatch kit may be purchased separately.

Radford, Penny. *Designer's Guide to Surfaces and Finishes*. New York: Whitney Library of Design, 1984.

Radford's book is a good first step in a long educational process for choosing and executing, or supervising, nonstructural, soft and hard decorative finishes for walls, ceilings, floors, and furniture. Opaque and translucent finishes, such as paint and glaze, and the techniques of applying and working them are her specialty. Good information on cleaning, preparing, and restoring surfaces. Residential applications.

Rees, Yvonne. *Floor Style*. New York: Van Nostrand Reinhold, 1989.

A tasteful, well-written, very basic introduction for students and laypeople to flooring materials, both structural and nonstructural. The book describes different floor coverings and then discusses the appropriateness of each for the various rooms of a residence. Good illustrations.

*Riggs, J. Rosemary. *Materials and Components of Interior Design*. 3rd ed. Englewood Cliffs, N.J.: Prentice Hall, 1992.

Basic introduction, with references to a limited number of brand- name products. Includes brief guides to installation and maintenance of finishes. Includes glossaries, bibliographies, and guides to manufacturers and associations. **NCIDQ**

Schoeser, Mary, and Celia Rufey. *English and American Textiles: From 1790 to the Present*. New York: Thames and Hudson, 1989.

Sumptuous illustrations, many in color, highlight this volume on "furnishing" fabrics. Fabrics, for both the wealthy and "common" person, are shown alone and in context. Useful, brief glossary of terms and processes in weaving and printing.

Teynac, Francoise, Pierre Nolot, and Jean-Denis Vivien. *Wallpaper: A History*. New York: Rizzoli, 1981.

Provides very good historic coverage of wallcoverings, primarily wallpaper, from 1509 to 1980. Numerous illustrations, both color and black-and-white, are identified and dated. Famous makers of wallcoverings and technological advances in the industry are covered. Very useful for relating wallpaper styles to specific periods.

Tortora, Phyllis B., ed. *Fairchild's Dictionary of Textiles*. 7ᵗʰ ed. New York: Fairchild Publications, 1996.

> This is a welcome update of the 1979 sixth edition. Each entry has been reexamined, resulting in extensive revisions. The latest developments in textile technology, all types of textiles, and many trademarked textiles are included.

Winkler, Gail Caskey, and Roger W. Moss. *Victorian Interior Decoration: American Interior 1830-1900*. New York: Henry Holt, 1986.

> The authors are fluent in the language of nineteenth-century design. Wall, window, ceiling, and floor treatments are addressed. Their very practical guidance may be relied upon, as their sources are the books, "ladies" magazines, and builders' guides of the Victorian period. The book is written for both laypeople and professionals. Glossary and bibliography.

*Yeager, Jan. *Textiles for Residential and Commercial Interiors*. New York: Harper & Row, 1988. have 2000, 2nd ed.

> This reliable student text covers the topic thoroughly, addressing fibers, construction, coloring, and fire safety. Analysis and specification of textiles for applications such as upholstery, window treatments, wall and floor coverings, and bath and bedding products are examined. The glossary and black-and-white illustrations are very good.

Detail, door handle. Total Communications. Manning Linder
& Associates. Photograph by Peter Vanderwarker.

Chapter 6

Building and Interior Systems

Building Construction, Materials, and Systems

In interior design, interior decorating, and interior architecture the building is the site. When the building is fully engaged as the site, the designer's thinking becomes holistic. The titles that follow treat the building in this volumetric manner, not as unrelated surfaces. These books are also useful to interior designers who are part of a team which may include architects, engineers, lighting designers, and acoustic engineers.

Allen, Edward. *Fundamentals of Building Construction: Materials and Methods.* 2nd ed. New York: John Wiley & Sons, 1990. 1999, 3 rd ed.

Allen's coverage of construction is more technical and more purely architectural than Ching's *Building Construction Illustrated* (see entry below). Only a small portion of the book deals with interior concerns, such as finishes and ceiling systems. Though an excellent book for architects, interior designers will probably find other titles more useful than *Fundamentals*. However, an extensive glossary of construction terms will be an asset to designers.

✗ *Ballast, David Kent. *Interior Construction & Detailing for Designers and Architects*. Belmont, Calif.: Professional Publications, 1994.

> Fuller descriptions of procedures and potential problems are needed to make this volume really useful. For example—what is the installation sequence for a wall panel? Again, Ballast says that one *can* wet-glaze, but does not say how. Despite this caveat, designers find this volume to be very useful. The bibliography of manufacturers' literature is of interest.

✗ *Building Air Quality: A Guide for Building Owners and Facility Managers*. Washington, D.C.: U.S. Environmental Protection Agency and U.S. Department of Health and Human Services, 1991.

> The EPA and the Department of Health and Human Services provide an authoritative guide to avoiding and remedying air quality problems in buildings. The volume is well organized and easily understood. The appendices provide information on common pollutants, definitions of terms and acronyms, pertinent government and private agencies, training institutes, a bibliography, and blank forms for review and analysis of IAQ (indoor air quality).

TH
146
. C52

*Ching, Francis D. K., with Cassandra Adams. *Building Construction Illustrated*. 2nd ed. New York: Van Nostrand Reinhold, (1991.) *have 1975*

> This excellent text is a must for students, providing a "quick read" for most building construction systems. Systems are represented by two- and three-dimensional illustrations in the wonderfully accessible graphic style for which Ching is famous. In addition to an overall understanding of structural systems, this reference provides good guidelines for lighting calculations. **NCIDQ**

✗ Egan, M. David. *Architectural Acoustics*. New York: McGraw-Hill, 1988.

> In this basic text, as in Egan's lighting book, the writing is straightforward and the illustrations (black-and-white photos and line drawings) are good. Bibliography.

✗ Flynn, John E., Jack A. Kremers, Arthur W. Segil, and Gary R. Steffy. *Architectural Interior Systems: Lighting, Acoustics, Air Conditioning*. 3rd ed. New York: Van Nostrand Reinhold, 1992.

> An essential text for students and professionals which discusses interior lighting, sound, and air handling systems for buildings. It is technically oriented only to the extent necessary for the designer to understand how

environmental systems may be utilized to the benefit of artful design. Energy conscious design is emphasized. Many line drawings and tables.

Guise, David. *Design and Technology in Architecture*. Rev. ed. New York: Van Nostrand Reinhold, 1991.

> Case studies of structural "types" of tall buildings, such as office buildings, laboratories, and museums offer interior designers comparisons of floor plans for interiors development. Structural design, code considerations, and HVAC design all influence both the exterior appearance and the interior function of buildings. This volume is not written for interior designers, but designers will benefit from its clear introduction to structural design. Plans and photographs are excellent.

*Ramsey, Charles George, and Harold Reeve Sleeper, eds. *Architectural Graphic Standards*. Edited by John Ray Hoke, Jr. [for] the American Institute of Architects. 9th ed. New York: John Wiley & Sons, 1994. 2000

> See **Chapter 1, Reference,** under **General References** section. (+CD-ROM)   1994-CIRC (also have 88/81)

Rupp, William, with Arnold Friedmann. *Construction Materials for Interior Design: Principles of Structure and Properties of Materials.* Drawings by Philip Farrell. New York: Whitney Library of Design, 1989.

> A valuable basic text detailing construction methods and materials for students. The layout is clear and pleasing, with many line drawings to illustrate construction details and material composition. No glossary. **NCIDQ**

*Salvadori, Mario, and Matthys Levy. *Why Buildings Fall Down: How Structures Fail*. New York: W. W. Norton, 1992.

> *Why Buildings Stand Up* provides basic information on structural design. *Why Buildings Fall Down* provides additional information and is written in the same accessible style.

*Salvadori, Mario. *Why Buildings Stand Up: The Strength of Architecture.* New York: W. W. Norton, 1990. have 1980

> As Salvadori says in his clearly expressed little book on structural theory, structure is unavoidable. He uses simple concepts and combines them to explain the workings of complex structures. Interior designers will enhance the quality of their work and their working relationships with other building professionals if they heed his advice. The book is acces-

sible to designers, has illustrations which are useful for classroom demonstrations, includes specific information about interiors, and addresses topics that are included in the NCIDQ exam.

NA
2840
• S73
1988

*Staebler, Wendy W. *Architectural Detailing in Contract Interiors*. New York: Whitney Library of Design, 1988.

Staebler offers the unusual combination of good detail drawings with quality color photos of the realized item. This reference manual provides an understanding of finished detailing which can be used by students and professionals. **NCIDQ**

X

*Staebler, Wendy W. *Architectural Detailing in Residential Interiors*. New York: Whitney Library of Design, 1990.

Residential Interiors follows the same format as *Contract Interiors*. Both volumes give full credits for designers, suppliers, and photographers. There is also a glossary in this volume.

TH
6010
• S74
2000

*Stein, Benjamin, and John S. Reynolds. *Mechanical and Electrical Equipment for Buildings*. 8th ed. New York: John Wiley & Sons, 1992. have 2000

This book has been a standard in the field since it was first published in 1937 and is used as both a text and a professional reference. The following section titles are dealt with in great detail, including numerous tables, illustrations, and appendices: Energy Overview, Thermal Control, Water and Waste, Fire Protection, Electricity, Illumination, Signal Equipment, and Transportation. It provides a common basis of communication among interior designers, architects, and engineers. It is very important to use the most recent edition. **NCIDQ**

X

Veitch, Ronald M. *Fundamentals: Detailing Fundamentals for Interior Design*. Winnipeg, Manitoba: Peguis Publishers, 1994.

In this very accessible student text, Veitch focuses on why specific details are used in specific instances, not on which materials are used. He covers basic joints, wood, case goods, cabinetry, floors/walls/ceilings, wood on walls, doors, frames, and glazing, glass, plastics, metals, and fixed seating. His line drawings are explicit and a bibliography provides further research for those who wish to pursue the topic.

X

*Wallach, Paul R., and Donald E. Hepler. *Reading Construction Drawings*. 2nd ed. New York: McGraw-Hill, 1990.

This concise, logical manual explains how to read a wide variety of construction drawings, thus aiding students in drafting and reviewing contract documents. Clear drawings illustrate details, and a comprehensive synopsis of symbols, abbreviations, elevation representations, and pictorial representations for plumbing, electrical, materials are included. **NCIDQ**

Lighting and Color Theory

Lighting

Lighting, like color, is both scientific and experiential. Each is dependent for its effect on the other. Without light, color cannot exist; therefore, the two elements have been grouped in the same chapter.

Interior designers typically do both the lighting design and specifications for a small project. On a larger project, an engineer would specify the general design established by the interior designer. Even larger, well-funded contract jobs are very much a team process, with a lighting designer working with the interior designer and the engineer.

Lighting books are written for this variety of readers—lighting designers, engineers, and architects or interior designers—although there are few lighting books that are comprehensive from an interior designer's point of view. By selecting from the titles below, interior designers should find the information they need. Please note the publication dates of books when looking for equipment and fixture information. This information is dated so quickly that it is only useful for two to three years after the date of publication.

Birren, Faber. *Light, Color & Environment.* 2nd rev. ed. West Chester, Pa.: Schiffer Publishing, 1988.

> Birren's concise volume combines comprehensible explanations of color and light theory with very specific recommendations for colors, complete with Munsell notations, to be used in different types of interiors. Commercial, office, hospital, school, and industrial interiors are addressed as well as computer facilities. Though the trend in color has moved away from some of his recommendations, his work is central to color theory.

X Block, Judith, and Rita Koltai. *Lighting Listings: A Guide to Lighting Publications, Research Organizations, Educational Opportunities, and Associations.* Troy, N.Y.: Lighting Research Center, Rensselaer Polytechnic Institute, 1992.

> This excellent little publication includes descriptions of English- language journals and names and addresses of foreign-language journals. Information regarding schools, government and nongovernment organizations, and trade associations is presented in a useful and concise manner.

X Boulanger, Norman, and Warren C. Lounsbury. *Theatre Lighting from A to Z.* Seattle: University of Washington Press, 1992.

> Techniques are frequently borrowed from theatrical lighting to create dramatic effects in contract and residential interiors. *Theatre Lighting* is a well-designed volume which presents lighting terms, illustrated with line drawings, in a dictionary format. A list of manufacturers and distributors and a bibliography provide interior designers with access to this related but less familiar territory.

X Brown, G. Z. *Sun, Wind, and Light: Architectural Design Strategies.* New York: John Wiley & Sons, 1985.

> This book is organized on the same "pattern" principle as Christopher Alexander's *A Pattern Language.* It deals primarily with daylighting, acoustics, how to use color, and shaping surfaces. Even though only a few of the patterns deal specifically with interiors, it is still valuable for interior designers.

TH
4915
.D8
E39
1986

Effron, Edward. *Planning & Designing Lighting.* Boston: Little, Brown and Company, 1986.

> This cohesive book is a stimulating introduction for students to electric lighting technique and lamp nomenclature. The color photos, all of residential applications, provide superb visual explication of the text. Additional line drawings illustrate the more technical elements of the text. A brief, helpful glossary is included.

X Egan, M. David. *Concepts in Architectural Lighting.* New York: McGraw-Hill, 1983.

> To the reader with some prior knowledge of lighting terminology and techniques, this volume will be readily comprehensible. Many line

drawings, but no color illustrations. Guidance on lighting and photo-graphing models.

Evans, Benjamin H. *Daylight in Architecture.* New York: Architectural Record Books, McGraw-Hill, 1981.

> Though interior designers may feel that their appropriate area of interest is artificial lighting, daylighting studies provide a basic understanding of how light behaves without the confusion of multiple types of artificial lighting. Evans' text for beginners includes good examples and illustra-tions and case studies. The first three chapters of the book are especially useful for students of interior design.

Gardener, Carl, and Barry Hannaford. *Lighting Design: An Introductory Guide for Professionals.* New York: John Wiley & Sons, 1993.

> The volume provides excellent color illustrations of current work in interior and exterior commercial lighting around the world. Basic explanations of the advantages and disadvantages of different types of lighting are given. Includes references, glossary, and a chapter on lighting and the environment. Technical information is biased towards British standards.

*Gordon, Gary, and James Nuckolls. *Interior Lighting for Environmental Designers.* 3rd ed. New York: John Wiley & Sons, 1995.

> This volume is thorough and reliable, addressing both the creative, subjective aspects of light and its equipment and components. However, it is written from a lighting designer's point of view in the language of a lighting designer. The text is appropriate for students of lighting design and advanced interior design students or experienced practitioners. The book is enhanced by charts, line drawings, and a good index. **NCIDQ**

Grosslight, Jane. *Light, Light, Light: Effective Use of Daylight and Elec-tric Lighting in Residential and Commercial Spaces.* Illustrations by Jeffery W. Verheyen. 2nd ed. Tallahassee, Fla.: Durwood Publishers, 1990.

> This is a basic, accessible book for design students and professionals. Rather than glossy color photos, it conveys information with clear diagrammatic drawings. The bibliography includes journal articles, which suggest magazine titles for perusal, and books. Grosslight's books are written for interior designers.

Grosslight, Jane. *Lighting Kitchens and Baths.* Illustrations by Jeffery W. Verheyen. Tallahassee, Fla.: Durwood Publishers, 1993.

> This focused volume is organized in the same orderly manner and illustrated by the same artist as the author's earlier, more general title listed above. Informative and thought-provoking, *Kitchens and Baths* will be valuable throughout the design process. Continuing education credits for certified designers are available when the completed workbook, which is available separately, is returned to the publisher.

Hopkinson, R. G. *Lighting: Architectural Physics.* London: Her Majesty's Stationary Office, 1963.

> The book represents studies conducted by the government's Building Research Station in the United Kingdom. The text is divided into two sections, a lucid introduction to light, design, measurement, and psycho-physics and, secondly, reprinted papers (1950-62) which expand upon basic information in part one. The book was written for first- and second-year architectural students and is still valid as a clear, concise introduction. Hopkinson is considered the father of modern lighting and his work is fundamental to later lighting designers such as Lam.

TH
7703
.H65
(1969)

Hopkinson, R. G., and J. D. Kay. *The Lighting of Buildings.* London: Faber and Faber, 1972. 1969

> Reiterates the principles stated in Hopkinson's *Lighting* book of 1963, then discusses lighting for specific building types, such as schools, hospitals, factories, residences, and buildings in the tropics.

REF
TH
4161
.I46
1983

*Illuminating Engineering Society of North America. *IES Lighting Handbook: Reference & Application.* 8th ed. New York: Illuminating Engineering Society, 1993. 5th - 1981

> See **Chapter 1, Reference,** under **Codes and Standards** section.

(3 v)

Jankowski, Wanda. *The Best of Lighting Design.* New York: PBC International, 1987.

> A well-designed book which presents award-winning lighting installations arranged by project type, i.e., hotels, museums, offices, retail, and outdoor spaces. All illustrations are large, color, and high quality. A concise text documents each project. A valuable idea book, written by a former editor of *Lighting Design + Application.*

✗ *Lam, William. *Perception and Lighting as Formgivers for Architecture.*
Edited by Christopher Hugh Ripman. New York: Van Nostrand Reinhold,
1992.

> The Van Nostrand Reinhold volume contains the same information as the
> McGraw-Hill title from 1977. Lam, as a member of the "perception"
> school of lighting, emphasizes the qualitative value of lighting rather than
> the laboratory-oriented quantitative approach as propounded by the
> Illuminating Engineering Society. Though Lam derides the quantitative
> approach in which "...there is rarely an attempt to articulate the desir-
> able, only an attempt to avoid or mitigate the intolerable.", he is very
> specific about the quantitative process. After detailing how one sees and
> perceives, he describes the process of design and applies his methods to
> specific cases. Well illustrated.

✗ Lighting Technologies. *Lumen Micro #7*. Boulder, Colo.: Lighting Technologies, current release.

> This is a Microsoft Windows-based computer software system which
> assists in specifying fixtures. The database contains over 15,000 fixtures
> and will be useful to anyone involved in fixture selection. The publisher
> plans to offer updates to owners for a nominal fee.

✗ Moore, Fuller. *Concepts and Practice of Architectural Daylighting*. New
York: Van Nostrand Reinhold, 1985.

> This student text provides full explanations of lighting terms, illustrated
> with excellent diagrams. The chapters on perception, how the eye sees,
> and lighting history are useful for interior designers.

✗ *Plummer, Henry. *Poetics of Light*. A + U: Architecture and Urbanism,
Extra Edition. Tokyo: A + U Publishing, December 1987.

> In exquisite photographs Plummer evokes the various possibilities of
> natural light as applied to both exteriors and interiors of buildings and
> streetscapes from many time periods. The text and photos provide an
> excellent introduction to the "feel" of light, something which few
> technically oriented books achieve. Pertinent quotations from designers
> such as Bernard Rudofsky and Louis Kahn further enhance an excellent
> publication. Text in English and Japanese.

✗ *Smith, Fran Kellogg, and Fred J. Bertolone. *Bringing Interiors to Light.* New York: Whitney Library of Design, 1986.

> Smith's book is both technical and readable, but does assume a basic knowledge of terms and techniques. The concepts are clear and presented from an interior designer's point of view. Good analysis of case studies. Unfortunately, the equipment section is outdated. **NCIDQ**

TH
7703
.S78
1990

*Steffy, Gary R. *Architectural Lighting Design.* New York: Van Nostrand Reinhold, 1990.

> Comprehensive, up-to-date, well-written book for the advanced student and professional, written by the president of the International Association of Lighting Designers. The book provides guidance for programming, documentation (i.e., specifications, shop drawings), concept development, and utilization of design tools. There is no glossary, so students will need another source for defining unfamiliar terms. **NCIDQ**

✗ *Stein, Benjamin, and John S. Reynolds. *Mechanical and Electrical Equipment for Buildings.* 8th ed. New York: John Wiley & Sons, 1992.

> This book has been a standard in the field since it was first published in 1937 and is used as both a text and a professional reference. The following section titles are dealt with in great detail, including numerous tables, illustrations, and appendices: Energy Overview, Thermal Control, Water and Waste, Fire Protection, Electricity, Illumination, Signal Equipment, and Transportation. It provides a common basis of communication among interior designers, architects, and engineers. It is very important to use the most recent edition. **NCIDQ**

✗ Whitehead, Randall. *Residential Lighting: Creating Dynamic Living Spaces.* Washington, D.C.: American Institute of Architects Press, 1993.

> Exquisite color photographs convey how lighting can enhance interior space. Lighting is treated as a design element, as part of the process, not an afterthought. Small line drawings and brief texts explicate the designs. All professionals are fully credited for their work.

Color

There are three distinct sources of color information for designers. Few, if any, single books answer the design teacher's need for a thorough text in teaching color. Scientifically based books are best for analyzing or explaining how color is manipulated by the light source (additive color). Color theory tends to focus on subtractive color, which is pigmentary. Most color theory books are intended for artists, not interior designers. It is necessary to study theory before moving on to an understanding of the effects of color in three dimensions—the application of color in interiors. In fact, color must be mixed or woven to be understood. Without this experiential understanding color will always be intimidating. The sheer quantity of color in an interior affects how it is handled, adding to the need for books which deal specifically with the use of color in interior design. Many fewer titles are written about the role of color in interior design practice than about basic color theory, such as those books written by Albers and Itten. The intensity of interest and research in color in design has fluctuated with alternating trends emphasizing either form or color. Publications have followed these trends. Fortunately, several good books on color from an interiors point of view have recently been published. Color as it is used by designers is also discussed in some of the general interior design books. John Pile's *Interior Design*, for example, is useful in understanding how to put a palette together.

Albers, Josef. *Interaction of Color*. New Haven, Conn.: Yale University Press, 1963. *have 1975, Rev. ed.*

> As a teacher of color and design at the Bauhaus and of color at Yale, Albers' theory of teaching color, as set forth in this volume, is particularly valuable.

Birren, Faber. *Color and Human Response*. New York: Van Nostrand Reinhold, (1984.) *1978.*

> Other titles by Birren are really more useful than this quirky volume which dictates what color should be used in what setting. **NCIDQ**

*Birren, Faber. *Principles of Color: A Review of Past Traditions and Modern Theories of Color Harmony*. 2nd ed. West Chester, Pa.: Schiffer Publishing, 1987.

> Essential basic book on color theory by an acknowledged authority. The book is concise and easily understood. In three sections Birren sets forth the history of color theory as propounded by mid-nineteenth-century Frenchman M. E. Chevreul; Birren's principles of "the harmony of color forms," as derived from Chevreul; and Birren's forward-looking, "new perception," in which the designer's knowledge of perception allows him to create qualities that do not exist externally, but are real in the mind's

eye of the viewer. The illustrations are precise and well integrated with the text.

Buckley, Mary, and David Baum. *Color Theory: A Guide to Information Sources*. Detroit: Gale Research, 1975.

> Though this volume is dated, it does provide concise annotations for color-related titles from a wide range of perspectives.

Chevreul, M. E. *The Principles of Harmony and Contrast of Colors and Their Applications to the Arts*. Rev. ed. with an introduction by Faber Birren. West Chester, Pa.: Schiffer Publishing, 1987.

> The first English edition of Chevreul, a chemist, was published in 1854 and several important color theorists have based their work on his treatise.

*Fisher, Mary Pat, and Paul Zelanski. *Color*. 2nd ed. Upper Saddle River, N.J.: Prentice Hall, 1994.

> *Color* provides a clear explanation of the process that leads from color theory to practice, which is the three-dimensional application of color. Although the book leans more towards the fine arts than interior design, it is not so specific as to lessen its value for practitioners. It is also valuable as a class text, covering a broad range of aspects of color, physics, history, paint and color mixing, lighting, and psychology of color.

Gerritsen, Frans. *Evolution in Color*. West Chester, Pa.: Schiffer Publishing, 1982.

> This title is specifically useful in color classes for its history of the development of color systems.

Gerritsen, Frans. *Theory and Practice of Color: A Color Theory Based on the Laws of Perception*. New York: Van Nostrand Reinhold, 1975.

> *Theory and Practice* is a good general class text, or as an added reference for a class.

Goethe, Johann Wolfgang von. *Goethe's Color Theory*. Edited by Rupprecht Mathaei; translated by Herb Aach. New York: Van Nostrand Reinhold, 1971.

110

Goethe is difficult to read and is read by color specialists out of respect for his groundbreaking work. This series of essays served as a catalyst for the work of Chevreul, Birren, and others.

*Halse, Albert O. *The Use of Color in Interiors*. 2nd ed. New York: McGraw-Hill, 1978.

Well-written, well-presented, and thorough coverage of color theory and its application in finishes, furniture, and furnishings. Includes a relevant discussion of historic precedents in the Ancient World, Europe, the United States, and the Orient. Excellent tables and glossaries. Description of paint includes both how paint is made and how different companies present, identify, and mix their colors and how a designer mixes his own colors. Practical and scholarly. The book is dated in several aspects—the illustrations and an excess of rules; for example, he insists that all ceilings be white.

*Holtzschue, Linda. *Understanding Color: An Introduction for Designers*. New York: Van Nostrand Reinhold, 1995.

This is the most broad-based of the current color books for interior design practitioners and students. Information for graphic designers and printers is included. The glossary, bibliography, and the 15-page student workbook add to the book's value as a textbook.

*Hope, Augustine, and Margaret Walch. *The Color Compendium*. New York: Van Nostrand Reinhold, 1990.

This excellent color reference for Western cultures is essential for schools of interior design. Published by Van Nostrand Reinhold, who has published important works on color for over 20 years, it includes authoritative encyclopedic entries, signed essays, palettes of historic colors, a list of international color organizations, descriptions of color specifying systems, a bibliography, and beautiful and pertinent illustrations.

Itten, Johannes. *The Art of Color: The Subjective Experience and Objective Rationale of Color*. New York: Van Nostrand Reinhold, 1973.

Itten summarizes the intuitive approach to teaching color which he developed at the Bauhaus. His color theory is based on seven color contrasts, or harmonies. Other authors may explain five of the seven well, but Itten is consistent and clear about all seven.

TEXTBOOK

ND
1493
.I8
I813
1970

Itten, Johannes. *The Elements of Color*. Edited by Faber Birren. New York: Van Nostrand Reinhold, 1970.

> This is a condensed version of the title listed above, providing fewer plates.

NK
2115.5
.C6
L39
1989

Ladau, Robert R., Brent K. Smith, and Jennifer Place. *Color in Interior Design and Architecture*. New York: Van Nostrand Reinhold, 1989.

> This comprehensive text for students and professionals explains how color is used in three dimensions to achieve both technical and behavioral results. High-quality photos, a glossary, and a bibliography enhance the text.

X Linton, Harold. *Color Consulting: A Survey of International Color Design*. New York: Van Nostrand Reinhold, 1991.

> Color forecasting is an important tool for interior designers. In addition to the many photos of installations, this volume discusses the educational preparation necessary for a career in color consulting, lists international color organizations, and contains useful references on a subject that is not well documented outside the technical literature of color. Bibliography.

BF
789
.C7
M24
1987

Mahnke, Frank H., and Rudolf H. Mahnke. *Color and Light in Man-made Environments*. New York: Van Nostrand Reinhold, 1987.

> The explanation of the psychology of color offered by the Mahnkes, who are architects, is the most useful one for current design practice. They speak to color and light in the three-dimensional sense, which is essential for interior design.

NA
2795
.M35
1996b

Mahnke, Frank H. *Color, Environment, and Human Response: An Interdisciplinary Understanding of Color and Its Use as a Beneficial Element in the Design of the Architectural Environment*. New York: Van Nostrand Reinhold, 1996.

> The Mahnkes have pursued the themes set out in their earlier volume. This is an important title for any school's color collection.

X Marberry, Sara, and Laurie Zagon. *The Power of Color: Creating Healthy Interior Spaces*. New York: John Wiley, 1995.

> The premise that humans have a physiological need for full spectrum colors in interiors and that utilizing full spectrum colors will enhance the healthfulness of an interior is explicated in a practical manner. The text

recounts the history of color in healing, covers color mixing and theory, and then provides application suggestions. A bibliography and list of additional resources are included.

Munsell, Albert H. *A Color Notation: An Illustrated System Defining All Colors and Their Relations by Measured Scales of Hue, Value, and Chrome*. 1905. Reprint, Munsell Color, 1947.

> Munsell charts are a crucial part of color theory, providing a means of consistently cataloging color. His sphere depicting colors through all their changes produces truer colors than the Ostwald system. The Munsell color notation system is used by historic finish consultants.

Munsell, Albert H. *A Grammar of Color*. Edited by Faber Birren. New York: Van Nostrand Reinhold, 1969.

> Ostwald was the first theoretician to systematize the cataloging of all colors. His color representations had the disadvantage of producing some colors that were muddy and disappeared. Munsell improved on the Ostwald model.

Poore, Jonathan. *Interior Color by Design: A Design Tool for Architects, Interior Designers, and Home Owners*. Rockport, Mass.: Rockport Publishers, 1994.

> Poore's visually delightful book is an excellent handbook for new professionals. He quickly goes through basic attributes of color, how colors mix, color scheme systems, and basic architectural applications. The book is philosophical and imaginative and goes well beyond the basics mentioned above.

Rossbach, Sarah, and Lin Yun. *Living Color: Master Lin Yun's Guide to Feng Shui and the Art of Color*. New York: Kodansha International, 1994.

> Those familiar with the authors' *Interior Design with Feng Shui* (see entry in **Chapter 2**) will know what to expect in this follow-up volume. Rossbach explains color theory, in philosophy and application, as practiced by Lin Yun, the spiritual leader of the Black Sect Tantric Buddists. Lin Yun is as specific about colors of individual rooms as was Faber Birren. This is not a particularly easy book to comprehend, but is essential for anyone interested in this area of study.

Sloan, Annie, and Kate Gwynn. *Color in Decoration*. Boston: Little, Brown and Company, 1990.

> Direct, well-written text with stunning, pertinent illustrations. "Colour portraits" and "Palettes" discuss color schemes associated with various periods in interior decor. Describes the "lineage" of colors with illustrations of daubs of pigment combinations. Recipes, bibliography.

Swirnoff, Lois. *Dimensional Color*. Boston: Birkhauser, 1989. Reprint, Van Nostrand Reinhold, 1992.

> The author emphasizes the three-dimensional approach to color and form. Philosophical in nature, the book includes wonderful experiments. Useful illustrations.

Varley, Helen, ed. *Color*. Los Angeles: Knapp Press, 1980.

> Color as it affects cultures, fine arts, decorative arts, and different industries is the focus of this atlas of color. It is an excellent general guide to color.

*Walch, Margaret, and Augustine Hope. *Living Colors: The Definitive Guide to Color Palettes through the Ages*. San Francisco: Chronicle Books, 1995.

> This is an excellent resource for both students in first or second semester design studios and practicing professionals. It is a self-described "visual thesaurus of color," which provides color samples, brief descriptions of the evolution of palettes, and color reproductions of original sources (such as paintings, tiles, and textiles) of the palettes for significant periods in Western design. The volume is thoroughly and beautifully designed and will undoubtedly be purchased for all design libraries and many personal collections.

Additional Resources

Lighting Research Center.

> See entry in **Chapter 14, Research Centers.**

Environmentally Conscious Design

Fortunately for all, awareness of the value of designing and building with a sensitivity to environmental concerns has increased dramatically over the past several years. The field is immature, as highlighted by the variety of terms, such as "green" design, "socially conscious" design, and "sustainable" design, applied to it. As might be expected, the literature is diverse, produced by a variety of sources and in a variety of media, and of uneven quality. The ability to practice knowledgeably requires effort, analysis, and common sense. Many guides focus on the qualities of materials; for example, how much energy is required to create the product, does the product emit fumes which are known to be harmful, how long can the product be expected to last? These questions lead to life cycle assessment, or "LCA." The *Environmental Resource Guide* listed below includes an excellent explanation of the complicated process of LCA and a good point of departure for further research. Many standards organizations (see **Chapter 13**) are addressing the need for common guidelines. ASTM's Green Building Subcommittee (E-50.06), ASHRAE, DOE Office of Building Technology, and the EPA are all working to achieve improved sustainable design and construction. This field is one in which information changes quickly, making Internet web sites, CD-ROM databases, and magazine articles particularly applicable and particularly difficult for the bibliographer to pin down. With this caveat in mind, the sources listed below are excellent starting points in the quest for responsible designs and materials.

Ecotourism Society. *The Ecolodge Sourcebook: For Planners & Developers*. North Bennington, Vt.: Ecotourism Society, 1995.

> See **Chapter 7, Project Types,** under **Hospitality** section.

Environmental Resource Guide: Subscription. Washington, D.C.: American Institute of Architects, 1993.

> A project of the AIA Committee on The Environment (COTE). Updated quarterly. The following topics are included: "site design and land use, energy, tropical rain forests, recycling, and building ecology." Of particular interest to interior designers will be the articles on products of tropical rain forests and indoor air pollution. There are updates on "EPA-funded *materials analyses*," case studies, and bibliographies of journals, newsletters, and books. This is a topic about which information changes

rapidly, which makes the subscription format particularly useful. The volume is well organized and provides a good list of other sources.

Harkness, Sarah P., and James N. Groom, Jr. *Building without Barriers for the Disabled*. New York: Whitney Library of Design, 1976.

> This brief, superb guide to designing interior spaces and aids for the physically disabled is still valuable. Some measurements are unchanged; for example, the reach of a person in a wheelchair. The excellent measured line drawings are all to a common scale. The photos and diagrams convey clearly and concisely to designers the effects on movement of various constraints.

Lebovich, William L. *Design for Dignity: Studies in Accessibility*. New York: John Wiley & Sons, 1993.

> The author, an architectural historian, emphasizes the high quality of design resulting from addressing not only the letter of the law, but particularly its spirit. Through case studies he presents a variety of accessible public and private buildings. His excellent list of associations includes those that are both broadly and specifically applicable to accessibility. Plans and functional black-and-white photographs illustrate the volume.

*Leclair, Kim, and David Rousseau. *Environmental by Design: A Sourcebook of Environmentally Conscious Choices for Homeowners, Builders, & Designers*. Vol. 1: *Interiors*. Point Roberts, Wash.: Hartley & Marks Publishers, 1992.

> This title is available in either a softcover binding or a three-ring binder with updates by subscription. The contents of generic building products are described, and methods of installation and maintenance are discussed. This introduction is followed with analyses of specific name brands of the generic type. Graphic symbols provide comparable guidelines for all products. A glossary and brief bibliography familiarize readers with new terms and concepts. The book received support from the Foundation for Interior Design Education Research.

Leibrock, Cynthia, with Susan Behar. *Beautiful Barrier-Free: A Visual Guide to Accessibility*. New York: Van Nostrand Reinhold, 1993.

> This book successfully integrates accessibility with high standards of design, covering everything from ventilation to telephones. Pleasing color illustrations and useful line drawings reinforce the text. Manufacturers' addresses are given, but specific products are not identified in the text or illustrations. Good bibliographic references included. **NCIDQ**

*National Audubon Society and Croxton Collaborative, Architects. *Audubon House: Building the Environmentally Responsible, Energy-Efficient Office.* New York: John Wiley & Sons, 1994.

> Not only have the designers created a cost-effective, ecologically sound office environment, but they have accomplished this in an 1891 building. Particularly useful to designers are the questions that were asked at each phase of design and the effective use of existing technology to develop environmentally responsible answers. The book is thorough and accessible, with excellent appendices.

National Park Service. *Sustainable Design and Construction.* Washington, D.C.: National Park Service, 1996.

> This database is available in its second edition on CD-ROM and online. It is organized in three sections: Environmentally Responsible Building Products, Construction Site Recycling Information, and Resource Information. Over 1,000 products are included and may be searched by CSI terms.

Pilatowicz, Grazyna. *Eco-Interiors: A Guide to Environmentally Conscious Interior Design.* New York: John Wiley & Sons, 1995.

> The author provides information in a clear and accessible manner, considering both cost and environmental appropriateness in evaluating building materials, products, and resources. The select group of references for each topic provides a means for the reader to update information in a field that changes quickly. Four very different projects are examined in case studies which apply the information and principles that precede them. Descriptions of organizations, legislation, and publications offer additional resources.

*St. John, Andrew, ed. *The Sourcebook for Sustainable Design: A Guide to Environmentally Responsible Building Materials and Processes.* Boston: Architects for Social Responsibility, Boston Society of Architects, 1992.

> This concise and practical guide to sustainable products is arranged according to the 16 divisions of the Construction Specifications Institute, but unfortunately does not include Division 12, Furnishings. Division 6, Wood and Plastics, and Division 9, Finishes, are useful. Valuable introductions to each section, lists of organizations, magazines, catalogs, and a bibliography round out the subject.

The Interface Group. Cambridge Seven.
Photograph by Peter Vanderwarker.

Chapter 7

Project Types

Healthcare

Most of the publications in this chapter reflect the current emphasis on humane health care. The usual constraints of well-ordered efficient space and sterile surfaces still apply, but to them is added the effects of the senses on healing. Light, color, sunshine, pleasant outdoor views, and music should be among the concerns of designers. "Green design" considerations are crucial so that vocs (volatile organic compounds) and other contributors to "sick building syndrome" are not introduced into a healing environment. Publications from the American Hospital Association and the AIA Committee on Architecture for Health provide only a portion of the information needed by designers. As in any area of specialization, information from sources in the professional literature of the subject field, such as medicine, are an essential part of design planning. Access to these sources will be found in the bibliographies of the books reviewed below.

*Bush-Brown, Albert, and Dianne Davis. *Hospitable Design for Healthcare and Senior Communities*. New York: Van Nostrand Reinhold, 1992.

> Doctors, designers, hospital human resource administrators, and marketing professionals discuss the psychological aspects of healthcare design.

119

Space, light, and landscape are some of the topics addressed through both theory and case studies. A glossary and a bibliography of journal articles are included.

*Calkins, Margaret P. *Design for Dementia: Planning Environments for the Elderly and Confused.* Owings Mills, Md.: National Health Publishing, 1988.

The author, who is noted in this field, interprets the research of behavioral and social scientists and psychologists for design applications. Plans, photos, and an extensive bibliography drawn from both books and journals supplement the text.

Carpman, Janet Reizenstein, Myron Grant, and Deborah A. Simmons. *Design That Cares: Planning Health Facilities for Patients and Visitors.* Chicago: American Hospital Publishing, 1986.

This book, by well-respected authors, is used consistently by professionals and students. Illustrations, checklists, references, and bibliographies enhance the thorough text.

Cohen, Uriel, and Kristen Day. *Contemporary Environments for People with Dementia.* Baltimore: Johns Hopkins University Press, 1993.

A thorough, sensitive volume which places the physical and emotional needs of people with dementia and their caregivers in a design context. Includes case studies, plans, and bibliography.

Goodman, Raymond J., and Douglas G. Smith. *Retirement Facilities: Planning, Design, and Marketing.* New York: Whitney Library of Design, 1992.

For students and professionals of design, architecture, marketing, and development. Offers a realistic appraisal of the needs and potential in this field. Goodman has a PhD in hotel administration from Cornell and Smith is an interior designer specializing in living environments for older adults. Color photos of retirement facilities around the United States. Excellent bibliographies in each chapter.

Guidelines for Construction and Equipment of Hospital and Medical Facilities. Washington, D.C.: American Institute of Architects Press and U.S. Department of Health and Human Services, 1996.

See **Chapter 1, Reference,** under **Codes and Standards** section.

Interior Design magazine. New York: Cahners Publishing Co., August 1993. ~~current 3 years.~~ This issue not available

>Entire issue devoted to "Design for Health Care." Glossary, pp. 114-15; bibliography, pp.116-17. Includes sources of additional information. Special issues of professional magazines are an excellent source of current information, as the editors assemble resources from many areas for the designer's easy use. For example, in this issue such varied sources as the Association for the Care of Children's Health and *Healthcare Forum Journal* are brought to the designer's attention.

*Malkin, Jain. *Hospital Interior Architecture: Creating Healing Environments for Special Patient Populations*. New York: Van Nostrand Reinhold, 1992.

>All projects included meet the author's criteria of achieving a "...true integration between architecture and interior design, and successful response to...a special patient population." Addresses the needs of, among others, children's, cancer, rehabilitation, Alzheimer's, and chemical dependency care facilities. Excellent organization and illustrations, superb bibliographies. The author is an authority in the field.

*Malkin, Jain. *Medical and Dental Space Planning for the 1990s*. New York: Van Nostrand Reinhold, 1990.

>This book reflects the author's 20-year study of, and experience with, the procedures, literature, and practice of the health care field. Color, interior finishes and furniture, lighting, construction, and codes are all addressed. Requirements for asepsis (an environment free of pathogens) due to HIV and Hepatitus B virus, as well as creating supportive environments for patients, are addressed. Photographs, plans, and sample questionnaires for space planning.

Regnier, Victor. *Assisted Living Housing for the Elderly: Design Innovations from the United States and Europe*. New York: Van Nostrand Reinhold, 1994.

>The author is both an architect and gerontologist and is involved in practice and research. His case studies come from the United States and Europe, where assisted living environments have been a topic of interest for many years. The book is profusely illustrated with black-and-white photographs and plans. The bibliography is international in scope and is drawn from gerontological, sociological, and design literature.

Toland, Drexel, and Susan Strong. *Hospital-Based Medical Office Buildings*. 2ⁿᵈ ed. Chicago: American Hospital Publishing, 1986.

> Though not written expressly for interior designers, this volume will familiarize designers with the concerns of hospital administrators regarding expansion of facilities and services. Contributors include accountants, attorneys, bankers, administrators, and doctors.

Hospitality

Trends in hospitality design, like retail design, change quickly. A very few "picture books" of installations are included here, as coverage of this sort is much better in the journal literature which can respond quickly to new work. The books by Davies, Rutes, and the Ecotourism Society contain information of relatively longer-lasting value, though in this field all publications are short-lived. Professional and trade organizations, magazines, specialty publishers, conferences, and schools, such as Cornell's School of Hotel Administration, are the best sources for up-to-the-minute ideas.

*Davies, Thomas D., Jr., and Kim A. Beasley. *Accessible Design for Hospitality: ADA Guidelines for Planning Accessible Hotels, Motels, and Other Recreational Facilities*. 2ⁿᵈ ed. New York: McGraw-Hill, 1994.

> The second edition, with its simple, clear text and illustrations, brings this essential publication up to date. The first edition was published by the Paralyzed Veterans of America and the American Hotel and Motel Association. Checklists provide detailed recommendations which are noted as ADAAG (*Americans with Disabilities Act Accessibility Guidelines*) requirements or the authors' suggestions. Black-and-white photos, line drawings, plans, brief bibliography.

Dorf, Martin E. *Restaurants That Work: Case Studies of the Best in the Industry*. New York: Whitney Library of Design, 1992.

> Well-organized and laid out, this volume combines history; analysis of concept development, budget, and design by restaurant consultants; code considerations, thorough case studies of 18 current, successful U.S. restaurants. Case studies include floor plans, comments by owners and designers, budgets, and design concepts. Sources are provided.

Ecotourism Society. *The Ecolodge Sourcebook: For Planners & Developers*. North Bennington, Vt.: Ecotourism Society, 1995.

> Although not written for interior designers, these proceedings from the first International Ecolodge Forum in 1994 are important for designers in the hospitality field. The guidelines and standards, case studies, and descriptions of additional resources on the topic provide a solid source of information in a field that has recently emerged.

Kishikawa, Hiro. *Great Hotels of the World*. 6 vols. Tokyo: Kawade Shobo Shinsha, Publishers, 1991; distributed by Books Nippan.

> Valuable picture books of a complete range of interior concepts, from resort, classic, and urban hotels to hotel restaurant design. The series provides an overview of a competitive market. Excellent photos.

Pacific Rim Information Network. *Hospitality Profiles*. Atlanta: Pacific Rim Information. Subscription service. (310) 305-7556.

> *Profiles* provides project descriptions and dates and key contact information for both renovations and new projects in three geographically oriented volumes. One volume covers hotels, resorts, and golf clubs in Asia and the Pacific Rim; another volume covers the same types of projects in Mexico, the Caribbean, and Latin America; and a third volume covers U.S. hotels, resorts, and assisted living projects. The U.S. volume is available in either eastern or western editions. Each volume is updated monthly and costs between $1,550 and $2,600 per year.

Restaurant Design 1–. Glen Cove, N.Y.: PBC International, 1986–.

> This series follows the format of many PBC books—vivid color photos, plans and elevations, brief text, and inclusion of "identity" graphics; in this case, menus and signs. Design credits, completion dates, square footage, and budgets complete the presentations. Three volumes have been published, the most recent in 1992.

Rutes, Walter A., and Richard H. Penner. *Hotel Planning and Design*. New York: Whitney Library of Design, 1985.

> A thorough, practical book with charts, floor plans, and numerous small black-and-white photos of hotel, resort, and condominium facilities around the world. The authors are both architects and Penner also teaches at Cornell's School of Hotel Administration. Provides a history of the building type, selected bibliography, analysis of the specialties involved (including ID) in design and construction, and description of hotel

operations. Another publisher, Books Nippan, provides large, glossy color pictures in this field, but this volume provides facts.

Office

Modern "professional" interior design really took off with open floor office planning in highrise buildings in the 1950s. The Quickborner team in Germany popularized the concept of the wall-less, flexible floorplan using moveable plants and screens to define space. The concept quickly came to the United States with the building of the Seagram and Pan Am buildings. Later, Herman Miller introduced the Action Office, which used moveable, interlocking parts like partitions and desks to create flexible office space. This concept of "office systems" has been developed further and now dominates the contract office market. Both Herman Miller and Steelcase continue to support and publish valuable research on the efficiency, ergonomics, and worker satisfaction of office design. This design specialty has a large dollar share of the interiors market.

Becker, Franklin. *The Total Workplace: Facilities Management and the Elastic Organization*. New York: Van Nostrand Reinhold, 1990.

> Becker has impressive academic and consulting experience. Both are apparent in this philosophical yet practical volume for architects, interior designers, facility managers, and senior management. Any professional whose responsibility is office design will benefit from careful consideration of *The Total Workplace*.

Brandt, Peter B. *Office Design*. New York: Whitney Library of Design, 1992.

> Brandt, who gained much of his experience at the successful and respected firm of Gensler and Associates/Architects, covers all phases of office design, including marketing, programming, furnishings, and contract administration. The book is well written and contains line drawings, sample forms, and a good selective bibliography.

Brill, Michael, with Stephen T. Margulis, Ellen Konar, and BOSTI. *Using Office Design to Increase Productivity*. 2 vols. Buffalo, N.Y.: Workplace Design and Productivity, 1985.

"This two-volume work presents the results of a large-scale, long-term research project on the effects of various aspects of the office environment on the employee's performance and ease of communication. The second volume provides a set of design guidelines for high-performance offices, and suggests useful procedures to better understand offices in the design process" (Richard Wurman, *Office Access*, San Francisco: HarperCollins, 1992, p. 88).

Cohen, Elaine, and Aaron Cohen. *Planning the Electronic Office.* New York: McGraw-Hill, 1983.

> Though now somewhat dated, this book's usefulness was never limited to computer planning. It covers the standard topics of space planning, systems furniture, environmental influences, ergonomics, lighting, acoustics, and the interaction of all these factors with requirements for computerization. The title is practical, but can no longer be considered a first choice. No bibliography or glossary.

Crane, Robin, and Malcolm Dixon. *The Shape of Space.* New York: Van Nostrand Reinhold, 1991.

> "Created by designers for designers, this book is 95% drawings, but they're extraordinarily helpful and comprehensible drawings" (Richard Wurman, *Office Access*, San Francisco: HarperCollins, 1992, p. 88). The series consists of four titles, all of which follow the same graphically based format.

Hamer, Jeffrey M. *Facility Management Systems.* New York: Van Nostrand Reinhold, 1988.

> Hamer explains the responsibilities of facility managers, such as cost containment, space allocation, and facilities systems. This understanding enhances the ability of designers to work successfully with facility managers.

Harris, David A., Byron W. Engen, and William E. Fitch, eds. *Planning and Designing the Office Environment.* 2nd ed. New York: Van Nostrand Reinhold, 1991.

HF
5547.2
.P58
(1981 ed)

> An exceptionally coherent, concise volume on office landscaping. Through clearly stated goals, the book integrates the various aspects of office planning—acoustics, lighting, HVAC, codes, power distribution, and systems selection. Each contributor to the volume is a respected

specialist and the editors have appropriately broad experience. The extensive glossary acknowledges the multidisciplinary nature of the text.

*Kleeman, Walter B., Jr., with Francis Duffy, Kirk P. Williams, and Michele K. Williams. *Interior Design of the Electronic Office: The Comfort and Productivity Payoff*. New York: Van Nostrand Reinhold, 1991.

A thorough, practical volume, which addresses building needs from systems for intelligent buildings, telecommunications, and CAD to indoor air pollution, interior furnishings and systems, and employee participation in design. Readers are introduced to studies, standards, and organizations pertinent to facility design and management. Black-and-white illustrations.

*Klein, Judy Graf. *The Office Book*. New York: Facts on File, 1982.

"This book may be 10 years old, but the information is still relevant. A practical guide to planning, designing, and decorating the modern office, it covers everything from choosing a desk to revamping the reception area. Written especially for the office planner with limited design experience" (Richard Wurman, *Office Access*, San Francisco: HarperCollins, 1992, p. 89). Of course, this book is now more than 20 years old, but Wurman's comments are still valid and the title still appears in most bibliographies. The history of office design, which is difficult to find, is particularly good in this volume.

Rappoport, James E., Robert F. Cushman, and Karen Daroff. *Office Planning and Design Desk Reference*. New York: John Wiley & Sons, 1992.

Written by attorneys, architects, developers, and designers, this very practical volume will be useful to anyone designing or leasing office space. The contributors represent consultants needed on an office facility team and, in their texts, emphasize how and when to work as a team. Included are many charts and forms and a selected bibliography.

Rayfield, Julie K. *The Office Interior Design Guide: An Introduction for Facilities Managers & Designers*. New York: John Wiley & Sons, 1994.

Rayfield's goals for this book are clearly defined—to introduce planning and design of commercial office space—and well executed. This practice-oriented title is valuable to beginning students and may be used by professionals as a quick reference for specific questions. She covers budgeting at the end of each phase of design, samples of requests for qualifications, requests for fee proposals, and a sample programming questionnaire. There is a good glossary and a bibliography which consists primarily of journal articles. The volume is illustrated with line drawings, plans, and charts.

Shoshkes, Lila. *Space Planning: Designing the Office Environment.* New York: Architectural Record Books, 1976.

> Good, brief history of the development of space planning, beginning with the Seagram, Time, and Union Carbide buildings. The buildings used as illustrations are owned by large New York City companies who use both in-house planners and outside consultants. The book is now most useful as a history of open space planning because its discussion of computer, electrical, telephone, and environmental needs is technically outdated.

Worthington, John, and Allan Konya. *Fitting out the Workplace: A Straightforward Guide for the Layman and Professional to the Specification of Workplace Interiors.* London: Architectural Press, 1988.

> The volume presents a practical analysis of designing or adapting interiors for business, high tech, or mixed industrial use. Also discussed are selection of a building shell and those elements which are not attached to the shell, at low-, medium-, and high-quality levels. The specifications are useful in principle only as they are based on the British system.

*Wurman, Richard. *Office Access.* San Francisco: HarperCollins, The *Understanding* Business, 1992.

> If *Office Access* looks familiar, it should. It is written and produced by the same people who write the very popular city access guides, such as *New York Access.* The small format and attention-getting page layouts offer concise information in a user-friendly approach. Though written for the office employee, designers will find it useful for themselves and in preplanning with office clients. Steelcase, continuing a happy publishing partnership between the design industry and designers, sponsors the volume. Excellent annotated bibliography, which is quoted in this section.

Residential

When laypeople think of interior design, they inevitably think of glamorous residences. Because interior design is an outgrowth of interior decoration, there are an incredible number of books about residential design, primarily for the layperson. More than in any other area of design, taste, which is certainly essential, can overshadow design principles. Because of the vast number of books devoted to this topic, this listing is limited to titles that emphasize design principles. So-called "stylebooks," which do not represent authentic period interiors, but strive to duplicate the ambiance, which may or may not be accurate, have been omitted. There are three areas of publishing in residential design: 1) housebuilding/planning guides by architects, which focus on a building's structure and the planning of space; 2) planning/design by interior designers, which focus on interior design components and decoration; and 3) specialty area emphasis, which focuses on kitchens and baths. All three types are included here. The **Product Sources** section in **Chapter 1, Reference,** may also be useful in conjunction with this section.

Cole, Jill. *California Interiors.* New York: Library of Applied Design, PBC International, 1991.

> Beautiful color photographs; plans; and a complete listing of designers, support staff, fabricators, suppliers, and photographers make this an excellent idea book for residential and commercial design of the West Coast.

Conran, Terence. *Terence Conran's Kitchen Book: A Comprehensive Source Book and Guide to Planning, Fitting and Equipping Your Kitchen.* Edited by Elizabeth Wilhide and Deborah Smith-Morant. Woodstock, N.Y.: Overlook Press, 1993.

> Conran's popular books are written for the layperson. However, designers may find that this is a good book to share with clients as it introduces them to terms and ideas that will facilitate the design process. Floor plans, enticing color photos, and discussions are offered for five different kitchens. Differing grades and qualities of materials and products are assessed and lists of sources are provided.

Gilliat, Mary. *The Complete Book of Home Design.* Rev. ed. Boston: Little, Brown and Company, 1989.

128

Gilliat has written numerous successful books relating to residential design. Though written primarily for knowledgeable laypeople, the practical tips, color plates, measuring guideline for windows and upholstery, lighting information, and notation symbols for room planning may be useful for designers.

Good, Clint, with Debra Lynn Dadd. *Healthful Houses: How to Design and Build Your Own.* Bethesda, Md.: Guaranty Press, 1988.

For laypeople, builders, and designers to assist in talking with clients who want a nontoxic environment. Arranged according to CSI Masterformat. Brand names of acceptable products are provided.

Grow, Lawrence, gen. ed. *The Old House Book of Bedrooms.* New York: Warner Books, 1980.

The history of the development of bedroom styles is described and illustrated in black-and-white photos of authentic interiors. The book is particularly useful in placing a particular object or convention in its appropriate timeframe. Unlike other *Old House* books, there is no list of suppliers of products and services.

Guild, Robin, with Vernon Gibberd. *The Victorian House Book.* New York: Rizzoli, 1989.

Both interiors and exteriors are represented in fresh color illustrations, line drawings, and plans. Covers furniture and finishes, reuse of fittings and fixtures, planning wiring and heating, and coding floor plans and furniture layout. Provides addresses of selected U.S. suppliers.

Hatje, Gerd, and Herbert Weisskamp. *Rooms by Design.* New York: Harry N. Abrams, 1989.

One can't go wrong with a book whose publisher, authors, designers, and photographers are all first class. A luxurious, refined idea book of international residences with a decidedly European point of view. Beautiful color photos are complimented by an intelligent text.

Lupton, Ellen, and J. Abbott Miller. *The Bathroom, the Kitchen, and the Aesthetics of Waste: A Process of Elimination.* Cambridge, Mass.: MIT List Visual Arts Center, 1992.

This lively and well-researched volume integrates contemporary images, plans, and writings with analysis of the development of these rooms from

1890 to 1940. The influence of the Modern movement, industrial design, and female "domestic theorists" are considered. Excellent illustrations and bibliography.

Madden, Chris Casson. *Interior Visions: Great American Designers and the Showcase House*. New York: Stewart, Tabori & Chang, 1988.

NK
2115
M315
.1988

Showhouses offer designers the unique opportunity to express their own tastes, rather than that of their clients, to a relatively large number of potential clients. This volume reflects their opulent character. It is arranged by room and includes designers' addresses and sources of furniture, fabric, and accessories. Excellent color photos.

Madden, Chris Casson. *Kitchens*. Photographs by Michael Mundy and John Vaughan. New York: Clarkson Potter/Publishers, 1993.

This book of fresh kitchen designs includes beautiful color photographs and layouts of designs. "Resources" provides small black-and-white photos of diverse styles of kitchen components, from flooring to lighting. Designers, manufacturers, and suppliers are credited.

*Moore, Charles, Gerald Allen, and Donlyn Lyndon. *The Place of Houses*. New York: Holt, Rinehart and Winston, 1974.

The purpose of the authors, all notable contemporary architects, is to provide a jargon-free treatise for people interested in building their own homes, with or without a designer. Their premise is that "anyone who cares enough can create a house of great worth—no anointment is required." The work is an invitation to designers and clients to reflect together on how houses can be shaped to the lives of their inhabitants and the places where they are built. Topics include the ordering and assembling of rooms, the relationships between rooms and machines (a concept inclusive of heating systems, kitchens, storage, and stairways), its interior ornamentation, and fitting the house to its site. The emphasis is on nurturing dreams, aspirations, and memory in patterning the house.

Mount, Charles Morris. *Residential Interiors: Architectural & Interior Details*. Glen Cove, N.Y.: PBC International, Architecture & Interior Design Library, 1992.

This idea book of opulent designs presents a diversity of styles, designers, and locations. Coverage of each project is broad enough to give a full impression of the work. Good color photographs, with some plans.

*National Kitchen & Bath Association. *The Essential Kitchen Design Guide*. New York: John Wiley & Sons, 1996.

> The NKBA's guide is a thorough introduction to specifying kitchen and bath design. The volume will be most useful to professionals who are new to this field, introducing information that could be expected to be acquired without its assistance with two years of fieldwork. Inclusion of measurements in centimeters and millimeters reflect the influence of cabinetry and appliances from Canada. Drawings, plans, and black-and-white photos provide ample illustrations of the text. This large (741 pages) volume is a condensation of the NKBA's own six-volume manual. Glossary.

*Nissen, LuAnn, Ray Faulkner, and Sarah Faulkner. *Inside Today's Home.* 6th ed. New York: Harcourt Brace College Publishers, 1994.

> The sixth edition is even more professional than the excellent previous editions. Though primarily written for residential designers, the principles and elements of design and explanations of support systems, floor plans, materials, furniture, and historic styles are so well expressed that all students would benefit from a careful reading of *Inside Today's Home.*
> **NCIDQ**

Pearson, David. *The Natural House Book: Creating a Healthy, Harmonious, and Ecologically-sound Home Environment*. New York: Simon and Schuster, A Fireside Book, 1989.

> In many ways a layperson's "lifestyle" book, this volume serves to introduce designers to all aspects of the "healthy" home. Household toxins and their nontoxic alternatives are listed. Each room of the house is discussed individually. Appealing illustrations.

Poore, Patricia, ed. *The Old-House Journal Guide to Restoration*. New York: NAL/Dutton, 1992.

> This volume is a compilation of technical and how-to information from the *Old-House Journal*, one of the few reliable sources for such information. It includes guidance for inspections, planning, plumbing, electrical, energy efficiency, and plaster work, all geared specifically for old houses. Photos and line drawings illustrate the text.

Raschko, Bettyann Boetticher. *Housing Interiors for the Disabled and Elderly*. New York: Van Nostrand Reinhold, 1991.

> A thorough, scholarly, yet accessible volume with a great deal to offer designers. Explicit definitions of terms, compilations of visual and written standards, results of international research, and selected state codes make this title essential. The bibliography and appendices may be easily updated by contacting the source agencies and publishers for the most recent editions. **NCIDQ**

Regnier, Victor. *Assisted Living Housing for the Elderly: Design Innovations from the United States and Europe*. New York: Van Nostrand Reinhold, 1994.

> See entry in the **Healthcare** section of this chapter.

Seale, William. *Recreating the Historic House Interior*. 2nd ed. Nashville, Tenn.: American Association for State and Local History, 1980.

> Seale, an authority on this subject, provides an excellent starting point for a designer embarking on an authentic recreation of an interior. His approach is both scholarly and accessible, covering research methods, reporting findings, selection of treatments and objects, planning, and finalizing the interior. Sixty-four illustrative plates with thorough explanatory text and an excellent subject bibliography complete this valuable work.

Wentling, James. *Housing by Lifestyle: The Component Method of Residential Design*. 2nd ed. New York: McGraw-Hill, 1996.

> Wentling, an architect, develops a system for planning and programming individual components of a house, then synthesizes the results. His process is practical rather than theoretical and takes emotion, function, and demographics into account. The emphasis is on space planning rather than design.

Retail

The number of titles published in the area of retail design is not so overwhelming as in other areas of design. By consulting the bibliographies in the books below, the reader will gain an accurate overview of the field. Publication dates should always be noted, as retail design is one of the fastest-changing fields of design. Retail designers seem to be blessed with an accessible number of well-written and well-presented volumes on the subject, as can be noted by the percentage of *highly* recommended titles. For the most up-to-date information and projections of trends, refer to the retail journals noted in **Chapter 11, Magazines.**

*Barr, Vilma, and Charles E. Broudy. *Designing to Sell: A Complete Guide to Retail Store Planning and Design.* 2nd ed. New York: McGraw-Hill, 1990.

> An excellent, practical book which focuses less on pretty pictures than useful information. Illustrations are primarily black-and-white, with many plans, line drawings, and charts. Provides graphic standards for retail design, legal information for designers, and a glossary. The authors teach seminars on the subject and this character, rather episodic, comes through in the book. **NCIDQ**

*Broudy, Charles E., and Vilma Barr. *Time-Saver Details for Store Planning and Design.* New York: McGraw-Hill, 1995.

> Good basic ideas about dimensioning are conveyed without stylistic overtones. This volume is designed to be a companion to *Designing to Sell* by the same authors, in addition to being another volume in the well-known McGraw-Hill publisher's *Time-Saver Standards* series. The presentations, covering 20 different store types from apparel to toys, are consistently organized with plans, tips, photos, and detail dimensioned drawings for each type. The two volumes are a distillation of 30 years of thoughtful, successful practice.

*Fitch, Rodney, and Lance Knobel. *Retail Design.* New York: Whitney Library of Design, 1990.

> A beautifully produced book in the tradition of the Whitney Library of Design. The authors, a founder of a successful retail design firm and a proficient writer in the design field, qualify as "experts." Large color photos of European, U.S., and Japanese stores and line drawings are well-integrated into the text. Brief history of retail design, bibliography, glossary, and index.

*Green, William R. *The Retail Store: Design and Construction.* 2nd ed. New York: Van Nostrand Reinhold, 1991.

> A well-organized book which covers the essential topics, including analysis of need, psychology and sociology of shopping, lighting,

133

display, security, and construction. "Checklist of program items," selective bibliography, glossary of retail "lingo," black-and-white photos, plans.

*Israel, Lawrence J. *Store Planning/Design: History, Theory, Process.* New York: John Wiley & Sons, 1994.

Israel, principal in the architectural firm Copeland, Novak, and Israel, has specialized in retail design from its beginnings as a design specialty after World War II. His lively and analytical presentation of both the history and the theory and elements of design is required reading for anyone in the field. Included are an excellent glossary of retail-related design terms, a valuable bibliography of books and journal articles, plans, and color and black-and-white photographs, with project analyses of 50 years of retail designs.

*Lopez, Michael J. *Retail Store Planning & Design Manual.* 2nd ed. National Retail Federation Series. New York: John Wiley & Sons, 1995.

See **Chapter 1, Reference,** under **General References** section.

Pegler, Martin, ed. *Home Furnishings: Merchandising & Store Design.* New York: Retail Reporting Corporation, 1990.

This is a good idea book offering an array of styles and techniques for retail presentation. Color photographs throughout. The editor has many years' experience in the field. Together, he and the publisher have produced several useful titles in this area. It is important to check the dates of publication of books on this topic as styles change very quickly.

Pegler, Martin, ed. *Storefronts & Facades/1–.* New York: Retail Reporting Corporation, 1986–.

Another visually stimulating series of idea books from Retail Reporting Corporation's *Visual Reference Library.* Excellent color photos of recently designed storefronts in international locations, minimal text, clear arrangement, knowledgeable editor. Credits for designers, developers, and contractors are not given consistently. No source credits.

Pegler, Martin, ed. *Stores of the Year/1–.* New York: Retail Reporting Corporation, 1979/1980–.

Large-scale color photos, small-scale floor plans, and several paragraphs of text comprise the coverage for each store selected by Pegler in this series. Men's, women's, and children's clothing shops, and homefashion, lifestyle, and department stores are shown. It is always worth looking at the most recent offering in this series, whose publisher is a major force in retail design.

Retail Reporting Bureau, 302 Fifth Ave., New York, NY 10001.

Retail Reporting offers two monthly subscription services of interest to retail designers. *Store Planning and Design Review*, approximately 52 pages for a three-ring binder, includes color photo prints with brief captions which highlight the latest and best in store design. *Use and Reviews* offers similar coverage for store window design.

Radiosity-based rendering, AutoCAD Release 12. St. Peter's, Rome.
Research project for the Palladio Museum, Rome. Diego Matho, 1993.

Chapter 8

Visual Communication Methods

Drawing and Rendering—Manual

Drawing is the essence of visual communication. Although one need not be an artist to be a designer, it is undeniably an asset, as legends of clients endorsing projects sketched on napkins exemplify. Students should remember that there are 20 different ways to achieve the same pictorial result and should experiment with different styles until comfortable with a technique. The books described below provide a variety of approaches and degrees of sophistication. Drawing can be part of the design thought process, as in Hanks' *Draw!* and *Rapid Viz,* or mathematically- and reference-oriented as in Rich's *Rendering Standards*. However, the types and techniques of drawings are not innumerable, so students do not need to feel overwhelmed. The books below, taken with their bibliographies, provide very good coverage of the subject. Most of the titles are for students, whether beginners or advanced, as professionals can be assumed to have already established their own techniques. For fine examples of manual and computer rendering, see publications of the American Society of Architectural Perspectivists, for whom there is a reference in **Chapter 13, Professional and Trade Organizations and Government Agencies,** under the **Professional Organizations** section.

Ballast, David Kent. *Interior Construction & Detailing for Designers and Architects*. Belmont, Calif.: Professional Publications, 1994.

> See **Chapter 6, Building and Interior Systems,** under **Building Construction, Materials, and Systems** section.

Burden, Ernest. *Entourage: A Tracing File for Architecture and Interior Design Drawing*. 2nd ed. New York: McGraw-Hill, 1991.

> "Entourage," in relationship to drawing, refers to the surroundings of a building. Such elements as furniture, people, or plants add a human scale to drawings and provide the observer with a sense of reality. For years renderers have been saving time by tracing these images into their drawings and Burden's books have been a primary source. "Clip art" for computer imaging has begun to take over this role.

Burden, Ernest. *Photo Entourage: A Tracing File Sourcebook*. New York: McGraw-Hill, 1991.

> This is a high-resolution tracing file which can be scanned into a computer database, or "digitized," and used in a drawing. This is also known as "clip art." Whether one uses printed or computerized entourage, it is important to control its use so that it is a resource, not a crutch.

*Ching, Francis. *Architectural Graphics*. 3rd ed. New York: Van Nostrand Reinhold, 1996.

> This is a universal text for beginning students. Perspective, shade and shadow, and rendering techniques are clearly explained. Finished drawings are shown in lower resolution, as high resolution would only frustrate a beginner. Ching's beautiful lettering and presentation are used by instructors to encourage their own students to do superior work.

*Diekman, Norman, and John Pile. *Drawing Interior Architecture*. New York: Whitney Library of Design, 1983.

> Diekman and Pile cover the manual and computer-aided techniques for creating presentation drawings.

*Diekman, Norman, and John Pile. *Sketching Interior Architecture*. New York: Whitney Library of Design, 1985.

> The book proceeds logically, addressing plans, sections, elevations, perspectives, concept, and field sketching. Drawings are low resolution and rather impressionistic and illustrate a broad range of graphic media

and drawings which vary from rough to finished. The title is only slightly dated regarding the tools of drawing.

Doyle, Michael E. *Color Drawing: A Marker/Colored-pencil Approach for Architects, Landscape Architects, Interior and Graphic Designers, and Artists*. Rev. ed. New York: Van Nostrand Reinhold, 1993.

> A popular how-to book for students with some knowledge of drawing. It is well organized, with textual illustrations by Doyle followed by a portfolio of work by professionals and students. Good glossary, selective bibliography, and cross-reference chart for color names from different marker manufacturers and Prismacolor pencils. Doyle provides advice on color mixing, introduces color composition, and gives examples of how to represent different materials through the use of color.

Drpic, Ivo D. *Sketching & Rendering Interior Spaces*. New York: Whitney Library of Design, 1988.

> This is specifically a guide for students, which includes techniques and uses of various sketching materials, one- and two-point perspective, rendering different surfaces, and shading. All drawings are by the author. Prismacolor pencil and Pantone numbers are noted on the drawings.

Hanks, Kurt, and Larry Belliston. *Draw! A Visual Approach to Thinking, Learning, and Communicating*. Menlo Park, Calif.: Crisp Publications, 1990.

> This volume by Hanks takes the student who has used *Rapid Viz* one step further into the drawing process.

Hanks, Kurt. *Rapid Viz: A New Method for the Rapid Visualization of Ideas*. Menlo Park, Calif.: Crisp Publications, 1990.

> *Rapid Viz* emphasizes drawing as part of the thought process in problem solving. He broadens the concept of drawing beyond drawing itself into the realm of communication.

*Jones, Frederic H. *Interior Architecture Drafting and Perspective*. Menlo Park, Calif.: Crisp Publications, 1989.

> This is a very valuable text for students as it anticipates no prior knowledge, moves through the basics of orthographic drawing to perspective and rendering, and is written specifically for interior design. It explains a wide variety of drawing types, provides many examples of real working

drawings, and may be used as a tracing file for beginners. Clear explanations and a bibliography are assets.

Lockard, William Kirby. *Design Drawing*. Menlo Park, Calif.: Crisp Publications, 1974. Reprint, 1993.

A strong architectural emphasis colors this volume which teaches individuals who are weak in drawing ability the basic drawing skills. A wide range of topics, from conceptual drawings to finished presentations, is addressed.

Lockard, William Kirby. *Design Drawing Experiences*. 6th ed. Menlo Park, Calif.: Crisp Publications, 1993.

An old friend of students, Lockard's book provides time-honored, generic good rendering. It is a quick reference manual for drawing basic elements in interiors, such as furniture, people, interior perspective, and sketching. All work is in the author's style, thus providing easy comparisons among different techniques. Lockard's techniques are very helpful in understanding the conceptual, schematic, and design development processes. This volume may be used with *Design Drawing Videotapes*.

Lockard, William Kirby. *Drawing Techniques for Designers: Advocating Line & Tone Drawing*. Menlo Park, Calif.: Crisp Publications, 1993.

This volume teaches drawing techniques to individuals who have minimal experience. It includes line techniques, reproduction methods, paste-up, using clip art, and night renderings.

Lockard, William Kirby. *Freehand Perspective for Designers: Including Shadow-Casting and Entourage*. Menlo Park, Calif.: Crisp Publications, 1993.

"User-friendly" describes this quick reference manual for perspective drawing dealing with interiors and exteriors. Includes shades and shadow techniques.

Lorenz, Albert, and Leonard Lizak. *Architectural Illustration Inside and Out*. New York: Whitney Library of Design, 1988.

Architectural and interior drawing and rendering presented for the novice. The book emphasizes visual rather than textual explanation of techniques. Well organized and clearly presented, a characteristic of any Whitney imprint.

Lorenz, Albert, and Leonard Lizak. *Trace: Three Thousand Drawings from the Al Lorenz Entourage File.* New York: Whitney Library of Design, 1993.

> More entourage! For an explanation of "entourage," see the entry above for Burden's *Entourage.*

Miller, William E. *Basic Drafting for Interior Designers.* New York: Van Nostrand Reinhold, 1982.

> Miller's straightforward presentation of the universal language and tools of graphic communication is a boon to beginning students. He includes chapter reviews and quizzes, tables of standard sizes, and a glossary.

Oliver, Robert S. *The Sketch.* New York: Van Nostrand Reinhold, 1979.

> Oliver teaches both how to quickly sketch while developing a thought one wishes to communicate and perspective development. The book is valuable for students and offices.

Pile, John, ed. *Drawings of Architectural Interiors.* New York: Whitney Library of Design, 1967.

> There are no instructions in this out-of-print volume, just pure examples of architectural rendering techniques as exercised by talented renderers from Piranesi to Paul Rudolph. An introduction puts the evolution and value of drawing into perspective.

*Pile, John. *Perspective for Interior Designers.* New York: Whitney Library of Design, 1985; reprinted as a paperback in 1989.

> Step-by-step guide to creating perspectives specifically of interiors. Includes several case studies of perspectives by well-known designers. Selected bibliography.

Porter, Tom, and Sue Goodman. *Design Drawing Techniques: For Architects, Graphic Designers, & Artists.* New York: Charles Scribner's Sons, 1991.

> This graphic reference manual provides assistance in preparing presentations and provides a good basis on which to develop one's own drawing techniques. It presents various graphic styles and explains the concepts of perspective, shade, shadows, and pencil techniques. The brief text enhances the illustrations. There is less coverage of interior design in this volume than in the earlier Porter and Goodman series below.

141

Porter, Tom, and Bob Greenstreet. *Manual of Graphic Techniques for Architects, Graphic Designers, & Artists*. Illustrated by Sue Goodman. New York: Charles Scribner's Sons, 1980.

This basic graphics manual begins with the mediums used in presentations—papers, pens, and pencils—and proceeds to the concept of perspective and the techniques of pen and ink, wash, and air brush.

Porter, Tom, and Sue Goodman. *Manual of Graphic Techniques 2: For Architects, Graphic Designers, & Artists*. New York: Charles Scribner's Sons, 1982.

Presents the technical aspects of visual awareness—how an individual sees an object, perspective, the concept of composition—and the mechanical aspects of visual elements, such as elevations and axonometrics.

Porter, Tom, and Sue Goodman. *Manual of Graphic Techniques 3: For Architects, Graphic Designers, & Artists*. New York: Charles Scribner's Sons, 1983.

This volume concentrates on lettering, line techniques, graphic techniques for photographic composition, screen printing, stenciling, and modelbuilding.

Porter, Tom, and Sue Goodman. *Manual of Graphic Techniques 4: For Architects, Graphic Designers, & Artists*. New York: Charles Scribner's Sons, 1985.

Excellent rendering techniques are demonstrated, including explanations of shades, shadows, and line types. Plans, elevations, isometrics, axonometrics, obliques, and night rendering are all explained. The series presupposes good freehand drawing ability.

Rich, Stephen W. *Rendering Standards in Architecture and Design*. New York: Van Nostrand Reinhold, 1984.

This book is designed as a text for students with drawing experience. Problems are included and an answer book is available. It is a meticulous reference manual for drawing. Includes definitions of terms.

Staebler, Wendy W. *Architectural Detailing in Contract Interiors*. New York: Whitney Library of Design, 1988.

See **Chapter 6, Building and Interior Systems,** under **Building Construction, Materials, and Systems** section.

Staebler, Wendy W. *Architectural Detailing in Residential Interiors.* New York: Whitney Library of Design, 1990.

> See **Chapter 6, Building and Interior Systems,** under **Building Construction, Materials, and Systems** section.

Szabo, Marc. *Drawing File for Architects, Illustrators, and Designers.* New York: Van Nostrand Reinhold, 1976.

> Szabo provides a high resolution tracing file.

Wakita, Osamu, and Richard M. Linde. *The Professional Handbook of Architectural Detailing.* 2nd ed. New York: John Wiley & Sons, 1987.

> This is a good basic refresher text for professionals and study text for students. Building construction techniques are shown in site, drawing, and model formats. Both wood frame and steel structures are detailed. The case studies can be used for exercises and there is a student handbook which can be purchased as a companion volume.

Drawing and Rendering—CAD

Written by Henry W. Cugno and Leo Murphy with Susan Lewis

Introduction

CAD, or computer-aided design, has fast become a design tool in many offices, not just a drafting tool. This transition began only recently. In 1987,

---

Henry W. Cugno, IBD, is a professional member of the Institute of Business Designers. He has been a member of the computer faculty at the Boston Architectural Center since 1990 and a principal at Angeli Design, Inc., since 1991, where he is responsible for design and production work. The firm has offices in Providence, Rhode Island, and Boston and provides commercial interior design services for corporate offices, research and development facilities, and health care facilities.

Leo Murphy, designer, currently works for Payette Associates, one of the largest architectural firms in Boston. He has been a CAD user, manager, and consultant since 1981 for various professions ranging from mechanical design to architecture.

CAD required a six-figure investment in bulky mainframe computers that ran programs difficult to understand and operate. Although much-improved versions of these original systems exist, relatively inexpensive personal computers have revolutionized the world of CAD by making it cost effective for the average design firm.

Conceptually, the computer is a tool used to enter, display, manipulate, store, and output information. Various types of software are used to do all of this. The type of software utilized depends on the type of task. Word processing puts words together into sentences, paragraphs, and pages. CAD puts designs together and allows the user to manipulate those designs into presentations and vector-based drawings. Although it is inevitable that there will be overlap in these functions, as yet no one product combines all functions. It is, however, becoming easier to combine or transfer the information from one software package to another.

Definitions

For those who are beginning to explore computers, it may be helpful to define some fundamental computer terms. These definitions have been placed at the end of this chapter. If you are new to CAD, you may want to look at this section before beginning the text that follows.

CAD Hardware and Software

For most CAD users the benefit of improved hardware is realized in speedier operation of existing software packages. There is a frequently overlooked bonus—the new top-of-the-line PCs (personal computers) now provide the power required to drive the new, more sophisticated 3-D (three-dimensional) CAD software programs. The software trend for the past several years has been toward user-friendly 3-D CAD. The new 3-D packages offer the design professional the marketing advantage of being both a *design* and a *presentation* tool that allows clients to view future spaces before any construction begins.

2-D vs. 3-D CAD

Recently, manufacturers of older 2-D software packages have released 3-D enhancements of their products. Unfortunately, most of these 3-D releases are very difficult to learn and operate. Often, the new 3-D supplements are afterthoughts to the original 2-D program. An improvement over these are the dozens of new 3-D modeling software packages which base the core of their design strategy on three- dimensional modeling, not two-dimensional concepts. These new products complement today's powerful new machines and offer the greatest cost/benefit potential to an office.

Specialization

A certain amount of specialization has begun to take place in CAD software products. This can be confusing as there are overlapping functions among software packages. For example, facility managers responsible for large companies have begun to utilize a combination of CAD and various business management software. The computer seems a natural for tracking furniture and equipment *graphically* as well as *numerically*. However, these functions require a sizeable commitment of the hard drive.

Occasionally large companies will turn to interiors firms for facility management. Many commercial interior design firms providing these services use specialized facilities management software programs that combine equipment inventory tracking, furniture inventory tracking, building systems records, drafting, and minor space planning. These products may or may not include 3-D capabilities.

Another rapidly growing use for computers in the interior design office is the storage and updating of Electronic Product Directories. These directories (usually on compact disks) are simply libraries of information about products used to create interiors. The categories include construction detailing products such as moldings; finishes such as carpets, wallcoverings, or paints; and furniture products such as chairs, tables, office panel systems, and files. Computer product directories offer information on style, color, price, and availability, and are beginning to include a color photo image of the item described.

Other specialized software applications, including electronic building codes, will be discussed later in this chapter.

Two-Dimensional CAD Drafting vs. Three-Dimensional CAD Designing

Electronic drafting has always been the most practical benefit of any CAD system. The first PC-based CAD packages made their marks by offering inexpensive 2-D drafting solutions. These 2-D functions take advantage of time-saving graphic libraries of information and eliminate repetition. The average CAD package works on a system of 2-D *layers* that behave much like the innovative manual *overlay drafting systems* in use just before CAD appeared. In a similar fashion, CAD layers efficiently produce many different drawings that share a *common base plan*. For example, a common base layer can be used for electrical plans, reflected ceiling plans, furniture plans, etc. This is one of the features that makes CAD systems cost effective as design changes are simultaneously executed on every type of plan. Another obvious advantage of CAD is the use of libraries of templates and details.

Many of the pioneering firms who originally purchased powerful 3-D-based CAD workstations ended up switching to less expensive 2-D-based PCs due to the simple fact that few designers had the time or skills needed to take advantage of 3-D capabilities. The learning curve for 3-D was very steep. Thus, most firms utilized only the 2-D features of these expensive systems for electronic drafting. The earliest, and still most common, approach to 3-D CAD requires the operator to build a *wireframe* model of a design. Every *edge* of all objects drawn (such as chairs, desks, lamps, casework, etc.) needs to be constructed one by one as if building with sticks or wire. A bird cage effect called a wireframe is the result. Later, this wireframe model must be covered with a skin or surfaces in a separate step. Surfaces are required for the computer to generate images that appear to be solid. The process of making wireframe look solid is called *hidden line removal*. Most wireframe CAD programs do not really recognize objects as being solid; instead, the model is really a hollow volume covered with a thin skin. True *solid modeling* is used in engineering to calculate stresses, centers of gravity, etc.; however, the term is often used to describe surfaced wireframe CAD images that have undergone hidden line removal.

The wireframe approach to CAD is still a time-consuming and tedious process. Building the wireframe model, applying surfaces to every face of the object (although this phase has enjoyed some automation), and waiting dozens of hours for the computer to calculate one picture does not boost office productivity. A design change creates a serious problem. Three- dimensional wireframe CAD has been around for quite some time and will probably never completely disappear. However, any software package that requires an operator to build a wireframe as a first step should be avoided.

Unfortunately, today's most popular PC CAD packages offer the older wireframe approach to 3-D, in spite of the fact that software research and design have undergone the same vast improvements as computer hardware. In the past several years newer 3-D software products based upon 3-D, not 2-D, have been developed. These packages allow a designer to create solid images quickly and easily without having to build a wireframe. It pays to investigate different CAD products.

Data Transfer between Software Programs

Many interior designers choosing CAD packages are also concerned about sharing CAD files with architects and engineers. Fortunately, exchanging drawings between different CAD packages is now a simple matter. Any CAD package that is considered professional in the industry can save its CAD drawings using DXF (data exchange format), a translation tool included in the software program. This common go-between format allows files to be shared among offices using different software, without sacrificing file integrity.

CAD Hardware

The older CADD systems were made up of large mainframe workstations that had specific environmental requirements and took up quite a bit of space. Special computer rooms had to be constructed to accommodate these machines. It was also necessary to retain the services of a programmer or system manager to develop computer standards for the office. In some firms this is still the case today.

Although the development of personal computer work stations has revolutionized the CAD station's position in the design office, there is only one basic element that has changed from old "CADD" systems to new "CAD" systems. This element is the capability to work in three dimensions.

Three-dimensional CAD has been available for quite some time, but has not been particularly affordable or easy to use until the late 1980s. The older 3-D systems required an operator who was well educated in computers. This operator was seldom a designer, but a computer programmer/draftsperson. The hardware needed to run 3-D software was very expensive. These systems created three-dimensional models of a design which could then be viewed from different angles or cut up to show sectional views.

Today, this and much more can be accomplished on a personal computer format. Programs that are easier to understand and operate have made it practical for designers to utilize the CAD programs themselves. The 3-D

147

models produced can be used to create walk-through animations. The addition of colors, shades, and shadows produces an animation leaving little to the client's imagination. The progress of photo-realistic technology in 3-D CAD has made the use of CAD presentations even more popular with interior designers. When colors, patterns, and textures are combined with photo realism in computers, the CAD presentation also becomes the finishes presentation.

CAD Management

The organization of CAD operations in the interior design office is as important as the design work itself. If CAD is not well managed, system operation becomes increasingly difficult. It should be remembered that CAD is a tool. Any tool, when used improperly, can cause more harm than good.

A good CAD program includes plans for CAD management, maintenance, and a yearly budget to keep up with new technology. Obviously, all of this does not occur on its own. An individual should be designated to manage these tasks.

Several basic principles of CAD management insure successful operation of the system. A procedures manual outlining the accepted office protocol should be written so that practice remains consistent from user to user. This keeps all the information generated looking uniform and allows different people to work on the same project. As in manual practice, drawings should be labeled and lettered uniformly. Details should be placed on sheets in the same locations. Documents should be part of a labeling procedure that allows for cataloging and filing. Information should be easy to find. In other words, much of the same reasoning used to create standards for drafting applies to CAD. Standards should be established regarding which information should be stored on the hard drive and which should be stored on removable storage media.

Layers

The efficient use of layers on the system is also crucial. Layers are used to separate information in much the same way that different drawing sheets separate information. This procedure need not be very complicated. It is as simple as naming a numbered layer with the type of information that will be placed on it. One basic example of a layering system is as follows:

Layer #1 = Building shell
Layer #2 = Interior Partitions
Layer #3 = Furniture
Layer #4 = Ceilings

The layering system can become more detailed depending upon the complexity of the project. Most CAD systems have upwards of 250 layers available to accept information, so layering can be as detailed as the user wishes.

It is convenient to have different information on different layers because the layers can be individually controlled. Each layer can be visible or invisible on the monitor. Most CAD systems offer a third option—visible/inactive. This means that the information is visible but cannot be acted upon. These three-layer conditions can apply to any layer at any time at the user's discretion. The value of this feature can be demonstrated through the following scenario.

Using the layering system example shown previously:

Layer #1 = Building shell : visible/inactive
Layer #2 = Interior partitions : visible/inactive
Layer #3 = Furniture : visible
Layer #4 = Ceilings : invisible

The above layer set-up would allow the user to move furniture around without affecting the building shell or interior partitions. The ceiling layer, which is invisible, is also unaffected, thus eliminating confusion when moving the furniture.

Learning Curve

An important part of CAD management is making sure that the policies and procedures of CAD operation are followed. When a CAD system is first introduced into a firm's operation, adequate time should be set aside for training personnel. Although this time is not billable, it is far from wasted. All too often, a firm purchases a CAD system which remains on a shelf because it has not committed time for its employees' training. If the CAD system is viewed as an investment, it is necessary to obtain a return on that investment as soon as possible. This can only be done through a regimented training schedule in which each individual who will work on the system spends at least one or two hours a day on the computer. If a firm makes this commitment, the return on the initial investment in hardware, software, and training will be realized through faster production and more impressive presentations. The firm's CAD manager will also need to monitor the way the CAD system is used during the training period. At first, there will be a fair amount of experimentation on the system. This "play" is healthy during training as it becomes a vehicle for learning. As users become more proficient on the CAD system, however, "play" can become addicting. It is up to the system manager to determine what is healthy experimentation and what is not. If, after full CAD training is complete, time savings are not realized, then the manner in which the computer is being used should be reevaluated.

CAD System Maintenance

CAD system maintenance consists of more than dusting the hardware and wiping the monitor. Software utility packages (in essence, maintenance tools) are valuable assets. These packages allow the user to get further efficiency from the system by providing such functions as disk optimization (a feature that ensures efficient storage and operation of documents and applications), disk partitioning (which manages disk storage space), and security access. These utilities can be considered preventive medicine and should be applied on a regular basis, not just when problems occur.

Hardware maintenance *is* fairly simple in that computers operate very efficiently and seldom break down. Keeping hardware clean and free from dust is usually all that is necessary. Follow the maintenance instructions enclosed with the equipment. The temperature and humidity of the room in which the computer will be stored represent another maintenance consideration. Once again, follow the manufacturer's instructions.

A yearly CAD budget should be established. A CAD system is an investment and is worth keeping up-to-date. This requires periodic expenditures on new software, hardware, and updates in order to stay close to the forefront of technology. Such investments are money well spent as they further improve the efficiency of the system already in place. Each firm, by selecting among the upgrades available in hardware and software, will, over time, customize the CAD system to its developing needs. The dollar amount in a CAD system annual budget will be determined by the amount the firm can afford as well as its level of commitment to development.

Before entering into a discussion about designing with CAD, it is worth mentioning that the computer can contribute to the needs assessment effort that begins each interior design project. Graphics produced on the CAD program can be merged with text generated by word processing software. This combination can create impressive needs analyses which may be revised and manipulated with ease. A firm's own graphic standards (typeface, logo, customized format) will further define and enhance the document.

Now that CAD history, hardware/software, and organization have been touched on, a discussion of designing with CAD can begin. The point at which CAD enters the creative process can be debated among users. Some designers start the creative process on CAD and some start with the traditional roll of trace paper. Although different designers bring CAD into the process at different times, all who have adopted the use of CAD would agree that it should be used as early in the process as possible.

Designing with CAD

Entering the Base Plan

No matter when the computer is brought into the creative process, a base plan will eventually have to be input. The schematic phase, which occurs after programming, cannot begin without a base plan in place. Base plans can be entered in several ways. The easiest way is to acquire a CAD floor plan created by either the client or another design professional and transfer it directly into your CAD system via disk. This approach assumes that the CAD package that created the plan can save the drawing in the DXF or other common language formats. In the past, the exchange of CAD plans was extremely rare because the translation process was far from satisfactory. Now, translating drawings is no longer an issue and exchanging CAD files has become commonplace. As long as both parties own professional CAD systems that support a common translator, there should be little cause for concern.

The most typical way to enter a base plan into a CAD system is manually. This means that an operator measures off a set of dimensioned prints and creates a CAD drawing from them. This method is similar to drafting and is a 2-D approach. If one uses a 3-D system, he or she may start with a 2-D floor plan and then build a 3-D model on top of it. It should be noted that different CAD packages treat 3-D differently. Some take two-dimensional elements and assign a third dimension (height) to them. In other words, they "pop up" or are *extruded* from 2-D to 3-D. Other CAD packages begin with three-dimensional solid elements. In either case, the result is a 3-D base plan or model which will then be used for space planning by the interior designer.

151

This method is also used to enter information from field dimensioning. As much of interior design work today involves renovation of existing buildings, designers often find it necessary to create information from scratch. If this is the case, it pays to determine the manner in which the field information is to be taken. Different CAD systems use different commands and tools to enter various forms of information into a document. The field information should be taken in a way that is consistent with system commands. Therefore, a procedure should be put in place which insures that every efficiency in a particular CAD software package is exploited when gathering this field information. If the procedure is well thought-out and is followed whenever field dimensioning is necessary, a substantial savings of time and effort can be realized.

The last way to enter information into a CAD system is to scan it. A scanner is a piece of hardware that allows the user to take an existing drawing and enter it into the computer. Scanners are driven by specific software applications. There are various types of scanners on the market. Some are hand-held and operated. Some are stationary. The way they work varies from one type to another, but is nevertheless quite simple. A hand-held scanner is simply rolled over the drawing after the proper commands are given through the software. As it passes over the drawing, the scanner records the information on the drawing onto a file document. This document can then be opened in the software used with the scanner and adjusted for entry into the firm's CAD software program.

Stationary scanners work in much the same way, but with the equipment providing the movement. A drawing is placed inside the stationary scanner and through software commands is scanned automatically by the piece of hardware. There are certain drawbacks with this method of entering information. First, the size of the drawing that can be scanned is limited. If the drawing is too large to be scanned into the system with one pass, then it must be "pieced" together. This process can be time consuming and extremely tedious. Second, the scanned image must be scaled once it is transferred into CAD software. This is also time consuming and tedious. Third, the cost of scanners (which varies from inexpensive to extremely expensive) may not be justifiable for many firms. In this case, a designer could contract with a scanning service to do the work. This type of service can be extremely expensive, with the cost of scanning a "D" size drawing in the vicinity of $200-$300. Scanning services frequently establish a minimum amount of work that they will accept from one client, so it may be advantageous to group work that is to be scanned.

Whatever method is used to enter information into a CAD system, care should always be taken to plan the most efficient path to follow. This is true not only for practical work flow reasons but also for financial reasons. The savings in time that are usually realized by CAD use should not be offset by the expense created by inefficient decision-making about how to enter and manage information. This may seem complicated, but just requires common sense. As long as procedures are developed and followed, CAD operation becomes second nature to most users.

Schematic Plan

Once the base information has been entered into the system, the schematic design process may begin. As mentioned earlier, this creative process can be accomplished directly on the CAD system or through the more traditional means of trace paper.

Taking advantage of three-dimensional capability in CAD, schematics that are prepared on the computer from the start of the process will inherently have more detail and dimension data than any design prepared on trace paper. This is true primarily because libraries of information, either commercially available or constructed in-house, may be drawn on. These libraries include detailed information, such as product dimensions, material, and pricing. This data can then be extracted and replicated as necessary, instead of being constructed from scratch each time it is required. For this reason, most CAD programs also offer the capability to create and enter new information into these libraries. If a complicated three-dimensional object is created for a specific project, it can be entered into a library and stored for future use on other projects. This practice, in time, creates vast libraries of information to draw on. If this concept is projected into the future, it is easy to see how the efficiency of the CAD system will continue to increase with use.

Starting the schematics process on trace paper does not eliminate efficiency as long as care is taken to use this process in conjunction with the computer. Many designers require the freedom of pen and paper to quickly jot down ideas and concepts. They feel that more options can be explored through the creative freedom offered by the absence of detail when using trace paper. Every designer knows, however, that one can become carried away with the flow of concepts resulting from this method. Details could enter into the process as by-products. Putting details on paper rather than into the computer dilutes the efficiency available to the CAD user. If a conscious effort is made to restrict the amount of work done on trace paper, the limited amount of work that is on trace can be transferred to computer. The use of libraries enters into the process at this point. When library items are used to create a schematic design conceived on trace paper, detail is automatically added to the design. This detail can then be used as-is or modified to suit the application. At this point, the use of trace paper in the process could be eliminated. This commentary is not meant to imply that "all" work that an interior designer does should be done on CAD. Rather, the emphasis is on efficiently using the computer tools that are available in conjunction with other means. If this cooperative attitude is adopted, then efficiency of time is realized.

A 3-D schematic design can be viewed from different angles to check that the desired design intent was successful. Skilled and talented designers can "think" and "see" in three dimensions. This skill is complemented by the use of CAD. The computer can be an effective presentation tool for the client's benefit and an effective verification tool for the designer's benefit. This is where the finer points of the design begin to be developed. Ideas can be inserted and manipulated with great speed, allowing the designer to make decisions faster and more easily. At any point during the process, the design can be checked to see if the ideas that are developed are successful as a three-dimensional image.

Client Involvement

The question of when CAD can be used to bring the client into the design process should be addressed at this time. Because the computer can generate the schematic information described in this section, it is tempting to bring the client into the process early. This may be done to impress a new client with the designer's capabilities. There are, however, numerous reasons why introduction of the client at this stage could be a great error. With the speed at which today's CAD programs can generate displays of information, it is easy for a client to get caught up in the instant gratification of seeing a revision take place. One result might be client and designer sitting side by side at a CAD workstation trying different ideas and seeing instantly how they work. Although this could be an effective process with some clients, it should be a general rule not to adopt this practice. Far too often, the client turns his or her excitement into "play" time and the designer in turn gets caught in a game difficult to escape. This also could lead to the client designing space rather than the designer. All in all, the client's role as it pertains to CAD should be one of spectator/audience and not director. The computer should be used to present information to the client. After all, before designers had CAD systems, they seldom invited the clients to sit with them at the drafting table.

Presentation Methods

Once schematic designs are placed on the CAD system and manipulated to the point that they require client feedback, a method of presentation is selected. Various methods are available to the designer. Some are two-dimensional in nature, while others are three-dimensional in nature.

Two-dimensional presentations are basically drawings extracted from the computer model created. These views could be floor plans, elevations, perspectives, axonometrics, or isometrics. The range of views available would depend on the CAD software package being used. The designer must request that the computer calculate each view desired. Once completed, the view can be placed with other views, text and title block are added, and a presentation sheet is born. Once the sheet is assembled, some clean-up work is usually required. Line weights are assigned, intersections are trimmed, etc. All that is left is to print the information. The scale is determined through the CAD software and depends on the capabilities of the output hardware selected. For instance, a drawing that requires a large format in order to preserve detail could not be output through a small printer. A plotter is used to print such a drawing at the desired scale and sheet size. This type of presentation can be made at either the client's location or the designer's office and would be conducted in the same way that most drawing presentations are made.

Three-dimensional presentations are much different. They require the use of equipment to make the presentation. Because this equipment may not be transportable, there may be no other choice than to make the presentation at the designer's location. The level of three-dimensional presentations that can be produced depends on the sophistication of the software used and the capability of the hardware used. There are two basic types of 3-D presentation. The first is conducted much like a slide show. Views taken from the three-dimensional model created through the schematics process described previously can be assembled in a linear fashion so that one view after another is displayed. Because this method of presentation uses the computer as the presentation medium, the views can be shown in color or even with shade and shadow added. This would obviously not be possible with a two-dimensional presentation. The "slide show" is simply run on the monitor while being narrated by the designer. The presentation can be run forward or backward and can also pause at views requiring more in-depth explanation. This is an effective way of presenting schematic ideas because the client can see many aspects of the concepts developed by the designer through the different views shown. Obviously, care should be taken to assemble the presentation in a way that maintains a fluid progression through the space. The insertion of floor plans or other views in key areas may help to orient the client within the space. The addition of color to shade and shadow provides a more realistic impression of the space.

The second type of three-dimensional presentation is extremely dramatic. It involves all of the aspects of the slide show with one addition—animation. The animated "walk-through" lets the client take a stroll through the space before it is constructed. These are actual movies constructed from the three-dimensional computer model. They can be initiated from any point in the space. They can take any path as well. The client can climb a set of stairs or fly around the space from above. The presentation works in much the same way as the slide presentation. The designer can set the animation in motion and narrate the entire presentation. Depending on the sophistication of the CAD system, shade and shadow can be added.

Shade and shadow can also be used to produce shadow studies. Software programs possessing the sophistication to produce shadow studies can demonstrate what will happen to a space during the course of any day at any time of year. These presentations look like time-lapsed photography. Besides being impressive to watch, shadow studies offer the designer insight into the level of detail required to protect against extreme lighting conditions. This is certainly an advantage not available to designers in the past. The time and money required to assess the effects of sunlight on space were exorbitant. With this method of presentation, a shadow study is a by-product of the three-dimensional computer model.

Until recently, the client would have to come to the designer's office to view such presentations since it was impractical to transport the necessary equipment. The cost of having the presentation transferred to videotape was prohibitive. Technology has developed, however, lower-cost equipment and software to create such a transfer of information. Depending on the CAD software and hardware used, the transfer of computer-generated animations from computer to videotape is now within the financial reach of many designers. With this advance in technology it is even easier to make animated presentations to clients. Music and/or voice can be added to the video, making it possible to send the presentation to the client and have the animation present itself. Though this may be extreme, it is possible.

Design Revisions

Now that the preliminary CAD presentation has been discussed, the most commonly used aspect of CAD can be approached—making revisions to the design. The same tools and commands that were used to create the three-dimensional computer model can be used to revise that model. Once revisions are made, new presentations can be prepared. When the impact of the presentation is compared to the amount of time involved to create it, and subsequent presentations, it is easily understood why the use of CAD has grown dramatically among interior designers.

The advantages to this type of presentation scenario include the following:

- Better client understanding of the designer's concepts.

- Reduced number of revisions.

- Reduced amount of time necessary to reach subsequent phases of design work.

These types of presentations involve the client in the design because he or she can understand it more easily and his or her requests for change can be accommodated more quickly. Every designer knows the importance of the client's confidence in the designer's abilities. The use of CAD in the presentation of schematic designs can strengthen this level of confidence.

Once the schematic design process has been brought to the stage of client sign-off, all information should be put into a drawing format, regardless of the presentation methods used. This will be a handy reference for the client as well as the designer. This is an important stage of CAD operation within the project as it is the first graphic documentation of the work completed and soon to be approved. Thus it is important to create these drawings as carefully as the original CAD presentation was created. The drawings will serve as a reference for both client and designer and as the springboard for the next phase of design.

Design Development

Using the documentation described above, the designer can now move on to design development. During the course of this phase, the designer normally refines all aspects of the schematics approved by the client. Details are developed and refined. Colors and textures are tested and determined and products are selected for use. During this process, all of the groundwork is done for the contract documentation of the design for construction. This means that all of the computer work done previously must be continuously updated with the information developed in this phase. This is where many designers feel that the computer has outlived its value to a project. After all, CAD cannot make color selections, or select products that possess the design qualities required by the designer. Nor can it develop the construction detailing necessary to enhance the characteristics of the designer's ideas. Nonetheless, if the three-dimensional model is updated with design development information, the computer can again be a useful tool in illustrating the designer's intent to the client and save time doing it. If this path is followed, there are several ways CAD can be useful.

First, any design detail that is added to the CAD 3-D model can then be viewed by the client in the same way as during the schematics phase. Every designer must keep his client abreast of the design process to gain client approvals. The computer can assist in making this task easier.

Second, with the progress of technology in CAD, software has been developed that allows designers to create photo realistic renderings of their projects. This technology has become available recently and is still in the process of becoming affordable and practical to use. Some software packages are more advanced than others. With this technology colors, textures, and lighting conditions can be depicted with realistic detail. Instead of seeking the client's approval of finish selections on a presentation board, one can see the actual finishes installed on the project, a factor that can expedite the approval process. This is not meant to suggest that presentation boards are to be replaced by such a process but rather that they should be used in conjunction with this technology.

Contract Documents

The last advantage of using CAD in design development is that the 3-D model can then be utilized to create virtually complete contract documents. This is accomplished by extracting from the model all of the necessary information required by each production drawing. If this process is completed efficiently, there will be less work required to finish each drawing.

Even the balance of work required to complete contract documentation can take advantage of CAD operation. In this phase, the three-dimensional portion of CAD is abandoned for the production efficiency of the two-dimensional aspect of the software.

Dimensioning is done automatically through the use of various tools and commands. This means that the computer can read the scale of the information on a document and determine dimensions by association. These dimensions can then be moved and modified as necessary.

Scaling can be modified to develop details that can be easily read. A detail can be extracted and enlarged or reduced as required and then dimensioned.

Hatching is a tool command that can be utilized to shade various areas to designate a particular material or apply a specific code. The hatching itself can be custom designed and entered into a library for future use. An example of the possible use of hatching is the designation of walls to be demolished, walls to remain, and new walls.

Symbol libraries can be utilized to place commonly used symbols such as elevation and section designations on drawings. These libraries either are available with the CAD software, or can be created by the user, or both. Libraries can be created for items such as doors, windows, toilet fixtures, lighting fixtures, furniture, etc. A symbol is created by drawing it and placing the drawing into a library via a code or a name. Many libraries are developed over time by the user so that a custom assembly of information takes place. These libraries of information can then become part of the standard procedure used to create construction documents.

Data Assembly

Once all of the information necessary for contract documentation is developed, it must be assembled onto sheets. Title blocks and text required for final notations can be added. Because information can be copied from one document to another and modified in the process, assembly of construction documents by CAD is speedier and easier than conventional drawing board methods. For this same reason, it is necessary to carefully catalog the completed document by each sheet so as not to confuse future CAD users.

Finally, the sheets can be output through a printer or a plotter. At this stage different line weights or different colored lines are identified with different pens in a plotter. It is a good practice to establish standards for lines also. This will insure that another individual will be able to create the same plot from a file without guessing at line weights or colors.

Here, it is worth entering into a short discussion about plotting media. There are various types of paper available for plotters. Bond paper is a white paper that will not reproduce in standard blueline machines. It can be used for color-coded presentations or single-color presentations. There are a number of reproducible types of paper including vellum and mylar film. Felt tip pens are usually the type of pens used with bond paper. Because of the wide range of pen selection available for reproducible media, it is necessary to experiment with pens until the right pen is found for the application.

There is one other form of documentation made possible by most CAD systems. Now that the interior designer's project has been documented through the CAD procedures described, information such as area, volume, and lineal dimensions can be selectively extracted. This information can then be linked to a spreadsheet or database software program. This means that all of the information necessary to create materials lists and their quantities can become available. Once placed into a database, this information can be manipulated into a *cost estimate* by adding the costs of materials and labor into the database. This is a more sophisticated use of computers in that it requires the integration of software programs. Although integration requires additional effort, it can be invaluable for generating preliminary budgets for clients quickly.

Data Exchange Between Professionals

The last item to be covered regarding CAD is the transfer of information between one professional's office and another. It is likely that on larger projects, practitioners representing a number of design professions may be required to complete the project.

If the same CAD software is used by cooperating professional offices, the transfer of information from one office to another is a simple task. It can be done by either transfer of removable disks or by modem on telephone lines. If the two offices are using different CAD software then the transfer of information is more complicated. In the event that an interior designer needs to share information with an architect or engineer using a different CAD software package, a common language between the two CAD systems is necessary. Most CAD software packages can write files in one or more of the common languages that have been developed for the purpose of exchanging information between different CAD systems. It is necessary, however, to develop the stored information carefully. Types of text and line weights should be compatible with the translating language used. Before any work is done on the project, it is good practice to establish guidelines for standard symbols, line weights, text, etc., among the parties sharing information. Some experimentation may be required to develop these standards. Without going through this process, the transfer of information from one CAD software to another can be extremely frustrating. The continuous research, development, and updating undertaken by CAD software manufacturers will continue to make it easier for users of different software to exchange information from one package to another.

Facilities Management

As mentioned earlier, interior designers have been offering facilities management services to small companies. Among the services offered are product/equipment inventory management, maintenance of building systems records, space planning, and drafting. The computer can be utilized to assist all such services.

It is obvious that CAD software could aid in space planning and drafting. The three-dimensional capabilities described earlier could be a further asset in this area. Facility management often includes standards programs for many items used by a particular company. One of these items could be employee workstations. Because of the nature of a standards program, typical workstations would be used repeatedly. It would then make sense to create a computer library of these workstations so that they would not have to be recreated each time they were used in a floor plan.

Product and equipment management can be handled on a spreadsheet/database program. If software programs are integrated, then a CAD program could work with a database to improve the efficiency of this service. Careful monitoring of inventories would insure efficient use of available items and early indication of depleted items. This information is also valuable to a company's accountant as depreciation formulas are employed for tax reasons.

Electronic Product Directories

Electronic product directories have grown more popular with increased computer use. These directories, such as *Sweet's* on CD-ROM, are nothing more than electronic catalogs representing a wide range of construction products, finishes, and furniture. They often include photographs and other graphic information relating to the products. Many of these directories are offered to interior designers at no charge by their manufacturers.

Electronic directories function like subscriptions. Once the manufacturer receives a request for a directory from a designer, that designer's name, address, and telephone number are entered into a customer file. As a result, the designer will receive constant updates on price, availability, and finish offerings. These directories must be kept up-to-date in a very consistent manner if an interior designer is to take advantage of them. Unfortunately, not every product manufacturer has made electronic product directories available to interior designers. Therefore, it is necessary to carefully evaluate the use of an electronic product directory before committing the time to maintaining it.

These directories can be very useful in creating specifications for products on projects. Often, they include information on installation and maintenance of the products along with fire retardancy figures.

In the future, all design-related products should be available in electronic directory format. Not only will they be available, but as technology progresses, enhanced in the following ways:

- automatic updating through a modem network

- audio descriptions of products

- video presentations on products

- instant information on manufacturers' inventories with delivery dates

Another related development will be instant order-checking by project. This means that if a project is listed with a manufacturer and orders are placed for products by that project name, designers will be able to check on the status of the orders and, in turn, the project, through their electronic directory link.

Specialized Computer Software

There are numerous software packages available for all types of tasks, among which are some specialized types appropriate to the average interior designer.

Building code software lists building code requirements developed by some of the leading code organizations in the country. Since most building codes are derived from these general codes they can be used as general references. However, building codes vary from one area of the country to another as well as from one town to the next. For this reason, building code software can only be used as a general reference until such time as a more comprehensive package can be assembled that encompasses particular areas of the country and individual towns.

Business software for the design professional is available for all types of business and accounting tasks. A number of software companies produce these programs specifically for designers. These programs offer the standard type of accounting functions plus design contract writing, design project progress tracking, designer time tracking, design-time billing, designer expenses billing, project profitability, payroll, and more. This type of software is useful in keeping the business end of the interior design profession organized.

Many of the procedures discussed previously in this chapter may require specialized software. Examples include scanning, animation, photorealistic rendering, etc. Further developments of specialized software programs to aid in the practice of interior design can be anticipated.

High Technology

Virtual reality is related to photo realistic rendering discussed earlier in this chapter. *Photo realism* is a process that creates images that are so close to photographs that it is difficult to tell that the image is computer-generated.

The difference between photo realistic rendering and virtual reality is another quantum leap. A photo realistic rendering is just a single picture that has been computer-rendered to simulate a photograph. Virtual reality is a computer-generated world which one can enter and move within. In the future, the interior designer will be able to create a 3-D computer layout of a space, and materials and surfaces will appear at the wave of a hand when the mouse has been replaced with electronic gloves that control interactive hands *in* the screen. These hands can build walls, ceilings, floors, and openings in seconds. Materials can be selected and changed through onscreen menus. One can move through this artificial space—opening and closing doors, looking closely at certain details, etc. In the near future there will probably be rooms in which a designer can assemble groupings of holographs to represent his designs. (A holograph is a two-dimensional projection that gives the illusion of three- dimensional appearance.)

Conclusion

Computers have become not only affordable, but also essential, for most interior design offices. The combination of lower costs, more powerful machines, more sophisticated software, and increased client demand for this technology has caused ever greater numbers of designers to turn to CAD.

CAD has grown beyond its role as a time-saving production tool; it is a sophisticated analysis and presentation medium as well. Through CAD, design changes are implemented and represented quickly and efficiently. Vivid, walk-through presentations utilizing animation and video are possible. These more comprehensive presentations enhance the client's ability to see the designer's ideas.

All phases of design work, including design development and contract documentation, can use such CAD features as information libraries and powerful drawing tools such as associative automatic dimensioning and hatching to increase productivity.

Information can be easily transferred from one design professional's office to another, thus enhancing design-time efficiency for every aspect of the project. With the wealth of specialized software available to interior designers, each designer can select and adopt one or more of these types of software to customize his work process.

The power and flexibility that CAD offers are valuable assets in a very competitive interior design market. Three-dimensional modeling offers unique opportunities to analyze and represent designs, opportunities which will grow with the development of virtual reality and animation. Combinations of software packages such as spreadsheet, word processing, graphics, and database with CAD effectively integrate many steps in the design, construction, and office management process. The result is an efficient, coherent interior design practice.

Definitions

For those who are beginning to explore computers, it may be helpful to define some fundamental computer terms. These "buzzwords" are associated with two basic categories, *hardware* and *software*.

Hardware

Hardware is the term used to describe the physical computer itself—the nuts and bolts. Hardware can include any piece of equipment used to assemble a computer workstation. The following are examples of hardware:

Monitor—Phosphorescent screen on which information is displayed. Monitors are available in different sizes and in black-and-white or color. Larger monitors allow more information to be legibly displayed on the screen at one time, thus minimizing scrolling and zooming. Monitors should be selected based on office needs. An appropriate screen for word processing is a low-cost black-and-white "portrait display" or single-page display screen. A color monitor is needed for CAD, with progressively greater sophistication and resolution required for more complex presentations. *Pixels* are small dots of phosphorescent light that create text and picture images on a computer screen much like the dots one sees in the Sunday comic pages. Most monitors have a screen resolution of 72 dots per inch (dpi).

CPU (Central Processing Unit)—The "brain" of the computer, consisting of a small microprocessing chip located on a printed circuit board. This main board is referred to as the "mother board." The mother board is usually the largest printed circuit board found in the cosmetic plastic box called "the computer." The plastic casing hides all the other circuit boards, chips, ports, slots, drives, etc. The computer also contains *storage* devices such as a hard disk drive and floppy disk drives (described below). The function of these "drives" is to store, copy, and transfer information (files) into and out of the machine. (More information about storage follows the "floppy disk" definition.)

Keyboard—Based on the typewriter keyboard. Keyboards also contain small numerical keypads which are set up like adding machines. Extended keyboards have extra keys which allow for "keyboard shortcut" commands on the computer (called "f" keys).

Mouse—A hand-controlled device attached to the computer used to point on the monitor for entering and modifying information. The mouse controls "cursors," "arrows," "crosshairs," and other types of gesturing symbols used to locate points on the screen.

Hard Disk Drive (Internal/External)—A machine that contains a fixed, rigid magnetic platter called a hard disk. Hard disks hold large amounts of information and are used for storing all the various software applications and files used daily in the office. Hard disks also run the computer's *operating system*. Internal hard drives are located in the computer's cosmetic plastic casing. External hard drives have their own casing and sit outside the machine. Hard drives are available in a wide variety of types and sizes and can now store hundreds of *megabytes* (one megabyte equals one million bytes) of information. The more software one has, the more hard disk space is required.

Floppy Disk Drive—A machine that *reads* floppy disks. Floppy drives are similar in function to hard drives except that they are much smaller in storage capacity and work much more slowly. Most floppy drives are internal. Their primary function is to load and unload small quantities of software and documents on and off the hard drive.

Floppy Disk—A small, round piece of magnetic tape enclosed in a plastic cover. Floppy disks come in 5 1/4" (now becoming obsolete) or 3 1/2" sizes. Their storage capacity also varies, but as of this writing the 1.4 megabyte 3 1/2" high-density diskette is the standard.

More about storage and computer disks: Keeping a duplicate of all software programs and files is mandatory. In general, the computer's hard drive is needed for the everyday use of all software programs. "Disaster" *backups* (copies) of all software and data (files) should be made on floppy disks. In addition to floppies, other new storage options include removable hard drive cartridges similar to floppy disks but with greater storage capacities, and tape drives, with varying storage capacities. Access speed, storage capacity, cost, and compatibility differentiate one from another.

Printer—Output device generally used to print letter- and legal- sized documents. Some printers produce 11 x 17 pages. Black-and-white dot matrix and laser printers are the most popular machines. Color "inkjet" printers are also now in popular use.

Plotter—Output device used to produce large format drawings. Plotters are available in different technologies such as mechanically driven pen plotters, electrostatic plotters, thermal plotters, or the more recent large format laser plotters. Most small firms use the less expensive and slower (yet high-quality) pen plotters with standard cut sheets. Reliable for the most part, pen plotters can suffer from clogged or dried-out pens. A highly detailed 34 x 22-inch drawing can take an hour or more to plot out. The alternative technologies are much faster, producing the same drawing in minutes. While line quality is somewhat compromised, the clarity of these nonmechanical plotters is improving and costs are rapidly decreasing. Drawing sizes in a plotter are usually referred to in engineering terms. "A" size drawings are approximately 8 1/2" x 11". "B" size drawings are approximately 11" x 14". "C" size drawings are approximately 18" x 24". "D" size drawings are approximately 24" x 36". "E" size drawings are approximately 36" x 48".

Software

Software is the term used to describe application programs that are used on a computer. Software programs are tools that allow people to enter, modify, and output information. The following are examples of types of software:

Operating System—In addition to the over-the-counter software products described below, all computers come with software that is necessary to start the computer and enable the use of the keyboard, monitor, mouse, hard drive, floppy drive, etc. This is the *operating system*—or electronic "infra-structure"—of a computer. Because the operating system controls the basic operation of the computer, it creates the look and feel of the user's interactions with the machine. Examples of operating systems are the Macintosh Finder, UNIX, and MS/DOS operating *platforms*, or basic operating software. These operating systems avail themselves of *icons*, *menus*, and *tools* manipulated by a mouse or keyboard.

Word Processing—Software that allows one to compose letters, reports, memos, and other documents traditionally created on a typewriter.

Spreadsheet—Software that performs mathematical calculations in a grid format. Examples of applications include critical path management, project management, budgets, cost tracking, sales projections, bar graphs, and charts, as well as routine accounting.

CAD (computer-aided design)—Software that allows one to create architectural or engineering designs, drawings, and details. These programs create *vector* geometry on the monitor such as lines, circles, and curves along

167

with vectorial lettering and dimensions. The word *vectorial* distinguishes CAD from other computer graphic products such as paint programs. Vectors are necessary in defining Cartesian (X,Y,Z) coordinates. The geometry in a CAD package has specific vector-coordinates attached to it, while a paint program simply turns pixels on or off on the monitor.

Books and Magazines

As in any subject area that is changing rapidly, magazines, which have a shorter lead time for publication, respond more quickly than books to new information. Therefore, magazines are an excellent resource for computer information. Journals in the fields of architecture, interior design, and computers (CAD, Macintosh, and IBM-style) are all pertinent. Some of these journals are listed below.

Books covering CAD topics must usually be as recent as possible in order to be of any value. For this reason, very few titles are included in this book, which is, in all other subject areas, an annotated bibliography. Some titles are listed below to provide a sample of what is available. There is no dearth of books published on computers. It is recommended that the reader verify the value of a book either through book reviews in professional magazines or from the direct personal experience of a respected colleague.

Interiors, Interior Design, IS, Architectural Record, and *Architecture* magazines contain sporadic coverage of computer applications for design. *Cadalyst* and *Cadence* are devoted to the topic. Bibliographic information for these titles is found in **Chapter 11, Magazines.**

CADD Management Institute (CMI), 12 S. Sixth St., Ste. 914, Minneapolis, MN 55402. (612) 333-9204; fax (612) 333-9210.

> David Jordani, executive director and founder. The newsletter, *Managing CADD*, is edited by B. J. Novitski. In addition to the newsletter, CMI offers research publications, educational seminars, and a directory of members. CMI is a member of the CADD Council, which will be developing standards for data exchange for the construction industry.

Kensek, Karen M., and Douglas E. Noble. *Software for Architects: The Guide to Computer Applications for the Architecture Profession.* Los Angeles: Center for Architectural Technology, 1996.

A comprehensive software shopping guide for all designers in professional practice. Approximately 20 percent to 30 percent of the entries are applicable for interior designers. Software is indexed by company name, function, and hardware platform.

Kirkpatrick, Beverly, and James Kirkpatrick. *AutoCAD for Interior Design and Space Planning.* New York: Macmillan, Merill, 1993.

A well-written tutorial for AutoCAD which is geared especially for interior design is most welcome. Objectives at the beginning of each chapter and review questions at the end support independent learning and true comprehension.

North American AutoCAD User Group (NAAUG), P.O. Box 3394, San Rafael, CA 94912-3394. (415) 507-6565, voice mail only. For quickest response, use the Web address, http://www.autodesk.com.

The users' group is sponsored by Autodesk. There are many options on the voice mail, including documents available by fax, current product information, locations of local user groups, and special interest groups, such as the A/E/C group. (A/E/C refers to architects, engineers, and contractors.)

*Vagts, Karen. *Managing AutoCAD in the Design Firm: A Manual for Architects and Interior Designers.* Reading, Mass.: Addison-Wesley Publishing Company, 1996.

The book lives up to its title. It is not a guide to how AutoCAD works, but rather a guide to making AutoCAD serve the needs of design firms of all sizes. The language is not technical and a glossary of terms is provided. Included are both approaches to thinking about using AutoCAD and painless descriptions for using special applications. Costs, payback, the differences between Releases 12 and 13, a short list of related organizations, and a bibliography all contribute to the book's overall usefulness. This book should be purchased by any office that uses, or wishes to use, AutoCAD.

Model Building

Interior models present more challenges to model builders than architectural models as they must convey volume, not just shapes in space. By necessity, they are in a larger scale than architectural models and therefore require greater detail. Color has scale and proportion and must be handled carefully or the interior will be misrepresented. Students should remember that materials boards, or story boards, are also three dimensional and form a sort of model in themselves. Books on model building provide both specifics, how-to-do-it, and new approaches to conceptualizing and expressing designs. Exposing oneself to a variety of designers' and builders' techniques will stimulate students to establish styles of their own. Very few books, good or bad, are available. Students should take every opportunity to examine work in exhibitions and that which is represented in current magazines.

Buckles, G. Matthew. *Building Architectural & Interior Design Models Fast*! Rancho Cucamonga, Calif.: Belpine Publishing Company, 1991.

> This guide for students and for designers who want to make their own models is well illustrated and clearly written. Conceptual, schematic, and presentation models are covered.

Cooper Union, Irwin S Chanin School of Architecture. *The Education of an Architect*. Edited by Elizabeth Diller, Diane Lewis, and Kim Shkapich. New York: Rizzoli, 1988.

> Excellent source of ideas for experimental techniques. The field of model building is in a new phase of exploration. This book has been a springboard for many current modelbuilders.

Hohauser, Sanford. *Architectural Interior Models*. Revised by Helen Demchyshyn. 2nd ed. New York: Van Nostrand Reinhold, 1984.

> Hohauser emphasizes more formal, finished models rather than models in progress. His approach is less "hands on" than, for example, Knoll. An appendix of suppliers of tools and materials provides an excellent source of information. Write or call for catalogs, most of which are free. Includes model photography.

*Knoll, Wolfgang, and Martin Hechinger. *Architectural Models: Construction Techniques*. New York: McGraw-Hill, 1993.

> Originally published in German, Knoll's book provides an imaginative and contemporary approach to building models and conceptualizing designs through models. Descriptive black-and-white photographs are combined with clear, well-written text. Measurements are metric but materials descriptions are generic and pose no translation problems to U.S. model builders. Excellent for students.

Kopelow, Gerry. *How to Photograph Buildings and Interiors*. New York: Princeton Architectural Press, 1993.

> Kopelow's pleasing book is designed to satisfy three different needs—assisting designers working with professional photographers, teaching designers how to photograph their own work, and enhancing the skills of professional photographers who want to photograph buildings and interiors. Techniques and equipment are discussed. Glossary.

Lucci, Roberto, and Paolo Orlandini. *Product Design Models*. New York: Van Nostrand Reinhold, 1990.

NA
2790
.L63
1990

> *Models* is a well-organized and visually pleasing addition to the literature. A wide variety of materials is presented in detail, including "found" objects. The materials are then applied to modeling various products. Fortunately for interior designers, these products include chairs, tables, lights, and several rooms. Black-and-white and color illustrations.

*Moore, Fuller. *Modelbuilder's Notebook: A Guide for Architects, Landscape Architects, and Interior Designers*. New York: McGraw-Hill, 1990.

> Moore's guide is exceptionally clear and well organized. He presents materials, tools, techniques, and scaling guidelines for creating models ranging in complexity from study models to presentation models. Techniques for rendering building and finish materials and a chapter on photographing models add to the book's value for both students and professionals. Illustrations are black-and-white.

*Porter, Tom, and Sue Goodman. *Manual of Graphic Techniques 3: For Architects, Graphic Designers, & Artists*. New York: Charles Scribner's Sons, 1983.

> This title and the following one are reviewed in this chapter under the **Drawing and Rendering—Manual** section, but they deserve another mention here in regard to model building. Thoroughness and practicality are hallmarks of the series. Theory, planning, construction techniques, and photography of models are all included in this volume.

Porter, Tom, and Sue Goodman. *Manual of Graphic Techniques 4: For Architects, Graphic Designers, & Artists*. New York: Charles Scribner's Sons, 1985.

> This volume advises students about photographing models.

Although most models of interiors are custom made, some elements of them are standard pieces which may be ordered. Several companies provide catalogs of such materials. Even if one does not order from the catalogs, they provide another source of ideas. Below are the names and addresses of several suppliers.

Plastruct, Inc.
1020 S. Wallace Place
City of Industry, CA 91748
(818) 912-7016; fax (818) 965-2036

Small Parts, Inc.
13980 N.W. 58th Court
P.O. Box 4650
Miami Lakes, FL 33014-0650
(305) 557-8222; fax (800) 423-9009

The company listed below provides a turn-key laser cutter that is compatible with CAD systems. It offers job shop services or machine sales.

Scale Models Unlimited
111 Independence Dr.
Menlo Park, CA 94025
(415) 324-2515; (800) 324-2515; fax (415) 324-2111

Thomson Financial. ADD Inc. Photograph by Peter Vanderwarker.

Chapter 9

Business and Professional Practice

Concerned with advancing the actual and perceived value of the profession in society, interior designers exhibit a high level of professionalism. Research and application to advance the causes of socially conscious and green design have received tremendous support in the design community. Productive partnerships with manufacturers such as Herman Miller and Steelcase have brought greater resources to bear in meeting design challenges. Examples of professional activity abound in the chapters on Competitions, Awards, and Scholarships and Professional and Trade Organizations. Running a business well and profitably is complex and time consuming. The titles in this chapter have been written by successful professionals to share their experiences and to assist others in the profession. In this chapter more than any other in this book, the appendices, sample forms, and glossaries found in the books listed are of great value. There is no point in reinventing a business practice or a form that has been repeatedly tested and can quickly be adapted to current needs.

American Society of Interior Designers. *Contract Forms*. ASID Service Corp., P.O. Box 1437, Merrifield, VA 22116-1437.

See **Chapter 1, Reference,** under **General References** section.

X *ASID: American Society of Interior Designers Professional Practice Manual.* Edited by Jo Ann Asher Thompson for the American Society of Interior Designers. New York: Whitney Library of Design, 1992.

> This relatively slim volume distills the knowledge and experience of the large number of respected professionals who contributed to it. The history and nature of the profession, its educational structure, its business practices, and the design and management of specialized projects are all addressed. Valuable forms and bibliographies are included.

X Berger, C. Jaye. *Interior Design Law & Business Practices.* New York: John Wiley & Sons, 1994.

> Basic information regarding accounting, contracts with clients and contractors, insurance, and litigation is outlined. Although it is not a substitute for financial and legal counsel, the volume alerts new professionals and students to areas requiring their attention. There is a useful appendix by Kerwin Kettler, a design educator, which describes the legal and professional requirements for design education and professional standing and the organizations that oversee these functions. Unfortunately, the book has no bibliography.

X *Downey, Joel, and Patricia K. Gilbert. *Successful Interior Projects Through Effective Contract Documents.* Kingston, Mass.: R. S. Means, 1995.

> As would be expected from this publisher, this volume provides accurate, well-organized information which assists in the practical application of design principles. New project managers and advanced students of design will find this volume invaluable. Included are a complete sample project manual, a concise bibliography, and 14 chapters of easily understood text which take the reader through the entire process from contract negotiations to contract administration and furniture specifications.

X *Farren, Carol E. *Planning & Managing Interiors Projects.* Kingston, Mass.: R. S. Means, 1988.

> Realistically details planning and execution of work for medium-to-large-scale commercial projects, with an emphasis on implementation. Includes sample forms for contracts, specifications, bids, budgeting, and proposals, as well as guidelines for moving offices. For professionals and students. **NCIDQ**

Friedmann, Arnold, John F. Pile, and Forest Wilson. *Interior Design: An Introduction to Architectural Interiors.* New York: Elsevier, 1982.

> Basic textbook for students written by experienced professors and practitioners. Excellent illustrated glossaries of technical terms. Annotated bibliographies flesh out the topics introduced. **NCIDQ**

Heuer, Charles R. *Means Legal Reference for Design & Construction.* Kingston, Mass.: R. S. Means, 1989.

> The author, a registered architect and attorney, addresses all aspects of design-related law. Valuable reference for professionals and useful for NCIDQ exam preparation. Extensive glossary.

IIDA (International Interior Design Association). *Forms and Documents Manual.* Chicago: International Interior Design Association, 1997.

> See **Chapter 1, Reference,** under **General References** section.

*Knackstedt, Mary V., with Laura J. Haney. *The Interior Design Business Handbook: A Complete Guide to Profitability.* 2nd ed. New York: Van Nostrand Reinhold, 1992.

> Thorough, professional coverage of interior design business considerations for both students and practitioners. Practical information—using ASID forms, employee relations, project management, understanding finances, and selecting consultants—is the core of the book. Includes bibliographies and references for design centers and trade associations.

Knackstedt, Mary V., with Laura J. Haney. *Marketing and Selling Design Services: The Designer-Client Relationship.* New York: Van Nostrand Reinhold, 1993.

> This is an insightful guide to marketing based on a win-win theory in which both the client's and designer's needs are met. It is clearly written and provides sensible suggestions for promoting design services and the design firm's reputation.

Morgan, Jim. *Marketing for the Small Design Firm.* New York: Whitney Library of Design, 1984.

> A well-written, well-presented book which is essential reading for designers. Its value is enhanced by its sensitivity to designers' emotional barriers to self-promotion. The principles recommended are illustrated

with examples drawn from 16 design firms of differing sizes and goals. **NCIDQ**

*Murphy, Dennis Grant. *The Business of Interior Design: Professional Practices Reference Guidelines*. Burbank, Calif.: Stratford House Publishing, 1975.

> Still a valuable introduction for students to the business and promotion aspects of the field. Written by a practicing professional and geared toward residential and small-scale commercial work.

*Piotrowski, Christine M. *Interior Design Management: A Handbook for Owners and Managers*. New York: Van Nostrand Reinhold, 1992.

> An up-to-date guide covering project management and the legal, planning, and business aspects of an interior design business. Includes sample forms, a bibliography, and glossary. Clear presentation of information makes the book a good choice as a classroom text.

Piotrowski, Christine M. *Professional Practice for Interior Designers*. New York: Van Nostrand Reinhold, 1989.

> Straightforward approach to professional practice. Especially useful chapters deal with employee relations (job descriptions, evaluation forms, benefits), marketing, contract documents, specifications, and career options. **NCIDQ**

Rose, Stuart W. *Achieving Excellence in Your Design Practice*. New York: Whitney Library of Design, 1987.

> Utilizes the author's expertise in design, management, and behavioral science to recommend concise strategies to improve both the designs and the personal service provided by a firm. Focuses on employee motivation and involvement. Discusses marketability as a direct result of the firm's attitude. **NCIDQ**

*Siegel, Harry, with Alan Siegel. *A Guide to Business Principles and Practices for Interior Designers*. New rev. ed. New York: Whitney Library of Design, 1982.

> Detailed guide to all aspects of business practices for designers, including liability and insurance. Many sample forms included. Written by a CPA and an attorney with many years' experience with interior design and decoration firms, especially New York City firms. **NCIDQ**

*Veitch, Ronald M., Dianne Jackman, and Mary K. Dixon. *Professional Practice: A Handbook for Interior Designers.* Winnipeg, Manitoba: Peguis Publishers, 1990.

NK
2116
. V45
1990

This compact paperback volume would serve well as the text for a professional practice course. It provides a clear and thorough description of the goals, education, organizations, and practice of the profession. Marketing, planning, programming, bidding, and specifications are detailed. Sample forms, excellent definitions. An index would have been useful.

Woodward, Cynthia. *Human Resources Management for Design Professionals.* Washington, D.C.: American Institute of Architects Press, 1990.

The author of the human resources chapter in *The Architects Handbook of Professional Practice* has written specifically for architects and engineers. She discusses all aspects of managing human resources in firms and includes sample forms, job descriptions, legal requirements, and a bibliography of books and articles.

Zweig, Mark C. *Human Resources Management: The Complete Guidebook for Design Firms.* New York: John Wiley & Sons, 1991.

A no-frills guide for professional managers and students of the subject. Includes checklists, forms, sample letters, and phone conversations in areas such as performance appraisal and recruiting. Be aware that the grammar in some examples is incorrect.

American Society of Interior Designers, Model Show House Specialty Award, 1995. Lee Bierly, ASID, and Christopher P. Drake, ASID, of Bierly-Drake Associates, Inc. Photograph by Sam Gray.

Chapter 10

Competitions, Awards, and Scholarships

Awards, grants, and competitions offer students and professionals an opportunity for recognition, publicity, and financial support. Although the competition for such rewards is usually stiff, and the submission process, as well as the ultimate jurying or decision-making, can be inconsistent, practitioners and aspirants with exceptional talent can gain immediate access to a wide audience. Coverage of winning competition entries can also indicate types of currently available work.

The focus of this listing is interior design. Therefore, when a competition is open to several professions, such as industrial design, interior design, and architecture, only interior design is mentioned. Conversely, when an interior designer sees a competition advertised in the professional literature as being for architects, or some other related profession, interior designers who are part of multidisciplinary design teams may very well be eligible. Programs cited and described below are also limited to those that are offered on a regular basis, usually annually; no competition or grant that is offered only once is included. Since submission dates will vary slightly each year, the sponsoring body should always be consulted for exact details. Unless otherwise noted, all quotes are taken from competition announcements written by the sponsors. Some awards may be applicable for both the Education and Research, and the Product Specialty headings. Please check in both sections for offerings.

The International Federation of Interior Designers has established guidelines for the organization and administration of competitions and endorses those sponsors who have applied for approval and whose competition structure satisfies IFI requirements. While lack of IFI endorsement does not indicate a poorly run competition, the federation's approval does insure a well-conducted competition worthy of an entrant's efforts. The IFI brochure, *Organising International Design Competitions & Award Schemes: Regulations and Guidelines,* is included in this book in **Chapter 1, Reference,** under the **General References** section.

Several serial publications are entirely devoted to announcing design competitions and awards. Other design magazines include such information in regular columns and often in editorial pages. Many sponsoring bodies will announce upcoming competitions, including detailed entry forms, jury members' biographies, submission requirements, etc., in professional design magazines and relevant industry-sponsored journals. Restrictive time deadlines usually preclude indexers from including competition announcements in their sourcebooks, but most do provide references to descriptions of winning entries published in the literature of the field. This can be useful when planning a strategy for entering a competition as it provides insight into successful entries. It is also helpful to know who the jurors will be for a specific competition. Thus the annotated listings of basic information sources that follow should be supplemented by scanning the professional periodical literature and its attendant indexes. (For complete publication data of magazines mentioned in this chapter, please see **Chapter 11, Magazines,** and for a listing of periodical indexes, please see **Chapter 1, Reference.**)

Winning grants, competitions, and awards is an art in itself! It is essential not only to submit an excellent design, but also to be thoroughly informed as to the members of the jury and the precise requirements for submission.

The grants, awards, and competitions listed in this chapter have been arranged according to the following divisions:

Professional Achievement Awards

Project Specialty
Healthcare
Historic Preservation
Hospitality
Religious
Residential
Retail

Education and Research

Product Specialty
  Accessories
  Fabrics and Finishes
  Flooring
  Furniture
  Glass
  Gypsum Board
  Lighting—Installation Design and Fixture Design
  Tile
  Signage, Graphics

Professional Achievement Awards

American Institute of Architects. *Institute Honors*. American Institute of Architects, 1735 New York Ave., NW, Washington, DC 20006-5292. (202) 626-7438; fax (202) 626-7421.

  For individuals or organizations who have executed an exceptional body of work in furniture design or a single work in interiors planning, preservation, or restoration. Must be nominated by an AIA member. Award: National recognition. Submission deadline: November 2nd.

American Institute of Architects. *Honor Awards for Interiors*. American Institute of Architects, 1735 New York Ave., NW, Washington, DC 20006-5292. (202) 626-7438; fax (202) 626-7364.

  Both new construction and renovations completed within the past two years are eligible. Design must be submitted by a registered architect. Award: National recognition, publication in *Architecture* magazine. Submission deadline: Fee, December 3rd; submission, January 7th.

American Society of Interior Designers. *ASID Design for Humanity Award*. ASID Design for Humanity, American Society of Interior Designers, 608 Massachusetts Ave., NE, Washington, DC 20002-6006. (202) 546-3480; fax (202) 546-3240.

  For "an individual or institution which has made a significant contribution toward improving the quality of the human environment through design-related activities." Award: Publication in *ASID Report*. Submission deadline: February 15th.

American Society of Interior Designers. *ASID Designer of Distinction Award*. ASID Designer of Distinction Award, American Society of Interior Designers, 608 Massachusetts Ave., NE, Washington, DC 20002-6006. (202) 546-3480; fax (202) 546-3240.

> For ASID professional members who have practiced at least 10 years and who have "made outstanding contributions toward achieving ASID's goal of design excellence." Award: Publication in *ASID Report*. Submission deadline: February 15th.

American Society of Interior Designers. *ASID Interior Design Project Awards*. American Society of Interior Designers National Headquarters, 608 Massachusetts Ave., NE, Washington, DC 20002-6006. (202) 546-3480; fax (202) 546-3240.

> Includes several categories in the contract and residential areas. Recently completed permanent installations are eligible. Multiple entries permitted, entry fee. Award: Publication in *ASID Report*. Submission deadline: Applications by March 15th, submissions by April 30th.

American Society of Interior Designers. *ASID Medalist Award*. American Society of Interior Designers, 608 Massachusetts Ave., NE, Washington, DC 20002-6006. (202) 546-3480; fax (202) 546-3240.

> Individual chapters may nominate outstanding chapter members for this highest of chapter honors. Recommendations are submitted to the national ASID board for its approval. Award: Recognition. Submission deadline: January 15th.

Architectural Record Magazine. *Record Interiors*. Record Interiors, *Architectural Record*, 1221 Avenue of the Americas, New York, NY 10020. (212) 512-2594.

> All projects must be recent and unpublished. Award: Publication in *Architectural Record's* special annual issue on interiors. No fee. Submission deadline: April 30th.

Builder Magazine. *Builder's Choice Design and Planning Awards*. *Builder's* Choice Awards Program, *Builder*, 655 15th St., NW, Ste. 475, Washington, DC 20005. (202) 737-0717; fax (202) 737-2439.

> Annual competition for professionals who have recently completed work in one of the following categories: light commercial construction, residential remodeling and new construction, kitchens, and baths. Entry

fee. Award: Feature in *Builder* magazine. Submission deadline: May 13th
for application fee and form; June 3rd for submission binder.

Contract Design Magazine. *New Faces issue.* New Faces Editor, *Contract Design*, 1515 Broadway, New York, NY 10036. (212) 714-1300.

Interior designers who have practiced design for fewer than 10 years may
enter projects completed within the past two years. Award: Publication
in the "New Faces" issue of *Contract Design*. Submission deadline:
October 19th.

Hospitality Design Magazine. *Platinum Circle Awards.* Bill Communications, Inc., 355 Park Ave. S., New York, NY 10010. (212) 592-6200.

This award honors those members of the profession who have made
outstanding contributions to the profession. Award: Publication in the
magazine. Submission deadline: Informal; selection made by January.

Interieur Foundation. *International Biennial Interieur.* Interieur Foundation, Groeningestraat 37, B-8500 Kortrijk, Belgium. 32-56-22-95-22 or
32-56-22-95-44; fax 32-56-21-60-77.

International biennial competition recognizing interior design creativity,
textile design, lighting objects, and furniture. Objects must not be in
production. Selection criteria include level of technical development and
feasibility for production, usefulness, and quality of presentation. Award:
International publicity, inclusion in exhibition and catalog. Submission
deadline: May 1st.

Interior Design Guild of South Florida. *Designers of the Year Award.*
Interior Design Guild, P.O. Box 370730, Buena Vista Station, Miami, FL
33137-0730. (305) 573-0404.

For licensed interior designers with recent installations in Florida.
Commercial, residential, and one special category which changes each
year. Award: Crystal palm, publication in national magazines. Submission deadline: Entry kits available in April.

Interior Design Magazine. *Interior Design Hall of Fame* Awards. Cahners
Publishing, 249 W. 17th St., New York, NY 10011. (212) 645-0067.

For professional interior designers whose "talent, commitment and vision
have contributed to the growth and prominence of the design field. Must

be nominated by a Hall of Fame member. Award: Publicity, prestige. Submission deadline: Nominations privately submitted.

Interiors Magazine. *Interiors* Magazine Competition. Awards Coordinator, The Interior Awards, *Interiors* Magazine, 1515 Broadway, New York, NY 10036. (212) 536-5153; fax (212) 536-5357.

> Contract design projects completed within the previous 20 months and located in the United States or abroad are eligible. Sixteen juried categories plus Designer of the Year. Entries may be submitted by designers, architects, clients, or manufacturers. Award: Publication in *Interiors*. Submission deadline: September 25th.

International Federation of Interior Architects/Interior Designers (IFI). *Nagoya International Design Competition.* Nagoya International Design Competition, c/o Secretariat/IFI'95, Nagoya, 6th floor Pola Nagoya Bldg., 9026, Sakae 2-chome, Naka-ku, Nagoya 460, Japan. =81-52-231-1351; fax +81-52-231-1355.

> The theme of the competition varies each year. In 1995, the subject was the application of environmental concerns to interior design. Award: grand prize of 3 million yen, a gold prize of 1 million yen, two prizes of 300,000 yen, and 5 honorable mentions of 100,000 yen. Submission deadline: initial inquiries by January 27th; preliminary judging April 14th; final submission August 4th.

International Furnishings and Design Association. *Trailblazer Award.* International Furnishings and Design Association, 1200 19th St., NW, Ste. 300, Washington, DC 20036-2422. (202) 857-1897; fax (202) 857-1106.

> The award is given to an individual who within the last five years has demonstrated leadership qualities and who "...has been responsible for an innovation that meaningfully alters the way some aspect of the furnishings and design industry functions or is perceived." Award: Trailblazer Award given at annual conference, conference expenses paid, publicity. Submission deadline: January 15th.

International Interior Design Association/*Interior Design* Magazine. *Contract Design Competition.* International Interior Design Association, 341 Merchandise Mart, Chicago, IL 60654-1104. (312) 467-1950; fax (312) 467-0779.

For any unpublished contract design project completed within the past two years. Entry fee. Award: $5,000 for winner, certificates to the next 10 winners. All winners will be published in *Interior Design* magazine. Submission deadline: April 1st.

International Interior Design Association. *Ron Wallin Distinguished Merit Award.* International Interior Design Association, 341 Merchandise Mart, Chicago, IL 60654-1104. (312) 467-1950; fax (312) 467-0779.

> The award recognizes an IIDA member who has made "outstanding contributions to the commercial design profession." Nominations may be made from the chapter level, but must be submitted by a board member or fellow of IIDA. Award: Professional recognition. Submission deadline: Mid-December.

International Interior Design Association. *Star Award.* International Interior Design Association, 341 Merchandise Mart, Chicago, IL 60654-1104. (312) 467-1950; fax (312) 467-0779.

> This award recognizes an individual (not necessarily an IIDA member) who has made an exceptional contribution to the industry. Nominations come from IIDA members and references are checked by the IIDA Board. Award: Industry recognition, national publicity. Submission deadline: Requests for nominations are sent to the chapters in August. The award is made in June.

Japan Design Foundation. *International Design Competition.* International Design Competition, Osaka, c/o Japan Design Foundation, 3-1-800, Umeda 1 Chome, Kita-ku, Osaka 530, Japan. 81-6-346-2611; fax 81-6-346-2615; cable DESIGNFOUND OSAKA.

> Broad-ranging biennial competition for recent, unpublished work in many areas, including interior design by students and professionals. Entries may encompass several areas in one submission. Two-stage judging. The submission must be in English or Japanese. Award: Total of $80,000, with $35,000 top prize. Submission deadline: Final judging for each competition is in July of odd-numbered years, for which initial inquiries must have been made by July 31st of the previous year. Endorsed by IFI.

Royal Oak Foundation. *The Royal Oak Competition in the Architectural Arts*. Royal Oak Foundation, 285 W. Broadway, Ste. 400, New York, NY 10013-2299. (212) 966-6565; fax (212) 966-6619.

> U.S. citizens who are students or not more than five years past graduation are eligible for this biennial competition. The problem written for the competition is designed to encourage collaboration among landscape architects, architects, and interior designers. The prize must be used for travel and study in the United Kingdom and utilize the resources of the National Trust. Award: $15,000. Submission deadline: May 1st.

Project Specialty

Healthcare

National Symposium on Healthcare Design and *Contract Design Magazine*. *Annual Healthcare Environment Awards*. National Symposium on Healthcare Design, 4550 Alhambra Way, Martinez, CA 94553-4406. (510) 370-0345.

> Categories for new construction and remodeling. Small entry fee. Award: Complimentary registration for Symposium on Healthcare Design and up to $1,500 reimbursement of expenses incurred to attend. Publication in *Contract Design Magazine* and *Journal of Health Care Design*. Submission deadline: August 1st.

National Symposium on Healthcare Design. *Annual Healthcare Design Competition*. National Symposium on Healthcare Design, 4550 Alhambra Way, Martinez, CA 94553-4406. (510) 370-0345.

> For students and professionals with "innovative design ideas." No entry fee. Award: Up to six $1,500 prizes and publication in the *Journal of Health Care Design*. Submission deadline: October 2nd.

Historic Preservation

American Society of Interior Designers. *Dora Brahms Award*.

> See **Education and Research** section of this chapter.

National Endowment for the Arts. *Presidential Design Awards*. Design Arts Program, Rm. 627, Nancy Hanks Center, 1100 Pennsylvania Ave., NW, Washington, DC 20506-0001. (202) 682-5437.

> Federal employees, contractors, state and local governments, and nonprofit groups that have completed design work for the federal government are eligible. Also eligible is work that has been sponsored, commissioned, or supported by the government. The work must have been completed and been in use within the previous 10 years. This award is in flux at the present time. It is hoped that this uncertainty will be resolved in the next several years.

National Trust for Historic Preservation. *Great American Home Awards*. National Trust for Historic Preservation, Center for Historic Houses, 1785 Massachusetts Ave., NW, Washington, DC 20036. (202) 673-4067.

> For preservation of residences built over 50 years ago in the United States and still used as residences. Categories include interiors and one special category which changes annually. Projects must have been completed within the past five years. Award: $2,500. Gift certificate from Sears and publication in *Historic Preservation* magazine. Submission deadline: June 30th.

National Trust for Historic Preservation. *Preservation Honor Awards*. National Trust for Historic Preservation, 1785 Massachusetts Ave., NW, Washington, DC 20036. (202) 673-4067.

> For individuals and organizations who have contributed to the preservation of the built environment. Fifteen awards may be given. Award: Publication in *Historic Preservation* magazine. Submission deadline: May 1st.

Hospitality

American Hotel & Motel Association in cooperation with the International Hotel/Motel & Restaurant Show. *Gold Key Awards for Excellence in Interior Design*. George Little Management, Media and Events Coordinator, Ten Bank St., Ste. 1200, White Plains, NJ 10606-1954. (914) 421-3315.

> Competition for professional designers who have exhibited excellence in hospitality design. Categories include lobby/reception areas, guest rooms, restaurants, and senior living facilities. Work must have been

completed during the prior 18 months. Entry fee $75. Award: Color coverage in *Hospitality Design* and *Lodging* magazines. Submission deadline: July 1ˢᵗ.

American Resort Development Association. *ARDY*. 1220 L St., NW, Ste. 510, Washington, DC 20005. (202) 371-6700; fax (202) 289-8544.

These awards for excellence are given for interior design of a timeshare resort unit and design or renovation of a resort common area. Criteria and categories vary slightly each year. Award: Statue. Submission deadline: Deadline changes each year.

Hospitality Design Magazine. *Platinum Circle Awards*.

See the **Professional Achievement Awards** section of this chapter.

James Beard Foundation. *James Beard Award for Best Restaurant Design*. James Beard Awards, c/o 77 Fifth Ave., Ste. 2CD, New York, NY 10003. (212) 620-7093.

The competition is open to architects and interior designers for projects completed in the United States or Canada. Judging is conducted by a volunteer committee of designers. Award: Certificate, bronze medallion, publicity. Submission deadline: September, with award announcement in May.

Religious

American Institute of Architects. *AIA Religious Art and Architecture Design Awards*. American Institute of Architects, 1735 New York Ave., NW, Washington, DC 20006. (202) 626-7586.

Interiors of religious buildings are included in this competition. Designers in North America who have substantially completed national or international projects begun within the past five years may submit work. Award: Citation, publication in *Architecture* magazine. Submission deadline: Entry forms due in late July 1995.

Residential

Mannington Builder Products. *In-step with Style Design Award*.

See **Product Specialty** section under **Flooring** category in this chapter.

Metropolitan Home Magazine. *Metropolitan Home Awards.* Awards Committee, Metropolitan Home, Hachette Publishing, 1633 Broadway, 41st floor, New York, NY 10019. (212) 340-9250.

Competition primarily for laypeople, though professionals who have designed residences of any sort (single family, multifamily, new construction, renovation, etc.) may enter. The focus is integrity and creativity of design. Laypeople will be given precedence over professionals. Award: Publication in the magazine. Submission deadline: August 10th.

National Kitchen & Bath Association. *NKBA National Design Competition.* National Kitchen & Bath Association, 687 Willow Grove St., Hackettstown, NJ 07840. (908) 852-0033; fax (908) 852-1695.

The competition is open to association members and qualified students in 13 categories whose projects have been completed in the year prior to the submission deadline. Categories include bathrooms and kitchens of specific sizes, showroom displays, special cabinetry applications, and "unique design solutions." Small entry fee. Award: Sculpture, national publicity. Submission deadline: September 14th.

Sub-Zero. *Sub-Zero Kitchen Design Contest.* Sub-Zero Freezer Co., Inc., 4717 Hammersley Rd., Madison, WI 53711. (608) 271-2233 or (800) 532-7820; fax (608) 271-1538.

Projects must have been designed and built within the nine-month period prior to the submission date and must include at least one full-size built-in Sub-Zero unit. Only professionals may submit entries. Award: $500 for local winners; $2,500 to $10,000 for national winners. Submission deadline: December 31st.

Retail

Display and Design Ideas Magazine. *Performance by Design Competition.* Display and Design Ideas, 6255 Barfield Rd., Ste. 200, Atlanta, GA 30328-4436. (404) 252-3381 or (800) 241-0934; fax (404) 252-4436.

Though cost of installation and appearance are criteria, the percentage increase in sales subsequent to installation is the primary factor in selecting a winner. Projects must have been completed within the current year. Award: Publication in this trade journal, which has a circulation of 18,000 visual merchandising professionals. Submission deadline: February 11th.

Institute of Store Planners and *Visual Merchandising + Store Design Magazine*. *Store Interior Design Competition*. International Executive Office of Institute of Store Planners, 25 N. Broadway, Tarrytown, NY 10591. (914) 332-1806; fax (914) 332-1541.

> Individuals or teams may enter projects completed within the past two years. Categories include shops under and over 5,000 square feet, food store, service retailer, mass merchant, specialty store, etc. Entrants must be members of ISP. $100 fee per entry. Award: Publicity. A winner and two honorable mentions selected. Submission deadline: October 15th.

Institute of Store Planners, Local Chapters. *Student Design Competitions*. International Executive Office of Institute of Store Planners, 25 N. Broadway, Tarrytown, NY 10591. (914) 332-1806; fax (914) 332-1541.

> Individual chapters, such as New York, Boston, and Los Angeles, sponsor student design competitions. All FIDER accredited schools in the region are notified. "Region" should be broadly interpreted. For example, students on the East Coast may enter the New York chapter competition. Award: Usually cash, but varies from chapter to chapter. Submission deadline: Contact the international office at the above address.

Institute of Store Planners and *Visual Merchandising + Store Design Magazine*. *Store of the Year Award*. International Executive Office of Institute of Store Planners, 25 N. Broadway, Tarrytown, NY 10591. (914) 332-1806; fax (914) 332-1541.

> Award: A "Store of the Year" will be chosen from the entrants in the *Store Interior Design Competition* listed above. Submission deadline: October 15th.

Education and Research

American Academy in Rome. *Rome Prize Fellowships*. American Academy in Rome, Fellowship Coordinator, 667 Madison Ave., New York, NY 10021. (212) 751-7200; fax (212) 751-7220.

> Fellowships for study at the Academy in Rome are designed primarily for U.S. citizens. "...excellence is the primary criterion for selection..." *Advanced Fellowships in the Design Arts* within the School of Fine Arts provide for study in interior design, architecture, historic preservation, etc., for currently practicing professionals with seven years' experience

and the equivalent of a bachelor's degree in the field. $50 application fee. Award: Six months of study at the academy in Rome, with accommodations and study/studio space. Submission deadline: November 15th.

American Society of Interior Designers. *ASID/Mabelle Wilhelmina Boldt Memorial Scholarship.* American Society of Interior Designers National Headquarters, 608 Massachusetts Ave., NE, Washington, DC 20002-6006. (202) 546-3480; fax (202) 546-3240.

Assists professional interior designers attend graduate school. Academic and creative abilities are emphasized. Applicants with an interest in design research are given preference. Award: One award of $3,500 given annually. Submission deadline: May 11th.

American Society of Interior Designers. *ASID/Steven Harris Memorial Scholarship.* Director of Education, American Society of Interior Designers National Headquarters, 608 Massachusetts Ave., NE, Washington, DC 20002-6006. (202) 546-3480; fax (202) 546-3240.

Financial need and academic and creative excellence are the criteria for this undergraduate scholarship. Award: Two scholarships of $1,500 each. Submission deadline: April 4th.

American Society of Interior Designers. *ASID/Wool Bureau Natural Fibers Fellowship.* American Society of Interior Designers National Headquarters, 608 Massachusetts Ave., NE, Washington, DC 20002-6006. (202) 546-3480; fax (202) 546-3240.

For practicing designers or educators working creatively with natural fibers in interior design. Award: $10,000 fellowship. Submission deadline: March 1st.

American Society of Interior Designers. *Dora Brahms Award.* American Society of Interior Designers National Headquarters, 608 Massachusetts Ave., NE, Washington, DC 20002-6006. (202) 546-3480; fax (202) 546-3240.

Available to schools to advance professional activities on behalf of their students in historic preservation and restoration. Award: Biennial award of $3,000. Submission deadline: May 11th.

American Society of Interior Designers Foundation. *ASID/Joel Polsky/ Fixtures Furniture Prize*. American Society of Interior Designers National Headquarters, 608 Massachusetts Ave., NE, Washington, DC 20002-6006. (202) 546-3480; fax (202) 546-3240.

> Written or visual presentations of scholarly contributions relating to education, behavioral science, business practice, design, or theory are recognized. Award: Annual award of $1,000. Submission deadline: January 14th.

American Society of Interior Designers Foundation. *ASID/Joel Polsky/ Fixtures Furniture Academic Achievement Award*. American Society of Interior Designers National Headquarters, 608 Massachusetts Ave., NE, Washington, DC 20002-6006. (202) 546-3480; fax (202) 546-3240.

> Rewards exceptional research or thesis projects by graduate or under-graduate students on the subjects of design education, behavioral science, business practice, design, theory, or another technical topic. Award: One $1,000 award annually. Submission deadline: January 14th.

American Society of Interior Designers Educational Foundation, Inc. *ASID/Steelcase Contract Design Scholarship*. Director of Education, American Society of Interior Designers National Headquarters, 608 Massachusetts Ave., NE, Washington, DC 20002-6006. (202) 546-3480; fax (202) 546-3240.

> Applicants must demonstrate superior design ability with an emphasis on contract design. Award: Two annual scholarships of $3,000 each. Submission deadline: April 1st.

American Society of Interior Designers Educational Foundation, Inc. *Yale R. Burge Award*. Director of Education, American Society of Interior Designers National Headquarters, 608 Massachusetts Ave., NE, Washington, DC 20002-6006. (202) 546-3480; fax (202) 546-3240.

> Portfolio competition for final-year students of degree or certificate programs in the United States and Canada. Professional presentation and design solutions for both residential and nonresidential interiors required. Award: One award of $500, one reserve award of $250, and five Certificates of Excellence. Submission date: February 1st for registration; April 4th for portfolio.

Center for Health Design. *Research Grant.* Center for Health Design, 4550 Alhambra Way, Martinez, CA 94553-4406. (510) 370-0345.

A grant will encourage research that will advance the design of health care facilities. Requests for proposals will be sent to schools of interior design, architecture, hospital administration, and nursing. Award: One grant of up to $10,000. Submission deadline: Requests for proposals will be sent to schools in March.

DuPont Flooring Systems. *Tony Torrice Educational Environments Graduate Fellowship and Research Award.* University of Tennessee, College of Human Ecology, Knoxville TN 37996-1900.

This annual fellowship is for graduate study in human ecology at the University of Tennessee-Knoxville which focuses on "...the effects of design on children's social, emotional or cognitive development." Award: $1,500 per annum. Submission deadline: Applications available in December; due February 15th.

Federal Interior Design Foundation (FIDF), now part of the International Interior Design Association. *Polsky/Fixtures Furniture/FIDF Grant.* International Interior Design Association, 341 Merchandise Mart, Chicago, IL 60654-1104. (312) 467-1950; fax (312) 467-0779.

Past grants have supported the establishment of the Council of Federal Interior Designers and research pertinent to the development of the field. Award: Varies with application. Submission deadline: Contact IIDA.

Fitch Grants. *James Marston Fitch Grants.* Beyer Blinder Belle, 41 E. 11th St., New York, NY 10003. (212) 777-7800; fax (212) 753-1284.

Mid-career professionals in historic preservation, decorative arts, architectural history, and other design fields may apply for research support. Award: Grants up to $10,000. Submission deadline: August 1st.

Foundation for Interior Design Education and Research. *Joel Polsky/Fixtures Furniture/FIDER Endowment.* Foundation for Interior Design Education and Research, 60 Monroe Center, N.W., Grand Rapids, MI 49503-2920. (616) 458-0400; fax (616) 458-0460.

Research grant supporting projects "related to current or future challenges facing interior design education, research, and/or the profession." Award: Up to $5,000. Submission date: January 3rd.

Furniture Library Association. *The Bernice Bienenstock Furniture Library Scholarships*. Furniture Library Association, High Point, NC 27262. (919) 883-4011.

Scholarships to aid students whose focus is furniture design, interior design, or a related subject. Schools must be accepted by the Furniture Library in order for their students to be eligible for scholarships. Once in the program, the schools themselves select award recipients. Award: Approximately 24 awards of $500 each. Submission deadline: New schools must apply to the Library scholarship committee prior to July each year.

Illuminating Engineering Society of North America. *Howard Brandston Student Lighting Design Education Grant*. Illuminating Engineering Society of North America, 120 Wall St., New York, NY 10005. (212) 248-5000.

See the **Product Specialty** section under the **Lighting—Installation Design and Fixture Design** category, in this chapter.

Interior Design Educators Council. *The Carole Price-Shanis, FIIDA/IDEC Foundation Endowment*. IDEC Foundation Grant Coordinator, 14252 Culver Dr., Ste. A-331, Irvine, CA 92714.

Educators and practitioners who have graduated from accredited interior design programs and who belong to a professional organization may apply for grants for professional development. Course tuition is eligible for support. Award: Grant of up to $1,500. Submission deadline: April 1st.

Interior Design Educators Council. *The Norman Polsky/Fixtures Furniture/IDEC Foundation Research Grant*. IDEC Foundation Grant Coordinator, 14252 Culver Dr., Ste. A-331, Irvine, CA 92714.

Interior design educators may apply for grants to support their research efforts in interior design education. Research undertaken to complete a degree is not eligible. Award: Grant of up to $5,000. Submission deadline: April 1st.

Interior Design Educators Council and the American College in London. *Summer Study Scholarship in Interior Design*. IDEC Scholarship Chair, 14252 Culver Dr., Ste. A-331, Irvine, CA 92714.

A winner will be selected from submissions of portfolios of two- and three-dimensional work and plans for contract or residential projects.

Students must be enrolled in an interior design program and must be sponsored by an IDEC member. Award: Tuition and room ($4,900). Submission deadline: December 15th.

International Facility Management Association Foundation.
IFMA/George Graves Scholarship.
IFMA/DuPont Carpet Fibers, Inc.
IFMA/Gensler and Associates Architects.
IFMA/Herman Miller.
IFMA/Teknion Furniture Systems.
International Facility Management Association, 1 E. Greenway Plaza, 11th Floor, Houston, TX 77046-0194. (713) 623-4362; fax (713) 623-6124.

Awarded to upper-level students enrolled in degree-granting facility management programs and based on grade point average, academic achievements, involvement in the field, and faculty recommendations. Award: Eleven $1,000 scholarships. Submission date: June 3rd.

International Facility Management Association Foundation. *Norman Polsky/Fixtures Furniture/IFMA Foundation Endowment for Education and Research.* International Facility Management Association, 1 E. Greenway Plaza, 11th Floor, Houston, TX 77046-0194. (713) 623-4362; fax (713) 623-6124.

Grants thus far have been for research reports. Award: Varies. Submission deadline: Contact IFMA.

International Facility Management Association Foundation. *Student Research Grant Program.* International Facility Management Association, 1 E. Greenway Plaza, 11th Floor, Houston, TX 77046-0194. (713) 623-4362; fax (713) 623-6124.

This grant supports students whose focus is facility management research and education. Award: Up to $1,000 per grant. Submission deadline: May 16th.

International Furnishings and Design Association Educational Foundation. *Student Scholarships.* International Furnishings and Design Association, 1200 19th St., NW, Ste. 300, Washington, DC 20036-2422. (202) 857-1897; fax (202) 857-1106.

Scholarships are available for students who are members of IFDA and who are enrolled full-time in design or related programs. Award: One grant of $1,500, or may be divided at judges' discretion. Submission deadline: October 15th.

International Furnishings and Design Association Educational Foundation. *Tony Torrice Professional Development Memorial Grant.* International Furnishings and Design Association, 1200 19th St., NW, Ste. 300, Washington, DC 20036-2422. (202) 857-1897; fax (202) 857-1106.

> The Torrice award assists professionals in the interiors furniture industry who wish to pursue academic study. Applicants may work in a variety of fields, some of which are design, education, retailing, marketing, or writing. Award: One per year of an unspecified amount. Submission date: January 15th.

International Interior Design Association. *IIDA Foundation/Lackawanna Leather Graduate Fellowship. IIDA Foundation/Steelcase Design Partnership Fellowship. IIDA Foundation/Wilsonart Graduate Fellowship. IIDA Foundation/Lester Johnson Graduate Fellowship. IIDA Foundation/Brayton Textile Collection Professional Fellowship.* International Interior Design Association National Office, 341 Merchandise Mart, Chicago, IL 60654-1104. (312) 467-1950; fax (312) 467-0779.

> Available annually to practicing interior designers who wish to pursue graduate-level work applicable to their practices, the profession, and the community. Award: $3,000-$5,000 per fellowship. Submission deadline: April 4th.

International Interior Design Association. *IIDA/Joel Polsky/Fixtures Furniture/Endowment.* International Interior Design Association, 341 Merchandise Mart, Chicago, IL 60654-1104. (312) 467-1950; fax (312) 467-0779.

> Funds "…research projects that will net a tangible product providing long-term benefits as well as education value to interior design professionals…" Award: Amount varies. Submission deadline: March 1st.

International Interior Design Association. *IIDA Scholarship.* (Formerly, International Society of Interior Designers *ISID Scholarship.*) International Interior Design Association, 341 Merchandise Mart, Chicago, IL 60654-1104. (312) 467-1950; fax (312) 467-0779.

One award available internationally to students of interior design. After students make their interest known to ISID, a specific project is assigned to the competitors. A winner is chosen based on the solutions. Award: $1,500, $1,000, & $500. Submission deadline: June 1st, but may vary.

International Interior Design Association College of Fellows. *IIDA Educator's Grant Competition.* (Formerly, International Society of Interior Designers College of Fellows *ISID Educator's Grant Competition.*) International Interior Design Association National Office, 341 Merchandise Mart, Chicago, IL 60654-1104. (312) 467-1950; fax (312) 467-0779.

Grant opportunity for a full-time instructor of interior design who is teaching in a degree program to develop "...educational course materials for undergraduate and graduate curricula in interior design." Award: $2,500 and publication. Submission date: June 1st.

International Interior Design Association Foundation. *Will Ching, IIDA Foundation Endowment.* International Interior Design Association National Office, 341 Merchandise Mart, Chicago, IL 60654-1104. (312) 467-1950; fax (312) 467-0779.

"This endowment honors the winner of the Will Ching, IIDA Foundation Design Award, a part of the IIDA/*Interior Design* magazine *Contract Design* competition. To qualify, projects must have been designed by designers employed by, or owning, firms of five designers or less." Any unpublished contract design project completed within the past two years is eligible. Award: $500. Submission deadline: April 2nd.

National Endowment for the Arts. *Project Grants for Design in Education.* National Endowment for the Arts, Design Arts Program, Rm. 627, Nancy Hanks Center, 1100 Pennsylvania Ave., NW, Washington, DC 20506-0001. (202) 682-5437; voice/T.T. (202) 682-5496.

Grants support organizations in "...a wide range of design education activities including the production of educational materials, the development of curricula integrating design with other subjects, teacher training programs, the testing of...evaluation methods and specific conferences...relating to design education." Award: Grants from $5,000 to $50,000, with matching funds. Submission deadline: September 16th.

National Endowment for the Arts. *Project Grants for Individuals.* National Endowment for the Arts, Design Arts Program, Rm. 627, Nancy Hanks Center, 1100 Pennsylvania Ave., NW, Washington, DC 20506-0001. (202) 682-5437; voice/T.T. (202) 682-5496.

> The grants encourage "...design as an art form that embraces aesthetic, economic and utilitarian issues." NEA encourages "projects that advance design practice, research, theory, and communication..." Proposals that address societal problems are encouraged. Award: Grants from $5,000 to $25,000. Submission deadline: July 15th.

National Endowment for the Arts. *Project Grants for Organizations.* National Endowment for the Arts, Design Arts Program, Rm. 627, Nancy Hanks Center, 1100 Pennsylvania Ave., NW, Washington, DC 20506-0001. (202) 682-5437; voice/T.T. (202) 682-5496.

> To support the "...practice of design as an art form that embraces aesthetic, economic and utilitarian issues." Projects that assist society while advancing design practice, research, theory, and communication are sought. Award: Grants from $10,000 to $50,000. Submission deadline: September 16th.

National Endowment for the Arts. *USA Fellowships.* National Endowment for the Arts, Design Arts Program, Rm. 625, Nancy Hanks Center, 1100 Pennsylvania Ave., NW, Washington, DC 20506. (202) 272-5427; fax (202) 682-5496.

> Fellowships for independent study and travel within the United States are awarded to professional designers whose work requires visits to sites of existing designs. Award: Fellowships from $5,000 to $20,000. Submission deadline: July 15th.

Nuckolls Fund for Lighting Education. Nuckolls Fund for Lighting Education, Inc., 70A Greenwich Ave., Ste. 411, New York, NY 10011. (212) 420-0377; fax (718) 769-7868.

> U.S. colleges and schools of design that currently offer courses in lighting design may submit proposals to support curricula and program development. Grants are available for programs designed for interior design and architecture professionals as well as for lighting majors. "The Fund does not provide financial support for technical research, equipment purchase, or student scholarships." Award: $10,000. Submission deadline: January 31st.

Society for Environmental Graphic Design. *Student Grant Program.*
Society for Environmental Graphic Design, One Story St., Cambridge,
MA 02138. (617) 868-3381; fax (617) 868-3591.

> Any student currently enrolled in a design program who wishes to study
> a specific area of graphic design for the built environment may apply for
> these research grants (*not* scholarships) from SEGD. Award: Two grants
> of up to $2,000 each. Submission deadline: Currently in January, but date
> is subject to change.

Steelcase Inc. and Steelcase Design Partnership. *Steelcase University.*
Steelcase University, CD-IN-02, P.O. Box 1967, Grand Rapids, MI
49501. (616) 698-4489.

> The four-week program has three goals: "encouraging students to link
> the physical environment to organizational effectiveness; helping them
> understand clients and their expectations; and providing them with
> knowledge that will help them compete in the global marketplace." The
> program is available to advanced students at FIDER-accredited schools
> on a competitive basis. Award: 25 scholarships covering housing, meals,
> and tuition. Submission deadline: January 1st.

Product Specialty

Accessories

American Society of Interior Designers. *ASID Product Design Awards.*
American Society of Interior Designers National Headquarters, 608
Massachusetts Ave., NE, Washington, DC 20002-6006. (202) 546-3480;
fax (202) 546-3240.

> Designers and manufacturers may submit recent market introductions for
> both residential and contract markets. Entry fee. Award: Publication in
> *ASID Report.* Submission deadline: March 15th for fee; April 26th for
> submission.

I.D.: The International Design Magazine. The I.D. Annual Design Review.
Design Review Editor, *I.D. Magazine*, 250 W. 57th St., Ste. 215, New York,
NY 10107. (212) 956-0535; fax (212) 246-3891.

> Professionals may submit any project or product for the North American
> market introduced or executed during the previous calendar year. Areas

of interest to interior designers are the following: contract interiors, contract or residential furniture, lighting fixtures, textiles, hard or soft floor finishes, and conceptual projects. Student entries are limited to product and graphic design. Award: Recognition and publicity. Submission deadline: February 1st.

Interior Design Magazine. *ROSCOE Awards*. Cahners Publishing, 249 W. 17th St., New York, NY 10011. (212) 463-6693.

Recognition of excellence in 30 different categories is given to designers, distributors, and manufacturers of interior furnishings for the residential or contract markets who have introduced products in the United States within the past year. One product will be selected as the year's Outstanding Interior Design Product. Entry fee. Award: Publication in *Interior Design* magazine. Submission deadline: February 15th.

International Interior Design Association. *IIDA Product Design Competition*. International Interior Designers Association, 341 Merchandise Mart, Chicago, IL 60654-1104. (312) 467-1950; fax (312) 467-0779.

This contract product competition has 35 categories, one of which includes desk and office accessories. Products must have been offered for sale during the past year. Award: *Contract Design* magazine will publish the winners. The Charles S. Gelber Best of Competition award is given. Submission deadline: July 2nd.

Maggi. *Maggi Edition*. Institut fur Neue Technische Form, "Maggi Edition," Eugen-Bracht-Weg 6, Darmstadt, Germany. 011-49-6151-480-08; fax 011-49-6151-465-53.

Maggi produces tableware and kitchen products and is interested in both creativity and function. The competition has several categories, is open to both students and professionals, and requires no entry fee. Award: 65,000DM to be divided among five prizes. Submission deadline: July 30th.

Fabrics and Finishes

American Society of Interior Designers. *ASID Product Design Awards*. American Society of Interior Designers National Headquarters, 608 Massachusetts Ave., NE, Washington, DC 20002-6006. (202) 546-3480; fax (202) 546-3240.

Designers and manufacturers may submit recent market introductions of surface coverings and textiles for both residential and contract markets. Entry fee. Award: Publication in *ASID Report*. Submission deadline: March 15th for fee; April 26th for submission.

American Society of Interior Designers. *ASID/Wool Bureau Natural Fibers Fellowship.*

See the **Education and Research** section of this chapter.

Amoco Fabrics and Fibers Company. *Student Design Competition.* Amoco, PO Box 66, Greenville, SC 29602. (800) 925-0668, ext. 337.

Design schools that have weaving programs may qualify for their students to enter the competition. The schools are given grants to support the competition and each school is given the same range and quantity of one of the company's yarns. The resulting fabrics are judged. The primary advantage to students is that all the winning designs are shown to manufacturers by an Amoco representative. Many designs are purchased by manufacturers, thus giving students exposure that would otherwise be difficult to achieve Award: $3,000 for 1st, $2,000 for 2nd, and $1,000 for 3rd places. Honorable mentions receive $100. Submission deadline: Late winter.

Carnegie Fabrics and the American Craft Council. *American Handweavers Competition.* Carnegie Fabrics, 110 North Centre Ave., Rockville Centre, NY 11570. (516) 678-6770; fax (516) 678-6848.

Biannual competition for handweavers meant to foster ties between handweavers and the American textile industry. Original textiles for upholstery and draperies are sought. Award: $750 to $3,000. Submission deadline: May 1st.

Chicago Athenaeum. *GOOD DESIGN Awards Program and Exhibition.* Deputy Curator/Manager of Exhibitions, Chicago Athenaeum, The Daniel H. Burnham Center, 1165 Clark St., Chicago, IL 60610. (312) 280-0131; fax (312) 280-0132.

Fabrics/textiles that have been designed or produced in the United States within two years prior to the submission date may be entered. Application fee. Award: Inclusion in exhibition at Chicago Athenaeum during NEOCON. Submission deadline: December 31st.

Interior Design Magazine. *ROSCOE Awards*. Cahners Publishing, 249 W. 17ᵗʰ St., New York, NY 10011. (212) 463-6693.

> Recognition of excellence in 30 different categories is given to designers, distributors, and manufacturers of interior furnishings for the residential or contract markets who have introduced products in the United States within the past year. One product will be selected as the year's Outstanding Interior Design Product. Entry fee. Award: Publication in *Interior Design* magazine. Submission deadline: February 15ᵗʰ.

International Interior Design Association. *IIDA Product Design Competition*. International Interior Designer Association, 341 Merchandise Mart, Chicago, IL 60654-1104. (312) 467-1950; fax (312) 467-0779.

> This contract product competition has 35 categories, some of which include hospitality textiles, wallcoverings, window coverings, upholstery textiles, and others related to finishes. Products must have been offered for sale during the past year. Award: *Contract Design* magazine will publish the winners. The Charles S. Gelber Best of Competition award is given. Submission deadline: July 2ⁿᵈ.

Wettbewerb I&I: Textile Design Competition. Design Center Stuttgart, Landesgewerbeamt Baden-Wurttemberg, Wettbewerb I&I, Willi-Bleicher-Strasse 19, D-70174 Stuttgart, Germany. +49-711-123-2536; fax +49-711-123-2228.

> The competition is international in scope and both mass-production and individual sample designs are eligible. Carpet, fabric, and bed linens will be evaluated in terms of aesthetic qualities, innovation, ability to be produced in quantity, and "green" characteristics. Award: Up to six winners will share DM60,000. Submission deadline: During the period July 1ˢᵗ-October 15ᵗʰ.

Flooring

Armstrong World Industries. *Elements of Style Commercial Flooring Design Competition*. Elements of Style Competition at Armstrong World Industries, P.O. Box 3001, Lancaster, PA 17604. (717) 397-0611.

> The judges look for "...innovative, creative and functional use of Armstrong resilient flooring within the context of the overall design theme." Projects must be located in the United States and have been

completed within the past two years. Award: $5,000, $2,000; feature in an Armstrong ad; national publicity. Submission deadline: January 1st.

DuPont Flooring Systems. *"Antron" Design Award*. DuPont Antron Design Award Center, Burson-Marsteller, 230 Park Ave. S., New York, NY 10003. (212) 614-4877.

For students and professionals in the following categories: offices, hospitality, health care, public spaces, and store planning. "All design entries must be for commercial projects in which carpet plays a significant role, and must incorporate carpets of 100 percent DuPont 'Antron,' 'Antron XL,' 'Antron Lumena' solution dyed or 'Antron Precedent' nylon." Awards: $10,000 top prize. Submission deadline: July 15th.

Interior Design Magazine. *ROSCOE Awards*. Cahners Publishing, 249 W. 17th St., New York, NY 10011. (212) 463-6693.

Recognition of excellence in 30 different categories is given to designers, distributors, and manufacturers of interior furnishings for the residential or contract markets who have introduced products in the United States within the past year. One product will be selected as the year's Outstanding Interior Design Product. Entry fee. Award: Publication in *Interior Design* magazine. Submission deadline: February 15th.

International Interior Design Association. *IIDA Product Design Competition*. International Interior Designer Association, 341 Merchandise Mart, Chicago, IL 60654-1104. (312) 467-1950; fax (312) 467-0779.

This contract product competition has 35 categories, one of which includes hard surface flooring. Products must have been offered for sale during the past year. Award: *Contract Design* magazine will publish the winners. The Charles S. Gelber Best of Competition award is given. Submission deadline: July 2nd.

Mannington Builder Products. *In-step with Style Design Award*. Mannington Builder Products, P.O. Box 30, Salem, NJ 08079-0030. (609) 935-3000; fax (609) 339-5813.

This "...contest is open to all designers of model home interiors who use a minimum of two (2) of Mannington's three (3) hard surface flooring products—ceramic tile, wood and resilient—for a model home design project." The judges include representatives of *Builder Magazine, House Beautiful* magazine, and ASID. Award: 1st prize, trip to Venice for Incontri Venezia (design show for wallcoverings and textiles) plus

$2,000; 2nd prize, $2,000; 3rd prize, $1,000. Submission deadline: October 31st.

Monsanto Contract Fibers. *DOC* awards. Monsanto, 320 Interstate North Parkway, Atlanta, GA 30339. (800) 543-5377.

These awards recognize outstanding contract installations which utilize Ultron nylon fibers. Award: Usually four first-place awards of $1,500 each, sculpture, trip to New York City, inclusion in national advertising campaign. Submission deadline: August 31st.

Furniture

American Society of Furniture Artists. *Furniture of the 90's*. American Society of Furniture Artists, P.O. Box 270188, Houston, TX 77277-0188. (713) 869-5600.

A biennial competition to identify the best in current "art furniture" by, among others, designers and students. Award: Three $1,000 prizes and inclusion in a traveling exhibition and the accompanying catalog. Submission deadline: September 15th.

American Society of Furniture Designers. *Outstanding Furniture Designer*. American Society of Furniture Designers, P.O. Box 2688, High Point, NC 27261. (910) 884-4074. Award: Recognition. Submission deadline: Call for information.

American Society of Interior Designers. *ASID Product Design Awards*. American Society of Interior Designers National Headquarters, 608 Massachusetts Ave., NE, Washington, DC 20002-6006. (202) 546-3480; fax (202) 546-3240.

Designers and manufacturers may submit recent market introductions for both residential and contract markets. Entry fee. Award: Publication in *ASID Report*. Submission deadline: March 15th for fee; April 26th for entry.

Chicago Athenaeum. *GOOD DESIGN Awards Program and Exhibition*. Deputy Curator/Manager of Exhibitions, Chicago Athenaeum, The Daniel H. Burnham Center, 1165 Clark St., Chicago, IL 60610. (312) 280-0131; fax (312) 280-0132.

Contract office furniture that has been designed or produced in the United States within two years prior to the submission date may be entered. Application fee. Award: Inclusion in exhibition at Chicago Athenaeum during NEOCON. Submission deadline: December 31st.

Chicago Merchandise Mart, cosponsored by the Summer and Casual Furniture Manufacturers Association. *Casual Furniture Design Excellence Awards*. Chicago Merchandise Mart, Chicago, IL 60654. (312) 527-7854.

Entry limited to Merchandise Mart tenants who are SCFMA members. Award recognizes excellence and innovation of design in this market. Award: Publicity. Submission deadline: September.

Concorso Spazio Design. *Spazio Design*. ADI, via Montenapoleone 18, 20121 Milano, Italy. 02/782044-798159; fax 02/76004937.

ICSID-sponsored competition for various furnishing items, such as lighting, sofa- and chair-beds, and kitchen furniture. ADI is a national organization representing Italian design nationally and internationally and is a member of ICSID and ICOGRADA. Contact ADI for information regarding additional competitions. Award: Contact ADI. Submission deadline: December 31st.

Doug Mockett & Co. *Doug Mockett Design Competition*. D. Mockett & Co., P.O. Box 3333, Manhattan Beach, CA 90266. (310) 318-2491; fax (310) 376-7650; telex 181872.

Designs are sought for furniture hardware, components, and parts for Mockett's line of office and laboratory furniture. Designs for domestic products that are not directly related to existing products are also encouraged. Award: $1,000 plus a royalty for items manufactured. Submission deadline: August 19th.

Furniture Library Association. *The Bernice Bienenstock Furniture Library Scholarships*. Furniture Library Association, High Point, NC 27262. (919) 883-4011.

See the **Education and Research** section of this chapter.

Industrial Designers Society of America with *Business Week. Industrial Design Excellence Awards (IDEA)*. Industrial Designers Society of America, 1142 Walker Rd., Great Falls, VA 22066. (703) 759-0100; fax (703) 759-7679.

> Furniture and fixtures comprise one of many categories in this well-established competition. Criteria applied to all entries are "innovation, benefit to user, benefit to client, ecological responsibility, and visual appeal." Entry fee. Award: Promotion and publication by IDSA. Some winners will be included in a lead story of *Business Week*. Submission deadline: Entry kit must be requested by February 18th; final submission by February 22nd.

Interior Design Magazine. *ROSCOE Awards*. Cahners Publishing, 249 W. 17th St., New York, NY 10011. (212) 463-6693.

> Recognition of excellence in 30 different categories is given to designers, distributors, and manufacturers of interior furnishings for the residential or contract markets who have introduced products in the United States within the past year. One product will be selected as the year's Outstanding Interior Design Product. Entry fee. Award: Publication in *Interior Design* magazine. Submission deadline: February 15th.

International Furnishings and Design Association Educational Foundation. *IFDA Local Chapter Student Design Competitions*. International Furnishings and Design Association, 1200 19th St., NW, Ste. 300, Washington, DC 20036-2422. (202) 857-1897; fax (202) 857-1106.

> Though the national organization no longer sponsors design competitions, many of its local chapters do, offering prizes as high as $3,000-$4,000. Contact IFDA national for a list of chapters and their addresses.

International Interior Design Association. *IIDA Product Design Competition*. International Interior Design Association, 341 Merchandise Mart, Chicago, IL 60654-1104. (312) 467-1950; fax (312) 467-0779.

> This contract product competition has 35 categories, some of which include furniture systems, tables, lounge furniture, and custom furniture. Products must have been offered for sale during the past year. Award: *Contract Design* magazine will publish the winners. The Charles S. Gelber Best of Competition award is given. Submission deadline: July 2nd.

International Woodworking Machinery & Furniture Supply Fair (IWF). *Competition for Student Furniture Designers.* IWF, 655 Engineering Dr., Ste. 150, Norcross, GA 30092. (404) 246-0608.

> Students must be matriculated in and sponsored by an accredited college in the United States. Six awards for different categories. Award: Top prize $2,000; awards total $12,000. Submission deadline: Schools must register with the IWF by January 10th; students must register with schools by March 4th.

Table, Lamp + Chair. *Table, Lamp + Chair.* Table, Lamp + Chair, P.O. Box 5906, Portland, OR 97228-5906. (503) 226-3556.

> International juried competition for "...original furniture and lighting design as industry and craft." Categories for students, professionals, and laypeople. Entry fee. Award: Grants to schools and professional organizations, recognition through an exhibition, and national media coverage. Submission deadline: June 19th.

Glass

National Glass Association. *Awards for Excellence.* National Glass Association President's Office, 8200 Greensboro Dr., Ste. 302, McLean, VA 22102. (703) 442-4890; fax (703) 442-0630.

> For professionals with recent commercial or residential installations that highlight the assets of glass in interiors. This competition was last held in 1989-90. It has not been canceled, but is on hold indefinitely.

Gypsum Board

Gypsum Association. *Excellence in Gypsum Board Design & Construction.* Gypsum Association, 810 First St., NE, #510, Washington, DC 20002. (202) 289-5440; fax (202) 289-3707.

> The competition is open to any member of a design/build team involved with a creative project-wide application of gypsum board. The project must be 90 percent complete by the end of the year in which the application is submitted. Award: $3,000 for each winning project team. Submission deadline: December 31st.

Lighting—Installation Design and Fixture Design

American Society of Interior Designers. *ASID Product Design Awards*.
American Society of Interior Designers National Headquarters, 608
Massachusetts Ave., NE, Washington, DC 20002-6006. (202) 546-3480;
fax (202) 546-3240.

> Designers and manufacturers may submit recent market introductions for
> both residential and contract markets. Entry fee. Award: Publication in
> *ASID Report*. Submission deadline: March 15ᵗʰ for fee; April 26ᵗʰ for
> entry.

CSL Lighting Manufacturing Inc. *Applie Awards*. CSL Lighting Manufacturing Inc., 27615 Ave. Hopkins, Valencia, CA 91355. (805) 257-4155.

> For designers who use CSL products in either contract or residential
> work. Award: Applie trophy and recognition. Submission deadline:
> October 31ˢᵗ.

Chicago Athenaeum. *GOOD DESIGN Awards Program and Exhibition*.
Deputy Curator/Manager of Exhibitions, Chicago Athenaeum, The Daniel
H. Burnham Center, 1165 Clark St., Chicago, IL 60610. (312) 280-0131;
fax (312) 280-0132.

> Lamps/lighting that have been designed or produced in the United States
> within two years prior to the submission date may be entered. Applica-
> tion fee. Award: Inclusion in exhibition at Chicago Athenaeum during
> NEOCON. Submission deadline: December 31ˢᵗ.

General Electric Company. *Edison Award Competition*. Edison Award
Competition, General Electric Company, Nela Park No. 4162, Cleveland,
OH 44112. (216) 266-2121.

> Open to any lighting professional who utilizes GE lamps in a project
> completed within the previous calendar year. Effective use of new
> products and techniques, aesthetic quality, and energy efficiency are
> examined. One of the judges is a representative of the American Society
> of Interior Designers. Award: A piece of Steuben crystal, plaques, and
> publicity. Submission deadline: February 25ᵗʰ.

Halo/Metalux. *Halo/Metalux National Lighting Competition*. Halo Lighting, 400 Busse Rd., Elk Grove Village, IL 60007. (708) 956-8400.

Annual competition sponsored in conjunction with ASID, emphasizing lighting as a design element. Technical expertise and creativity in the use of Halo Lighting Power-Trac, Halo down lighting, and Metalux florescent lighting are sought. Award: $750-$2,000 prizes, recognition. Submission deadline: June 1st for early submittal bonus; July 1st final deadline.

Halo/Metalux. *Halo/Metalux Product Design Competition*. Halo Lighting, 400 Busse Rd., Elk Grove Village, IL 60007. (708) 956-8400.

Categories for contractors, students, and designers. Award: $2,000, manufacture of winner with design credit. Submission deadline: June 1st for early submittal bonus; July 1st final deadline.

Illuminating Engineering Society of North America. *Howard Brandston Student Lighting Design Education Grant*. Illuminating Engineering Society of North America, 120 Wall St., New York, NY 10005. (212) 248-5000.

The award "was established to encourage and recognize students who have evidenced high professional promise through the presentation of an original and ingenious solution to a supplied lighting design problem." Award: Plaque and free registration at IESNA annual conference plus $1,000 to defray travel expenses to convention. Submission deadline: May 1st.

Illuminating Engineering Society of North America. *International Illumination Design Awards, Aileen Page Cutler Memorial Award for Residential Lighting*. Illuminating Engineering Society of North America, 120 Wall St., New York, NY 10005. (212) 248-5000.

Installation must have been completed within the previous two years. Judging progresses through local and regional levels to reach the national level. Competition is administered by IIDA committee. Award: Certificates at local and regional levels; certificates and sculpture at national level. Submission deadline: January 1st at section (local) level.

Illuminating Engineering Society of North America. *International Illumination Design Awards, Edwin F. Guth Memorial Awards*. Illuminating Engineering Society of North America, 120 Wall St., New York, NY 10005. (212) 248-5000.

Installation must have been completed within the previous two years. Judging progresses through local and regional levels to reach the national level. Competition is administered by IIDA committee. Award: Certificates at local and regional levels; certificates and sculpture at national level. Submission deadline: January 1st at section (local) level.

Illuminating Engineering Society of North America. *International Illumination Design Awards, Electric Power Research Institute (EPRI) Energy Efficiency Award.* Illuminating Engineering Society of North America, 120 Wall St., New York, NY 10005. (212) 248-5000.

This award "recognize(s) quality lighting applications in commercial buildings that demonstrate dramatic energy savings while improving the overall quality of the installation." Award: Crystal obelisk, certificate, national publicity. Submission deadline: January 1st at section (local) level.

Illuminating Engineering Society of North America. *Richard Kelly Grant.* Illuminating Engineering Society of North America, Lighting Research and Education Fund, 120 Wall St., New York, NY 10005. (212) 248-5000.

For those "35 years of age or younger working or studying in the United States, Canada or Mexico..." The program seeks "New and innovative work in the conceptual or applied use of light..." Award: $1,500 and $500. Submission deadline: January 31st.

Interior Design Magazine. *ROSCOE Awards.* Cahners Publishing, 249 W. 17th St., New York, NY 10011. (212) 463-6693.

Recognition of excellence in 30 different categories is given to designers, distributors, and manufacturers of interior furnishings for the residential or contract markets who have introduced products in the United States within the past year. One product will be selected as the year's Outstanding Interior Design Product. Entry fee. Award: Publication in *Interior Design* magazine. Submission deadline: February 15th.

International Association of Lighting Designers, cosponsored by *Interiors* magazine. *IALD Lighting Awards.* IALD Awards Program, International Association of Lighting Designers, 18 E. 16th St., Ste. 208, New York, NY 10003-3193. (212) 206-1281; fax (212) 206-1327.

Anyone who has recently completed a permanent installation that "displays high aesthetic achievement backed by technical expertise and exemplifies a synthesis of the architectural and lighting design processes" is eligible. Small entry fee. Award: Certificates of Excellence and Honorable Mention, worldwide publicity. Submission deadline: March 1st.

International Interior Design Association. *IIDA Product Design Competition.* International Interior Designer Association, 341 Merchandise Mart, Chicago, IL 60654-1104. (312) 467-1950; fax (312) 467-0779.

> This contract product competition has 35 categories, some of which include furniture integrated task/ambient lighting, portable lamps, and general lighting. Products must have been offered for sale for the first time during the past year. Entry fee. Award: *Contract Design* magazine will publish the winners. The Charles S. Gelber Best of Competition award is given. Submission deadline: July 2nd.

Koizumi Sangyo Corporation. *Koizumi International Lighting Design Competition for Students.* Mark Shan, Shan Exhibit, 395 Broadway, 7B, New York, NY 10013. (212) 274-8348; fax (212) 274-8434.

> A two-stage competition inviting students to examine alternative methods of creating light that conserve energy and preserve the environment. Finalists will be given a 50,000 yen subsidy to assist in construction. Award: Three awards totaling 1,400,000 yen, recognition in industry publications, inclusion in exhibition in Tokyo. Submission deadline: January 31st.

National Lighting Bureau. *National Lighting Awards.* National Lighting Bureau, 2101 L St., NW, Washington, DC 20037. (202) 457-8437.

> Installations completed within the past 22 months that represent the value of new or updated lighting to productivity and safety are eligible. Award: Publication in national trade or professional journal with the winner's byline. Submission deadline: October 15th.

Nuckolls Fund for Lighting Education.

> See the **Education and Research** section of this chapter.

Tile

Assopiastrelle. *Assopiastrelle Design Award.* Italian Tile Center, division of Italian Trade Commission, 499 Park Ave., New York, NY 10022. (212) 980-1500. Competition administered by Abbate Communications, 222A 6th Ave., Brooklyn, NY 11215. (718) 783-3160; fax (718) 398-2591.

> "The award was created to honor an American interior designer or architect whose creative use of ceramic tile has helped to enhance the

image of the material." A designer's entire body of work is examined to select a winner. Award: $5,000. Submission deadline: Late winter, early spring for award at "Coverings," tile and surface treatment show.

Mannington Builder Products. *In-step with Style Design Award.*
See **Flooring** category in this section.

Tile Promotion Board. *Spectrum International.* Spectrum Competition, c/o Tile Promotion Board, 900 E. Indiantown Rd., Ste. 211, Jupiter, FL 33477. (800) 495-5900 or (561) 743-3150; fax (561) 743-3160.

For professionals and ceramic tile trade members. Awards highlight excellence and creativity in new residential construction, residential remodeling, new commercial development, and commercial remodeling projects completed within the previous two years anywhere in the world. Award: Wide publicity in shelter, trade, and professional magazines; crystal award designed by Tiffany. Submission deadline: January 31st.

Signage, Graphics

James Beard Foundation. *James Beard Award for Best Restaurant Graphics.* James Beard Awards, c/o 77 Fifth Ave., Ste. 2CD, New York, NY 10003. (212) 620-7093.

The competition is open to architects, interior designers, and graphic designers for projects completed in the United States or Canada. Judging is conducted by a volunteer committee of designers. Award: Certificate, bronze medallion, publicity. Submission deadline: September, with award announcement in May.

Society for Environmental Graphic Design. *SEGD Design Awards.* Society for Environmental Graphic Design, One Story St., Cambridge, MA 02138. (617) 868-3381; fax (617) 868-3591.

SEGD recognizes exceptional design in many categories; among them are wayfinding, signage, storefronts, directories, showrooms, exhibits, and unbuilt projects. Entry fee. Award: Honor and Merit awards, publicity. Submission deadline: Spring or fall; call for specific date.

Journals

The following journals are devoted to coverage of competitions.

The Competition Project. *COMPETITIONS*. *COMPETITIONS*, P.O. Box 21445, Louisville, KY 40250. tel./fax (502) 451-3623. $28/two titles published at six-week intervals.

> *COMPETITIONS* and *CompetitionHotline* announce competitions for architects and designers that "require the design of products...which have not yet been in production" or which are "site specific." Competition results are published with illustrations. Includes interviews with well-known designers. Stimulating publication, but direct coverage of interior design competitions is limited.

*Deadlines. Deadlines, P.O. Box 3449, Arlington, VA 22302. tel./fax (703) 578-4918. $26/12 times per year.

> Well-organized, accessible newsletter announcing competitions for interior design, architecture, the arts, landscape design, and urban planning. Pamphlet format, no illustrations. Provides the most comprehensive listing of interior design competitions.

The following journals include coverage of interior design competitions.

Architecture (Incorporating Architectural Technology). BPI Communications, Inc., 1130 Connecticut Avenue, NW, Suite 625, Washington, DC 20036.

> Submission deadlines listed in "Events" column.

Architectural Record. McGraw-Hill Publications, Subscription Department, P.O. Box 564, Hightstown, NY 08520-9885.

> Competitions listed in the "Letters/Calendar" column under the "Competitions" subheading.

Casabella. Elemond spa, Via D. Trentacoste 7, 20134 Milano, Italy. Tel. 02/215631, fax 02/21563260.

> Lists only winners, not announcements.

Domus: *Architettura Arredamento Arte*. Editoriale Domus, Via Achille Grandi 5-7, 20089 Rozzano, Milano, Italy.

> Lists architectural and design competitions (concorsi di design) in the back of each issue. Only countries whose language is English have listings in English, though this is not consistent. German and Italian competitions, for example, are described in Italian.

Interior Design Magazine. Cahners Publishing, 249 West 17th St. New York, NY 10011. (212) 463-6693.

> Competition announcements listed in "Forum" column.

Interiors Magazine. 1515 Broadway, New York, NY 10036. (212) 536-5152.

> Competition submission dates listed under heading "Industry Dates." Additional information is in "In the News."

IS, the magazine for Interiors & Sources. L.C. Clark Publishing Co., 840 U.S. Highway One, Ste., 330, North Palm Beach, FL 33408-3878.

> "Business Briefs; Honors, Awards and Competitions" column lists competitions and winners. Additional information is in the "General News" column.

L'architettura: Cronache e Storia. Instituto Poligrafico e Zecca dello Stato, Piazza Verdi, 10-00198 Roma, Italia. Tel. 06/85081, fax 06/85082517.

> Lists themes, qualifications, due dates, sponsors, and prizes for international and European competitions in each issue in the column "Rubriche/news, concorsi." More detailed information regarding new competitions is in an adjacent column. Competitions are primarily for architecture and urban planning. Listings are in Italian.

Progressive Architecture. 600 Summer St., P.O. Box 1361, Stamford, CT 06904.

> See "Events" listing for competition deadlines; "News" for announcements of competition winners.

"THE STUDIO,,
YEAR-BOOK
OF DECORATIVE ART

A REVIEW OF THE LATEST DEVELOPMENTS IN THE ARTISTIC CONSTRUCTION DECORATION AND FURNISHING OF THE HOUSE

1915

OFFICES OF ,THE STUDIO' 44, LEICESTER SQUARE LONDON

"The Studio" Yearbook of Decorative Art, 1915.
Photograph courtesy of the Boston Athenaeum.

Chapter 11

Magazines

Written and compiled by Margaret Peterson Bartley and Susan Lewis

Journals, or magazines, are the source of the most current information in any field and a crucial form of professional communication. Interior design makes the most of the attributes available in this area of publishing. Journals provide a constant flow of visual stimuli, sources for new and desirable products, the latest in code and licensing requirements, economic information, and professional support and acknowledgement. Many journals devote one issue per year to either a special subject or a compilation of resources and references which provide invaluable current information for designers. Design journals represent an area of the highest production quality of all magazines, making them attractive to both professionals and laypeople. The journals included in this volume have been selected for professionals and students in the field and include non-English language titles, as their visual nature renders them intelligible to all designers. In each entry the address given is that of the editorial office. It is followed by the current or approximate cost of a one-year subscription in dollars and the frequency of publication. The magazine's focus and special offerings are then detailed. When publishers have included particularly good content descriptions, those comments are included in quotations and not footnoted. At the end of the magazine listing are the titles of indexes that may be used to access information in the journals. Full descriptions of the indexes are found in **Chapter 1, Refer-**

ence. Following the list of indexes is a citation for the book *Directory of International Periodicals and Newsletters on the Built Environment*, which may be consulted for coverage of additional journals relating to the built environment and suggestions to individuals and firms for subscribing to magazines.

Abitare. Editrice Abitare Segesta S.p.A., Corso Monforte 15, 20122 Milan, Italy. U.S. contact: Virginia Gatti, 6725 Allot Ave., Van Nuys, CA 91401. $115/11 issues.

> This excellent Italian magazine appeals to a general design audience, bringing the important Italian design aesthetic to architecture, interiors, product design, and industrial design. Imaginative special features, plans, elevations, reviews of international exhibits, and parallel English translations enhance its value.

Aesclepius. The Official Publication of the National Symposium on Healthcare Design. National Symposium on Healthcare Design, 4550 Alhambra Way, Martinez, CA 94553-4406. $48/three issues.

> Written for design professionals who specialize in healthcare design, this brief newsletter provides news, a calendar, and articles on current topics. The board of directors of the National Healthcare Symposium is made up of well-respected professionals.

American Furniture. Chipstone Foundation, Milwaukee, WI; distributed by the University Press of New England, 23 S. Main St., Hanover, NH 03755-2048. $45/one issue.

> Stanley and Polly Stone collected furniture that was made or used in America from Colonial times to the present. They created the Chipstone Foundation for the "dual purpose of preserving and interpreting their collection and stimulating research and education in the decorative arts." This scholarly journal, first published in 1993, includes such topics as furniture history, technology, connoisseurship, and conservation. Articles are approximately 20 pages in length and include end notes. Scholarly book reviews, black-and-white and color illustrations, and a bibliography of recently published books and articles about American furniture make this a significant resource for furniture history.

APT: Association for Preservation Technology, Communique and *Bulletin.* Association for Preservation Technology International, P.O. Box 8178, Fredericksburg, VA 22404. (540) 373-1621. (Voice mail only; the office is no longer staffed.) *Communique*—four/year, *Bulletin*—four/year. Subscriptions with membership, which ranges from $25 to $115.

> *Communique* is a nontechnical newsletter of approximately 15 pages which keeps the profession current on news and projects. The *Bulletin* provides guidance for conservation techniques. The organization itself is interdisciplinary and is "dedicated to the practical application of the principles and techniques necessary for the care and wise use of the built environment." Book reviews.

Architectural Lighting. Miller Freeman, One Penn Plaza, New York, NY 10119. $24/four issues.

> Guided by an editorial advisory board of distinguished designers, lighting engineers, and educators, *Architectural Lighting* provides excellent coverage of all aspects of lighting relevant to interior designers. In addition to product information, reports on technology, and features on professional techniques and practice, each issue documents and analyzes at least three to four exemplary interior projects, either by typology or application.

*Architectural Record. McGraw-Hill, 1221 Avenue of the Americas, New York, NY 10020. $59/14 issues.

> Increasing interest in the interrelations of interiors and architecture is reflected in this premier American architectural magazine, which now has an editor specifically for interiors. An annual issue is devoted to award-winning interiors projects. As of January 1, 1997, *Record* will be the official organ of the American Institute of Architects.

Architectural Review. 33-39 Bowling Green Lane, London EC1R ODA, UK. $85/12 issues.

> Based in London, *Architectural Review* offers a British perspective on the design activities within the built environment. With the April 1993 issue, the editors introduced a monthly interiors feature to replace the defunct *Designers Journal*. It showcases projects notable for the innovative use of light, color, and materials. An entire issue is annually devoted to interiors projects in Britain, Europe, and North America. Documentation includes drawings, richly colored photographs, and succinct project description.

*Architecture (Incorporating Architectural Technology). BPI Communications, 1130 Connecticut Ave., NW, Ste. 625, Washington, DC 20036. $42/ 12 issues.

> Even though its treatment of interior design is slight, the up-to-date coverage of developments in building design and technology offered by this publication is informative. One issue per year is devoted to interior design and there is increasing coverage as the monetary value of interior design becomes apparent. Interior designers may profit also from the regular features on facility management, office practice, and computers in design practice, as well as book reviews, news notes, and legislative updates. The magazine may change after December 30, 1996, when it ceases to be the organ of the American Institute of Architects.

Cadalyst: the Autocad Authority. Avanstar Communications, Inc., 7500 Old Oak Blvd., Cleveland, OH 44130. $39.95/12 issues.

> The editorial direction of this magazine makes it particularly valuable for students. The editor is an architect rather than an engineer, which influences the content. There is little overlap between *Cadalyst* and *Cadence* and the two together provide very good coverage.

Cadence. Miller Freeman, 600 Harrison St., San Francisco, CA 94107. (800) 289-0484. $39/12 issues.

> The magazine is written for users of computer-aided design, specifically AutoCAD.

Canadian Interiors. CI Publishing, Crailer Communications, 360 Dupont St., Toronto, ON M5R 1V9, Canada. (416) 966-9944; fax (416) 966-9946. $32/six issues in Canada; $75/six issues outside Canada.

> *Canadian Interiors* fulfills the role of interiors trade publication for the Canadian market as *Interior Design* and *Interiors* do in the United States. An annual source directory is published in the July/August issue.

Construction Specifier. Construction Specifications Institute, 601 Madison St., Alexandria, VA 22314. $36/12 issues for non-members; $30/12 issues for members.

> The *Specifier* is the official publication of CSI, presenting technical but readable articles for construction technology and practices in commercial design. Authors are drawn from education, industry, and government. Code applications, specification of materials, and legal applications in

design are some of the topics covered. Designers should browse the table of contents on a regular basis.

BACKWARDS IN OUR LIST. [handwritten]

*Contract Design (formerly *Contract*) Miller Freeman, One Penn Plaza, New York, NY 10119. $35 for professionals; $65 for all others/12 issues.

1-FB 2000 [handwritten]
2000 → [handwritten]
The magazine strives to illuminate the relationship between design and its constituents—corporations, health care facilities, education, government, etc.—via the case study method, including interviews with both clients and designers. Professional news and listings of CAD products are regular features. Recent installations and new products are highlighted.

D & W C: Draperies & Window Coverings. L. C. Clark Publishing, P.O. Box 13079, North Palm Beach, FL 33408. $33/13 issues.

D & W C is a trade publication "for the American Window Coverings Professional," which highlights designers, workrooms, techniques, business strategies and trends, and new products.

Design. Design Council, 28 Haymarket, London SW1Y 4SU, United
1-89 [handwritten] Kingdom. $99/12 issues.
SUND [handwritten]

Product design, corporate communication, and design management are the central topics of this journal. Funded by the British government, *Design* is clearly oriented toward the advancement of British design. The magazine's mission is being reexamined and advertising will be excluded in future issues. It should resume publication for the 50th anniversary of the Design Council. This publication was suspended in May 1994.

Design Solutions. Architectural Woodwork Institute, 1952 Isaac Newton Sq., Reston, VA 20190. $18/four issues.

Technical solutions to architectural woodwork problems are the focus of this journal, an official publication of the Architectural Woodwork Institute. Most of the feature articles are concerned with the use of casework, fixtures, paneling, and flooring for office, retail, residential, and civic interiors, as well as various restoration projects. Presentations are well illustrated and include detailed drawings of solutions. Includes new product listings.

X *Developments.* American Resort Development Association, 1220 L St., NW, Ste. 510, Washington, DC 20005. Membership only/12 issues.

> This is a narrowly focused newsletter for the resort/recreation and community development sector of the industry. Those designers actively involved in this market will want to subscribe.

X *Display and Design Ideas.* Shore-Varrone, 6255 Barfield Rd., NE, Ste. 200, Atlanta, GA 30328-4300. (404) 252-8831; fax (404) 252-4436. $60/12 issues.

> Information is presented in a newspaper tabloid format. The journal includes many ads for lighting, new products, and display ideas which are an excellent resource for retail designers. In addition, an annual buyer's guide is published.

1980-86
BOUND
Domus: Architettura Arredamento Arte. Editoriale Domus, Via Achille Grandi 5-7, 20089 Rozzano, Milano, Italy. $175/11 issues + $30 for two issues of *Domus Dossier* (each issue devoted to a single architectural topic).

> Premier Italian design journal, covering architecture, furnishings, equipment, art, and interiors. Superb illustrations and ads. Book reviews in Italian. Indexed in *Art Index*, *Avery Architectural Periodicals Index*.

X *Earthword, the Journal of Environmental and Social Responsibility.* EOS Institute, 580 Broadway, Ste. 200, Laguna Beach, CA 92651. $20/four issues without membership. Membership in the institute is $30 and includes a subscription.

> *Earthword* is a substantial publication which examines both practical and philosophical considerations of sustainable design on local and global levels. Book reviews, lists of additional resources appended to articles, and product reviews are a part of each issue. See entry for EOS Institute in **Chapter 13, Professional and Trade Organizations and Government Agencies,** under the **Professional Organizations** section.

X *Facility Management Journal.* International Facility Management Association, 1 E. Greenway Plaza, Ste. 1100, Houston, TX 77046-0194. $75/six issues.

> This is the primary magazine for facility managers. Issues of interest to interior designers include indoor air quality, computer-aided management, and security.

FDM: Furniture Design and Manufacturing. Cahners Publishing, 1350 E. Touhy Ave., Box 5080, Des Plaines, IL 60018-5080. $55/12 issues; free to qualified personnel.

This title, which represents the furniture manufacturing industry, is appropriate for those designers actively involved with furniture design. Technical tips and finishing technology are among the topics covered.

Fine Homebuilding. Taunton Press, 63 S. Main St., P.O. Box 5506, Newtown, CT 06470-5506. $29/six issues + one special issue.

Aimed at master craftspeople and inspired amateurs alike, *Fine Homebuilding* provides some of the most comprehensive and well-documented coverage of residential construction methods and materials available in the periodical literature. All aspects of housebuilding are covered, from foundations and framing to the care and use of tools. Each issue includes features on interior renovation and remodeling; the selection and installation of fixtures, kitchen cabinets, flooring, etc.; and case studies of energy-efficient, barrier-free, or affordable homes. The general aesthetic tone is an elegant vernacularism.

Fine Woodworking. Taunton Press, 63 S. Main St., P.O. Box 5506, Newtown, CT 06470-5506. $32/six issues.

The format and high quality found in *Fine Homebuilding* are also evident here. Beautiful illustrations, including excellent details, of furniture construction make the magazine a valuable reference for custom furniture design.

GA Houses. A.D.A. Edita Tokyo, 3-12-14 Sendagaya, Shibuya-ku, Tokyo, Japan; distributed by GA International Company, 594 Broadway, 3rd Fl., New York, NY 10012. $23.50/issue; three issues/year.

Aimed toward architects and "those who wish to master the art of living," the purpose of *GA Houses* is to document "outstanding" new residential architecture as well as past masterpieces throughout the world. Documentation includes plans, elevations, and photographs. High-quality interior views provide insight into many architect-designed interiors.

Health Care Construction Report. American Hospital Publishing, 737 N. Michigan Ave., Ste. 700, Chicago, IL 60611. $350/12 issues.

Approximately 80 planned and current projects for both renovations and new construction are profiled each month. The names, titles, and telephone numbers of persons to contact for each project are included, as well as the areas of construction where contracts have not been let. This is an excellent source of potential work.

X *Healthcare Forum Journal: Leadership Strategies for Healthcare Executives*. Healthcare Forum, 425 Market St., San Francisco, CA 94105. $45/ six issues.

> Although this journal is written for healthcare managers, design firms that specialize in healthcare facilities will probably want to follow its coverage of current and projected issues.

X *Historic Preservation: The Magazine of the National Trust for Historic Preservation and Historic Preservation News*.

> See entry for *Preservation* below.

X *Hospitality Design* (formerly *Restaurant & Hotel Design*). Bill Communications, 355 Park Ave. S., 3rd Fl., New York, NY 10010-1706. $45/six issues.

> The magazine is a showcase for hotel, restaurant, and senior living design and is written for designers, developers, and owners. Trade show and source information is included.

✓ *Hospitals and Health Networks* (formerly *Hospitals*). American Hospital Publishing, 737 N. Michigan Ave., Ste. 700, Chicago, IL 60611. $65/26 issues for members.

> Although the focus of this journal is management, there is enough coverage of construction, design, and products to make it worthwhile for firms that specialize in healthcare design.

X *I.D.: The International Design Review*. 440 Park Ave. S., 14th Fl., New York, NY 10016. $60/seven issues.

> Product design, including furniture, fixtures, and fabrics, is the primary focus of this beautifully produced journal. *ID* is especially attuned to the intersections of design and commerce and offers informative, practical articles on such topics as negotiating corporate cultures, client psychology, marketing, and other aspects of professional practice and office management. The July/August issue contains an "Annual Design Review" with awards for various product categories.

Interior Architecture. Ypma Publications, 4 Davies St., Surry Hills, 2010 Australia. (02) 319 2588; fax (02) 318 0149. U.S. subscription agent: Speedimpex, USA Inc. (718) 392-7477.

> Beautifully designed and exquisitely presented, the goal of this journal is to contemplate the relationship between architecture and interiors, both contract and residential. Includes book reviews. Unfortunately, publication has been suspended. It is included here to encourage readers to look at back issues and promote the rebirth of this title or another based on similar aesthetic standards.

*Interior Concerns Newsletter: A Newsletter for Environmentally Concerned Designers, Architects & Building Professionals. Interior Concerns Environmental Resources, P.O. Box 2386, Mill Valley, CA 94942. (415) 389-8049; fax (415) 388-8322. $35/six issues.

> Victoria Schomer, ASID, produces this information-packed 15-page newsletter. Topics cover all areas of interest from sources of wood, ecologically sound products, and eco-tourism to the argument that support of the environment costs jobs. Concise and timely, the newsletter also offers telephone numbers and addresses for further information at the conclusion of each article.

*Interior Design. Cahners Publishing, 249 W. 17th St., New York, NY 10011. $47.95/18 issues.

> A primary professional magazine in the United States, *Interior Design* is sound, informative, and businesslike. It is geared primarily toward the contract market. Regular features include fairs and new products, a calendar, juried coverage of new products, installations, awards, current and prospective jobs, and well-written commentary on the design world. A large-format monthly supplement, *Interior Design Market*, vividly illustrates a variety of product types and provides their sources.

*Interiors. BPI Communications, 1515 Broadway, New York, NY 10036. $35/12 issues.

> Well-documented and richly illustrated features on exemplary projects in hospitality, office, healthcare, and residential interiors are the central focus. Thoughtful monthly coverage of design trends and practice as well as developments in technology, product sources, industry events, and competitions make this journal an important vehicle of professional communication.

International Lighting Review. P.O. Box 721, 5600 AS Eindhoven NL, The Netherlands. NLG 65 (airmail)/four issues.

> Crisp and handsomely produced, *ILR* provides much-needed international coverage of all aspects of lighting. Each issue concentrates on a central theme or applications problem with richly illustrated reports on outstanding projects from all over the globe. There are also regular features on new products, publications, and industry conferences and events. Self-indexed.

Interni.

> See entry for *Rivista dell'Arredamento* below.

IS, the Magazine for Interiors & Sources. L. C. Clark Publishing, 840 U.S. Highway One, Ste. 330, North Palm Beach, FL 33408-3878. $27/nine issues.

> This well-organized and graphically pleasing magazine provides excellent coverage of industry events, topics of interest, awards, commercial and residential installations, and, of course, sources. Practical financial and business information and the inclusion of floor plans are also useful. Individual practitioners may find valuable mentors through this publication.

Journal of Healthcare Design. National Symposium on Healthcare Design, 4550 Alhambra Way, Martinez, CA 94553-4406. $75/one volume.

> Each issue contains the proceedings of the annual Symposium on Healthcare Interior Design. Topics have included "Design Solutions for Special Populations" and "Innovative Technologies in Health Care Design."

*Journal of Interior Design Research (formerly *Journal of Interior Design Education and Research*). Interior Design Educators Council, c/o Denise Guerin, editor, University of Minnesota, 240 McNeal Hall, 1985 Buford Ave., St. Paul, MN 55108. $35 or free to IDEC members/two issues.

> This "...scholarly, refereed publication (is) dedicated to issues related to the design of the interior environment," and includes reviews of books, software, and videos. It is the only regularly published journal devoted to interior design research.

*LD+A (Lighting Design & Application). Illuminating Engineering Society of North America, 120 Wall St., 17th Fl., New York, NY 10005. $35 nonmembers/12 issues.

> Published by the Illuminating Engineering Society of North America as a "popular magazine" for all those concerned with illumination, *LD+A* is essential for designers and students concerned with design and illumination technology. The journal offers clear and succinct articles by experts on a variety of current lighting applications as well as reports on products, technology, and industry activities. An equipment and accessories guide is published annually. (See also **Chapter 10, Competitions, Awards, and Scholarships,** under **Product Specialty** section, **Lighting** category, for IESNA entries.) It is available both in hard copy and online.

Lighting Dimensions. 32 W. 18th St., New York, NY 10011-4612. $48/nine issues.

> Although *Lighting Dimensions* is oriented largely toward lighting professionals in the arts and entertainment industry, frequent features on architectural interiors, new product information, and updates on technology make this journal informative and inspiring for interior designers as well. The recent appointment of an architecture editor should strengthen the magazine's appeal to all design professionals concerned with architectural interiors and lighting. Subscription includes annual "Buyers Guide" and "Industry Resources" issues.

Living Architecture. Living Architecture Magazine ApS, P.O. Box 2076, Bredgade 34, DK-1260 Copenhagen, Denmark. $78/four issues.

> This magazine offers glossy images of new and traditional Scandinavian design, furniture, and architecture. It exposes students to a different aesthetic than that readily found in the majority of design journals.

Lodging: The Management Magazine of the American Hotel & Motel Association. American Hotel Association Directory Corp., 1201 New York Ave., NW, Washington, DC 20005-3931. $35 nonmembers/11 issues.

> Only designers in this specialty area would gain any benefit from this journal, and then the usefulness is limited. Announcements provide names of prominent professionals. There is a regular "Design & Renovation" supplement which is directly applicable to interior designers. *Allied Voices,* a monthly newsletter for allied members, will be more valuable to designers for its inclusion of information regarding future design opportunities.

1985 -89 *md* (formerly *md: Moebel Interior Design*). Konradin Verlag, Robert
Bou v9 Kohlhammer GmbH Anschrift, Ernst-Mey-Strasse Be 8, 70771
Leinfedden - Echterdingen, Germany. (0711) 7594-0; fax (0711) 7594-
390. DM.240/12 issues.

> This international trade journal of interior furnishings, interior design,
> and design planning has been published for 40 years and has correspon-
> dents in Finland, Spain, Australia, and Switzerland. English translations
> parallel Finnish and French. European professional activities, products,
> articles, and ads present residential and commercial design and installa-
> tions in a stylish layout. Black-and-white and excellent color photos
> illustrate the magazine. Indexed in DAAI.

Metropolis. 177 E. 87th St., New York, NY 10128. $28/10 issues.

> A lively and provocative journal dedicated to scrutinizing current trends and
> innovations in design from furniture and textiles to urban parks, with an
> emphasis on events and issues in New York City. Each issue includes an
> interview with a prominent designer, articles on special themes—for
> example, "the geography of the home"—and coverage of national and
> international design events, product fairs, and exhibitions; the illustrated
> advertisements are also a good source for information on unique products.

EBSCO
ACADEMIC
SEARCH
O LTLY96

*Modern Healthcare: The Newsmagazine for Administrators and Manag-
ers in Hospitals, and Other Healthcare Institutions*. Crain Communications, 740 Rush St., Chicago, IL 60611. $125/52 issues; $63/52 issues,
students.

> This is an essential periodical for designers of healthcare facilities. The
> coverage is national and very current.

Old-House Interiors. Dovetail Publishers, The Blackthorn Tavern, 2
Main St., Gloucester, MA 01930. $18/four issues.

> The publishers of the well-established, architecturally-oriented *Old-
> House Journal* recognized a need for an interiors magazine of the same
> high caliber. While *Interiors* is a pleasant magazine with good color
> illustrations, it is more decorative than design-oriented, without some of
> the nitty-gritty articles which characterize the older journal. Of greatest
> value are its advertisements and product listings.

Old-House Journal. Dovetail Publishers, The Blackthorn Tavern, 2 Main
St., Gloucester, MA 01930. $27/six issues.

Clem Labine made information about the inside, outside, and structure of old (not always historic) U.S. houses readily available when he founded the excellent *Old-House Journal* in 1973. *The* magazine for designers and informed laypersons who restore and renovate pre-1939 houses in the United States, *OHJ* includes case studies of successful projects; excellent "how-to" guides for problems; a question-and-answer column; and valuable lists of books, products, and artisans. The classified ads provide excellent specialty resources.

Perspective. International Interior Design Association, 341 Merchandise Mart, Chicago, IL 60654. Subscription with membership/four issues.

This is the official organ of the International Interior Design Association and essential for those who wish to be aware of new ideas and events from that source. It includes coverage of professional practice, undergraduate and continuing education, scholarships and competitions, and both philosophical and practical topics of current interest. Some articles are sponsored or written by industry manufacturers and are so noted. Beginning in December 1996, the newsletter *Advantage* will be published eight times per year, in the months when *Perspective* is not published.

Preservation: The Magazine of the National Trust for Historic Preservation. National Trust for Historic Preservation, 1785 Massachusetts Ave., NW, Washington, DC 20036. $20 for Trust membership/six issues.

Preservation now also incorporates *Historic Preservation News*. The goal of this organ of the Trust, which is chartered by Congress through the Interior Department, is to stimulate the preservation of "…sites, buildings, and objects significant in American history." *Preservation* provides well-illustrated and well-written coverage of significant sites, book reviews, a calendar, monuments open to the public, and classified ads for real estate. A primary goal of *Preservation* is to champion beleaguered buildings.

Professional Services Management Journal. Practice Management Associates, 10 Midland Ave., Newton, MA 02158. $195/12 issues.

PSMJ is directed primarily at A/E/C managers, but is a high-quality management newsletter. The company also offers seminars and publications, also of high quality and often with money-back guarantees. Its information for sole practitioners is particularly useful.

Progressive Architecture. 600 Summer St., P.O. Box 1361, Stamford, CT 06904. $48/12 issues.

Due to its excellent coverage of professional issues, technology, and sustainable design, *PA* has long been an important professional forum for American architects. In early 1993 the editors initiated a shift in focus from isolated buildings to design processes and social context. Unfortunately, this thought-provoking journal ceased publication with the December 1995 issue.

Record: The IDEC Newsletter. Interior Design Educators Council, 9202 N. Meridian St., Ste. 200, Indianapolis, IN 46260-1810. $35 or IDEC membership/three issues.

This IDEC organ lists activities, seminars, competitions, and available faculty positions.

Retail Store Image. Intertec Publishing Corp., 6151 Powers Ferry Rd., NW, Atlanta, GA 30339-2941. $55/eight issues + directory.

Store managers, interior designers, architects, and store planners can follow such topics as lighting trends, new products, professional activities, and successful installations. The Institute of Store Planners has a regular column.

Rivista dell'Arredamento. Interni. Elemond Periodici s.p.a., Via D. Trentacoste 7, 20134 Milano. $120/10 issues; annual supplement available.

This glossy, color magazine presents first-rate residential interiors and high-fashion products similar to those shown in *Domus*. Features and columns include new products and their sources; events; product evaluations; interiors, including one celebrity interior; and high-quality ads. It is available in an international edition with a full English translation. The magazine is associated with the three foremost Italian publishers, Electa, Einaudi, and Mondadori.

Skylines. Building Owners and Managers Association (BOMA) International, 1201 New York Ave., NW, Ste. 300, Washington, DC 20005. $95; $75 for members/10 issues.

Skylines is the organ for BOMA and as such is an important source of information and publicity for individuals and companies in the commercial real estate business. Security, indoor air quality, "green" design, and legislation affecting the industry are representative subjects addressed in the publication.

X *Vanguard: A Publication of the International Interior Design Association.* International Interior Design Association, 341 Merchandise Mart, Chicago, IL 60654. Subscription with membership/four issues per year.

This is a well-written and graphically pleasing newsletter which provides professionals with information regarding pertinent events and dates, such as competitions and awards and continuing education courses.

X *VM & SD: Visual Merchandising & Store Design.* S T Publications, 407 Gilbert Ave., Cincinnati, OH 45202. $39/12 issues.

VM & SD is known as one of the premier magazines for retail designers due to its excellent coverage of national and international retail installations, window and product display design, and products related to retailing.

Indexes and Abstracts

See the **General References** section of **Chapter 1, Reference,** under individual titles. For the reader's convenience, the titles are listed below. It should be remembered that few indexes include every single item in a magazine. For example, "News" and "Events" columns are seldom indexed.

AIA*Online*
Architectural Index
Artbibliographies Modern
Art Index
√ Avery Index to Architectural Periodicals
Construction Index
Design and Applied Arts Index
SEARCH

Additional Resource for Information Regarding Design Periodicals

*Gretes, Frances C. *Directory of International Periodicals and Newsletters on the Built Environment*. 2nd ed. New York: Van Nostrand Reinhold, 1992.

> This book is a must for any academic library or large professional office. It is an up-to-date, annotated compilation of journal titles which includes address, cost, and coverage, with access by title, subject, and country of origin. Indexes and online services are also described.

Periodical Subscriptions

Several of the magazines listed above are sold only to professionals and are not available on newsstands. The most expeditious way to subscribe is to locate a subscription card in a library or colleague's copy. If a copy of the magazine is unavailable, call the publisher.

Single copies or subscriptions to foreign design titles can be difficult. If one wishes to purchase a single issue, a sophisticated newsstand in a metropolitan area is the first place to inquire. If this fails, consult one of the bookstores or dealers listed in **Chapter 12, Publishers and Bookstores.**

To obtain a subscription to a foreign journal, either consult one of the bookstores in the Publishers chapter or fill out and mail a subscription card from an issue of the magazine. The subscription card may or may not receive a response. The publisher may accept payment in U.S. dollars or may require a bank draft in the currency of the country of origin. There is a charge for the foreign currency draft. Most U.S.-based magazine subscription services—vendors who will place multiple subscription orders for journals of any country of origin and provide the purchaser with one invoice—deal only with institutions. An exception to this rule is EBSCO, whose address is listed below. It has international agents to smooth the frequently tortuous path of international subscriptions. Of course one pays a fee for this, but the service received is excellent.

EBSCO Subscription Services
1163E Shrewsbury Ave.
Shrewsbury, NJ 07702-4321
(908) 542-8600; (800) 526-2337; fax (908) 544-9777

Archivia, the Decorative Arts Book Shop, 944 Madison Ave., New York.
Photograph by Andrew Bordwin.

Chapter 12

Publishers and Bookstores

Written and compiled by Sarah W. Dickinson

The citations in this chapter provide the interior design practitioner with sources for books, old and new, on interior design and related topics. While no publisher and few bookstores specialize solely in interior design, this list attempts to identify those sources that can be relied upon to provide titles oriented towards the professional market.

Although many trade publishers produce interior design titles, they are often aimed at the homeowner or amateur decorator. The publishers included here are limited more to those who regularly offer titles with professionals in mind. Each entry gives the address, phone number and fax number, if available, for the order department, as well as a summary of the publisher's focus, and any special subject catalogs available. It should be noted that many catalogs only list the most recently published or "best seller" titles. Older publications are often still available: a telephone call to the publisher will confirm a title's availability.

Sarah W. Dickinson has been a librarian at the Boston Architectural Center since 1987. She is a member of the Art Libraries Society of North America, and is the past chair of the New England chapter. As a member of the Association of Architectural Librarians, she organized the 1992 national meeting which met in Boston and was hosted by the Boston Design Librarians.

In some instances a publisher's scope is so broad that to include the publisher in this chapter would misrepresent the extent of its offerings in interior design; McGraw-Hill is an example. Relevant titles from publishers who fall into this category will often appear throughout the general bibliography.

Sales catalogs or brochures from well-stocked specialty bookstores are also a valuable source of information, often including abstracts or brief descriptions of new titles in stock. Some subject specialists stock foreign publications that might otherwise be very difficult to track down and purchase. As with publishers, bookstore catalogs do not necessarily list all books that are in stock.

Several sources for out-of-print, foreign, code-related, and U.S. government titles are also cited at the end of the chapter.

Publishers

Abbeville Press
Special Sales
488 Madison Ave.
New York, NY 10022
(800) 278-2665; fax (212) 644-5085

> Abbeville Press now offers a special catalog listing all of its published titles in architecture, interior design, and the decorative arts. Titles include international home style books, historic surveys of interior decoration, the *Interior Design Yearbook*, and *International Contract/ Interior Design* series.

Harry N. Abrams Inc.
100 Fifth Ave.
New York, NY 10011
(800) 345-1359; fax (212) 645-8437

> This well-known art publisher has produced some beautiful historic interiors, furniture, and design titles over the years. A backlist is available, complete with a subject listing of previously published titles.

American Institute of Architects Press

> See entry in this chapter under AIA Bookstore.

Antique Collectors' Club
Market Street Industrial Park
Wappingers Falls, NY 12590
(800) 252-5231; fax (914) 297-0068

> The club is a publisher and distributor of informative texts on furniture,
> textiles, metalwork, and collectibles, as well as art reference books and
> architecture and gardening books, all of which are published in the
> United Kingdom. It also distributes Sotheby's publications and the Miller
> price guides and checklists.

Books Nippan
1123 Dominguez St., Ste. K
Carson, CA 90746
(800) 562-1410; fax (310) 604-1134

> A good U.S. source of bilingual Japanese publications from Graphic-sha,
> Process Architecture, and other Japanese publishers. Relevant titles focus
> on international hotel, restaurant, and store design, and well as graphic
> and rendering titles. Backlist includes a subject listing of all titles.

Chronicle Books
85 Second St.
San Francisco, CA 94105
(800) 722-6657; fax (800) 858-7787

> Architecture, style, and design books include good selection of Califor-
> nia style, furniture, color, and period detail titles. Chronicle is also the
> U.S. distributor of Phaidon Press publications from London.

Dover Publications Inc.
31 E. 2nd St.
Mineola, NY 11501

> No phone/credit card orders. Dover publishes well-made and inexpensive
> paperback books that reprint out-of-print titles in many topics. The Dover
> Complete Catalog of Books on Architecture includes titles on antique
> furniture, interior design, historic interiors, and design. The Pictorial
> Archive catalog lists the titles Dover has published for permission-free
> use, including clip art, color art and design, Art Deco and Art Nouveau
> illustrations, and historic ornamentation.

GA International Co. Ltd.
180 Varick St., 4th Fl.
New York, NY 10014
(212) 741-6329; fax (212) 741-6283

> This address is for the mail-order distribution of Global Architecture titles, including GA Document, GA Houses, GA Architect, and other beautifully photographed and well-documented titles from this Japanese publisher. Its catalog also lists other titles it distributes, with an emphasis on twentieth-century architecture and design.

R. S. Means Company
100 Construction Plaza
Kingston, MA 02364
(800) 334-3509; fax (617) 585-7466

> Means publications include annual cost data guides and estimating reference titles, as well as facilities management, ADA compliance, and other planning and management titles.

Monacelli Press
10 E. 92nd St.
New York, NY 10128
(212) 831-0248; fax (212) 410-2059

> Founded by the former president of Rizzoli Books, and publisher of Rizzoli International Publications, Monacelli Press produces beautifully illustrated and conceived titles, including five to ten interior design or decorative arts titles a year. Previous titles include the exquisite *American Colonial* and *Shaker Built*.

PBC International Inc.
One School St.
Glen Cove, NY 11542
(800) 527-2826; fax (516) 676-2738

> Design book publisher that produces well-illustrated titles on residential and commercial interior design, often with floor plans, as well as volumes on exhibit, furniture, product, and lighting design.

Preservation Press

> See John Wiley & Sons.

Professional Publications
1250 Fifth Ave.
Belmont, CA 94002-3863
(800) 426-1178; fax (415) 592-4519

> Published titles include license exam review guides for the NCIDQ
> examination, general professional reference books, and building code
> guides.

Retail Reporting Corporation
302 Fifth Ave.
New York, NY 10001
(800) 251-4545; fax (212) 279-7014

> The volumes from this New York publisher, covering stores, window and
> storefront design, signs, catalogs, and food market design, are amply
> illustrated with large color photographs and, in most cases, small floor plans.

Rizzoli International Publications
St. Martins Press
175 Fifth Ave.
New York, NY 10010
(800) 221-7945; fax (800) 258-2769

> Rizzoli's beautifully produced and amply illustrated biannual catalog
> includes several interior design titles each year, as well as many architec-
> ture, decorative arts, and fine arts titles. St. Martins Press has taken over
> distribution of all Rizzoli titles as well as the titles published by the
> Vendome Press.

Van Nostrand Reinhold
7625 Empire Dr.
Florence, KY 41042-2978
(800) 842-3636; fax (606) 525-7778

> VNR publishes a special annual catalog listing all new and bestselling
> design titles, including architecture, interior, landscape, urban, and
> professional reference volumes. Catalog entry for each title includes a
> summary description of the book as well as a contents listing and
> publication date, a courtesy not found in all catalogs.

Watson Guptill Publications
P.O. Box 2014
Lakewood, NJ 08701
(800) 451-1741; fax (908) 363-0338

> Watson Guptill is one of the best sources for interior design titles,
> including the beautifully produced publications of the Whitney Library
> of Design, timely visual arts annuals published by Rotovision S.A., and
> other reference and survey volumes. The informative catalog, produced
> twice a year, includes a comprehensive backlist. Watson Guptill now
> distributes Editorial Gustavo Gili titles as well.

John Wiley & Sons
Distribution Center
1 Wiley Dr.
Somerset, NJ 08875-1217
(800) 225-5945; fax (908) 302-2300

> Well known for publications on architecture and engineering, Wiley is now
> one of the major publishers for interior design professional practice titles. In
> recent years Wiley has published titles on color, codes, specifications, office
> design, and business and professional practice, as well as several publications
> from the National Kitchen and Bath Association. Wiley now publishes titles
> formerly available from the Preservation Press, the publishing arm of the
> National Trust for Historic Preservation, including the Historic Interiors
> series, preservation, and style survey books.

Specialty Bookstores/Mail Order Catalogs

AIA Bookstore
2 Winter Sport Ln.
Williston, VT 05495
(800) 365-2724; fax (800) 678-7102

> The phone and fax numbers listed are for the order department that
> serves both the American Institute of Architects Press and the AIA
> Bookstore, located at 1735 New York Ave., NW, Washington, DC 20006.
> The bookstore carries all AIA Press titles, including monographs on
> architectural firms, professional practice reference titles, AIA and joint
> AIA/ASID forms, NCIDQ exam preparation material, and other AIA
> publications, including guidelines and reviews of medical and hospital
> facilities.

Archivia: The Decorative Arts Book Shop
944 Madison Ave.
New York, NY 10021
(212) 439-9194; fax (212) 744-1626

> This small specialty bookstore stocks in print, out-of-print, and foreign titles in interior design, the decorative arts, architecture, and garden design. Its annual fall catalog is supplemented by brochures highlighting recent additions to its stock.

Art Book Services, Inc.
P.O. Box 360
Hughsonville, NY 12537
(800) 247-9955; fax (914) 297-0068

> Mail-order catalog sells art, auction, and antique price guides and reference volumes, including Kovel's, Miller's, period checklists, and historical guides.

Art Consulting: Scandinavia
25777 Punto de Vista Dr.
Monte Nido, Cakabasas, CA 91302-2155
(818) 222-2088; fax (818) 222-2577

> U.S. distributor of books on Scandinavian art, architecture, and design, including the applied and decorative arts, interior design, and furniture and industrial design. Catalog lists new books, backlisted, and close-out titles.

Builders Booksource
Ghiradelli Square
900 North Point
San Francisco, CA 94109
(415) 440-5773; fax (415) 440-5772

> There is a Builders Booksource in San Francisco and one in Berkeley. They produce a catalog that is representative of their extensive stock of books on codes, finishes, renovation, design theory, and business and legal issues.

Building News Bookstores
129 Highland Ave.
Needham, MA 02194
(800) 873-6397; fax (617) 455-1493

> While BNI has bookstores in Needham (near Boston), Los Angeles, and the Washington, D.C., area, its catalog, produced quarterly, offers "one stop" shopping for building codes and standards, some state and city codes, estimating books and software, construction-related titles, ADA information, and construction industry forms and documents.

Construction Bookstores
Box 7029
Dover, DE 19903
(800) 253-0541; fax (800) 676-3299

> The quarterly catalogs from this construction-oriented bookstore chain are a good, comprehensive source for national and state codes, the Code of Federal Regulations, AIA contract documents, and a wide range of construction and management titles. Publications from IEEE, NFPA, BOCA, and other regulatory organizations are available, and special orders are accepted. The catalog includes a good subject index.

*Richard Hilkert, Bookseller Ltd.
333 Hayes St.
San Francisco, CA 94102
(415) 863-3339; fax (415) 863-3339

> This small San Francisco bookstore specializes in interior design and related titles, and has been recognized by the ASID as "the best supplier of interior design books in the country."

Peter Miller Bookstore
1930 First Ave.
Seattle, WA 98101
(206) 441-4114; fax (206) 441-1501

> Bookstore holdings include titles on interior design, graphic standards, pricing guides, showcase and exhibit design, lighting, and furniture. The catalog includes a subject breakdown of titles in stock.

Old-House Bookshop
Two Main St.
Gloucester, MA 01930-9942
(800) 931-2931; fax (508) 283-4629

> As the title implies, this catalog features books focussing on the preservation and restoration of old houses and gardens, including historic style books, how-to books, reference books, and publications from *Old-House Journal*. The editor has included useful in-depth descriptions for each book in the catalog, as well as a selection of out-of-print or low- stock titles.

Prairie Avenue Bookshop
418 S. Wabash Ave.
Chicago, IL 60605
(800) 474-2724; fax (312) 922-5184

> Prairie Avenue prints a substantial catalog biannually that, while predominantly architectural, lists titles in interior design and decorative arts, drawing and technical manuals, building codes, and domestic and foreign periodicals. Four newsletters are produced throughout the year advertising new acquisitions to the store.

William Stout Architectural Books
804 Montgomery St.
San Francisco, CA 94133
(415) 391-6757; fax (415) 989-2341

> Comprehensive architectural bookstore in San Francisco stocks several thousand titles in interior design. A catalog is produced twice a year listing over 1,000 new and out-of-print titles. Domestic and foreign journals are also available.

Superintendent of Documents
U.S. Government Printing Office
P.O. Box 371954
Pittsburgh, PA 15250-7954
(202) 512-1800; fax orders (202) 512-2250; fax order inquiries (202) 512-2168; *GPO Access* <http://www.access.gpo.gov/su_docs>

> U.S. government publications and subscriptions are available for purchase through the office listed above. Orders may be placed in writing or over the phone with a credit card or by setting up a deposit account. Most government publications are identified by either a stock number (#S/N)

for books, or a List ID number for subscriptions. This office can also assist callers who only have title information, and will direct callers to other agencies when appropriate. A subject bibliography, and subscriptions to new government book and serial listings, are also available through this office, or from one of the 24 U.S. government bookstores located throughout the country. *GPO Access* became a free Internet site in December 1995. Available at the site are the *Congressional Record*, the *Federal Register*, Congressional bills, and a growing number of databases.

Out-of-Print Book Dealers

Acanthus Books
54 W. 21ˢᵗ St., Rm. 908
New York, NY 10010
(212) 463-0750; fax (212) 463-0752

> While specializing in predominantly rare and out-of-print decorative arts titles, this mail-order business has started importing new, in-print titles from Europe, and reprinting design classics from the nineteenth and twentieth centuries under the title "Acanthus Press." Catalogs are mailed twice a year, with additional flyers listing new stock. Special requests are welcomed.

Archivia
944 Madison Ave.
New York, NY 10021
(212) 439-9194; fax (212) 744-1626

> See entry under **Specialty Bookstores** section of this chapter.

J. M. Cohen Rare Books
2 Karin Ct.
New Paltz, NY 12561
(914) 883-9720; fax (914) 883-9142

> The focus of this mail-order antiquarian and rare book business is on fashion, the decorative arts, and twentieth-century interior design and ornament. Catalogs are produced four to six times a year, listing 100-120 titles. Judy Cohen, the proprietor, will search for out-of-print titles and welcomes special orders in her field.

National Fire Protection Association, Quincy, Massachusetts. Benjamin
Thompson Associates, 1981. Photograph by Steve Rosenthal.

Chapter 13

Professional and Trade Organizations and Government Agencies

Professional and trade organizations are excellent sources of information, support, and promotion. They frequently provide "quality control" by establishing standards that practitioners must meet before they may be licensed or titled to practice, such as the NCIDQ does for interior designers. Both trade and professional groups may publish membership lists, conduct research, establish standards that are used in specifications, hold conferences and seminars, and publish newsletters and magazines. They are the unifying elements among individuals and companies which might otherwise have little contact. As such, they are one of the first resources to employ when entering an unfamiliar field of information or endeavor.

There are several good sources of descriptive information regarding organizations. The *Encyclopedia of Associations*, which is described in **Chapter 1, Reference,** under the **General References** section, can be found in most libraries. In addition, *Interiors*, *Interior Design*, and *Interiors & Sources* magazines publish resource issues which include some basic information on this topic. The Professional Organizations and Trade Association sections are followed by a brief list of pertinent U.S. government departments and organizations.

Professional Organizations

Acoustical Society of America
500 Sunnyside Blvd.
Woodbury, NY 11797
(516) 576-2360; fax (516) 349-7669

> The society publishes a scholarly technical journal (*Research + Measurements*), industry standards, and reprints of acoustics books.

American Association of Textile Chemists and Colorists (AATCC)
P.O. Box 12215
Research Triangle Park, NC 27709
(919) 549-8141; fax (919) 549-8933

> Membership requires a degree or five years of experience in the field. The technical publications on test methods are collected annually and published as the *AATCC Technical Manual*.

American Hospital Association (AHA)
1 N. Franklin, 28th Fl.
Chicago, IL 60606
(312) 422-3000; fax (312) 422-4700

> A large catalog of publications provides some titles of interest to architecture and interior design professionals. See *Health Care Construction Report*, in **Chapter 11, Magazines,** which provides a list of upcoming jobs. It should be noted that reference questions will be accepted from AHA members only.

*American Institute of Architects (AIA)
1735 New York Ave., NW
Washington, DC 20006
(202) 626-7300

> One must be a registered architect for full membership. The institute sponsors a bookstore, a library, committees in many areas of interest (including interior design), publications, and online reference. A description of AIA*Online* may be found in **Chapter 1, Reference,** under the **General References** section.

*American National Standards Institute (ANSI)
11 W. 42nd St., 13th Fl.
New York, NY 10036
(212) 642-4900; fax (212) 302-1286

> ANSI coordinates voluntary standards development and approves standards
> as American National Standards. Although there are over 8,000 ANSI
> standards, only about 30 of them are cited in model building codes.

*American Society for Testing and Materials (ASTM)
1916 Race St.
Philadelphia, PA 19103-1187
(215) 299-5400; fax (215) 299-5511

> ASTM's primary goal is to establish tests and specifications for materi-
> als. Committees on textiles (which includes home furnishings), paint, and
> resilient floor coverings are pertinent for interior designers. ASTM
> publishes, among other titles, a listing of all laboratories that test materi-
> als. Membership is open to both individuals and other organizations.

American Society of Architectural Perspectivists (ASAP)
52 Broad St.
Boston, MA 02109
(617) 951-1433, ext. 225

> ASAP, despite its name, has expanded into an international organization.
> The group has an annual show of its work, at which the work is judged;
> the show "goes on the road" and is then published as a catalog. The Hugh
> Ferriss Memorial Prize is the highest honor given to a competitor.

American Society of Civil Engineers
1015 15th St., NW, Ste. 600
Washington, DC 20005
(202) 789-2200

> This well-established organization publishes codes, standards, contract
> documents, journals, and newsletters. It supports research and offers
> recognition for outstanding members.

American Society of Heating, Refrigerating, and Air-Conditioning Engineers, Inc. (ASHRAE)
1791 Tullie Circle, NE
Atlanta, GA 30329
(404) 636-8400; fax (404) 321-5478

ASHRAE develops standards, compiles research specific to this field, and publishes essential information. *ASHRAE Standard 62: Ventilation for Acceptable Indoor Air Quality* is of particular interest to designers. Affiliate membership is open to interior designers. The organization also publishes *ASHRAE Journal* and *ASHRAE Insights*.

*American Society of Interior Designers (ASID)
608 Massachusetts Ave., NE
Washington, DC 20002
(202) 546-3480; fax (202) 546-3240; e-mail network@asid.noli.com

ASID is the largest (30,500 members) professional organization in the United States for interior designers. The group's mission statement is two-pronged, to promote expansion of interior design markets and to advance professionalism through continuing education. The organization writes contract forms (most recent edition 1996) for use by designers, offers continuing education courses which fulfill registration requirements, publishes newsletters and magazines for the profession, and supports research and awards.

American Society of Mechanical Engineers (ASME)
22 Law Dr., Box 2900
Fairfield, NJ 07007-2900
(800) 843-2763; fax (201) 882-1717

ASME sells a large number of publications regarding codes and standards. Of particular interest to designers will be the codebook on dimensioning and tolerancing.

American Society of Plumbing Engineers (ASPE)
3617 Thousand Oaks Blvd., Ste. 210
West Lake Village, CA 91362
(805) 495-7120; fax (805) 495-4861

Technical booklets describe plumbing installations, including the *ASPE Data Book*.

Architects/Designers/Planners for Social Responsibility (ADPSR)
1807 W. Sunyside Ave., Ste. 300
Chicago, IL 60640
(312) 275-2498 or (312) 275-1807; fax (312) 275-1858

As stated in its literature, the organization endorses "...arms reduction, protection of the natural and built environment, and socially responsible development." The group operates on national, international, and chapter levels. Among other efforts, it publishes bibliographies and a quarterly newsletter, organizes conferences, and maintains professional relations with ASID, IIDA, and AIA.

Association for Preservation Technology (APT)
APT International
P.O. Box 8178
Fredericksburg, VA 22404
(703) 373-1621; fax (703) 373-6050

This multidisciplinary group holds an annual conference, gives technical seminars, and publishes on such topics as decorative finishes and windows. The broad focus is preservation of the historic built environment. The publications are authoritative and reasonably priced. Unfortunately, the office is no longer staffed; there is an answering machine.

Building Officials and Code Administrators International, Inc. (BOCA)
4051 W. Flossmoor Rd.
Country Club Hill, IL 60478-5795
(708) 799-2300; fax (708) 799-4981

BOCA publishes a bimonthly magazine, *The Building Official and Code Administrator*, which contains both news of professional activities and coverage of current topics and proposed code changes.

Building Owners and Managers Association International (BOMA)
1201 New York Ave., NW
Washington, DC 20005
(202) 408-2662; fax (202) 371-0181

BOMA is a major force in the commercial real estate field. It publishes a newsletter (*Skylines*), research reports, and a membership directory; holds college-level educational seminars; tracks industry performance; and accredits facility managers. The organization issues reliable standards and works with other groups to respond to real needs for standards. Titles that may be of interest to interior designers include market trend information, tenant needs studies, and the *Standard Method of Measuring Floor Area in Office Buildings*.

Construction Specifications Institute (CSI)
601 Madison St.
Alexandria, VA 22314-1791
(703) 684-0300; (800) 689-2900; fax (703) 684-0465; e-mail, csimail@csinet.org; web site, http://www.csinit.org

> A working knowledge of how to specify materials and products in a uniform manner is essential for any designer. CSI format is one standardized method for accomplishing this. *Sweet's Catalog File* of products is arranged by CSI's classification system and many firm libraries use the system to arrange product literature. On large projects, a professional spec writer may be part of the design team. On smaller projects, the designer will write the specs himself or herself. CSI publishes, among other titles, the *Manual of Practice*, *MASTERSPEC*, and *SPEC-DATA*, which provides manufacturer's information with the specific technical information required to write specs, and specific format documents. Many other services and educational programs are offered.

Council of American Building Officials (CABO)
5203 Leesburg Pike, Ste. 708
Falls Church, VA 22041
(703) 931-4533; fax (703) 379-1546

> This national organization was formed by the three model building code organizations, BOCA, ICBO, and SBCCI. In addition to the code work described in the **Codes and Standards** section of **Chapter 1, Reference,** CABO created the National Evaluation Service (NES) to review new construction materials and methods.

Eastern Paralyzed Veterans Association (EPVA)
75-20 Astoria Blvd.
Jackson Heights, NY 11370-1177
(800) 444-0120

> EPVA has been a leader in providing information to individuals with handicaps and for designers regarding the needs of those with handicaps. It sponsors, and usually provides single copies for free, many valuable publications.

EOS Institute for the Study of Sustainable Living
580 Broadway, Ste. 200
Laguna Beach, CA 92651
(714) 497-1896; fax (714) 494-7861

> The institute was founded in 1990 "for the study of ecologically balanced living...[it] promotes the creation of sustainable human environments through its educational resource center, publications, lectures, workshops and programs." Additional services include design consultations and student internships. The journal, *Earthword*, is included in **Chapter 11, Magazines.**

*Foundation for Interior Design Education Research (FIDER)
60 Monroe Center, NW, #300
Grand Rapids, MI 49503-2920
(616) 458-0400; fax (616) 458-0460

> The organization's mission statement is as follows: "FIDER promotes excellence in interior design education through research and the accreditation of academic programs which prepare interior designers to create interior environments for improving the quality of human experience." It provides grant support for research into educational topics and is the accepted accrediting body for programs of interior design instruction in the United States and Canada. A list of all schools accredited by FIDER is available from the organization. There are no individual members, only other organizations.

Human Factors and Ergonomics Society (HFES)
P.O. Box 1369
Santa Monica, CA 90406-1369
(310) 394-1811; fax (310) 394-2410

> The group publishes a number of research-oriented journals. The quarterly *Ergonomics in Design* emphasizes environmental and workplace design. Full members are usually psychologists or engineers, but affiliate membership, which includes all publications, is available. Technical subgroups publish newsletters on specific design problems, such as aging or disability-related design. HFES worked with BIFMA and ANSI to develop standards for computer workstations.

*Illuminating Engineering Society of North America (IES)
120 Wall St., 17th Fl.
New York, NY 10005
(212) 248-5000; fax (212) 248-5017

> IES sponsors courses, publications, awards, an annual conference, and lighting standards, which are available in hard copy or on CD-ROM. It also publishes *LD+A*, an excellent magazine for designers, and the technical *Journal of the IESNA*. Professional, student, and associate memberships are available. Mission statement: "To advance knowledge and to disseminate information for the improvement of the lighted environment to the benefit of society."

Industrial Designers Society of America (IDSA)
1142-E Walker Rd.
Great Falls, VA 22066
(703) 759-0100; fax (703) 759-7679

> IDSA is an international industrial and product design group and is the premier industrial design association in the United States. It sponsors important and well-publicized annual competitions and strives to uphold the standards of design.

*Institute of Store Planners (ISP)
25 N. Broadway
Tarrytown, NY 10591
(914) 332-1806; fax (914) 332-1541

> This retail design group has over 1,000 members and issues a quarterly newsletter and a membership directory. It also sponsors design competitions for students and professionals and operates an employment referral service. Professional membership is based upon strong store planning experience and education. There are strong local chapters throughout the country.

Interior Design Educators Council (IDEC)
9202 N. Meridian St., Ste. 200
Indianapolis, IN 46260-1810
(317) 816-6261; fax (317) 571-5603

> IDEC's focus is education, research, and building a body of knowledge relating to "quality of life and human performance in the interior environment." IDEC is a member of the International Federation of Interior Architects/Interior Designers.

Interior Design Society (IDS)
Market Square, Space 400
P.O. Box 2396, 305 W. High St.
High Point, NC 27261
(800) 888-9590; fax (910) 883-1195

> The National Home Furnishings Association is the parent organization of
> the IDS. The NHFA seeks to establish two-tiered licensing, with separate
> exams and titles for residential and contract designers. ASID and IIDA
> are opposed to this concept, saying that the residential exam ignores life
> safety codes. It is also said that retail furniture dealers favor this differen-
> tiation so that they can call their decorators and sales staff "residential
> interior designers." IDS publishes *Portfolio* newsletter quarterly.

Interior Designers of Canada/Designers D'Interieur du Canada (IDC)
260 King St. E.
Ontario Design Centre, Ste. 414
Toronto M5A 1K3, Canada
(416) 594-9310; fax (416) 594-9313

> IDC represents Canadian designers with the federal government of
> Canada, is a member of FIDER, is associated with NCIDQ, and works
> with its U.S. counterparts on the Interior Design Continuing Education
> Committee. The group publishes the *Communique* newsletter twice a
> year and *Newswire* six times per year. Membership requires successful
> completion of the NCIDQ exam. IDC supports title legislation that
> restricts use of the title Interior Designer to qualified designers.

International Association of Lighting Designers (IALD)
1133 Broadway, Ste. 520
New York, NY 10010-7903
(212) 206-1281; fax (212) 206-1327; e-mail IALD@iald.org

> IALD represents lighting designers, or architectural lighting designers,
> while the Illuminating Engineering Society represents lighting engineers.
> Upper-level membership requires that the member not represent any
> lighting manufacturer or sell any specific lighting equipment, in order to
> assure the members independence. Membership includes practitioners in
> North America, Western Europe, and the Far East. It publishes a newslet-
> ter and an annual membership directory.

International Conference of Building Officials (ICBO)
5360 S. Workman Mill Rd.
Whittier, CA 90611
(310) 699-0541; fax (310) 692-3853

In addition to publishing the *Uniform Building Code*, ICBO publishes its
own *Book of Standards* which is similar in nature to NFPA, ASTM, or
Underwriters Laboratories standards. ICBO is now acting as the official
publisher of titles that were published by individual code organizations,
such as BOCA and SBCCI.

*International Facility Management Association (IFMA)
1 E. Greenway Plaza, 11th Fl.
Houston, TX 77046
(713) 623-4362; (800) 359-4362; fax (713) 623-6124

IFMA is a strong organization which offers education, publications for
sale, research reports, library services, conferences, a journal and
newsletters, a national certification program, and employment services.
An annual list of members is available to members only. Bureaus are
located in Canada and Europe.

International Federation of Interior Architects/Interior Designers (IFI)
P.O. Box 19126
1000GC Amsterdam, The Netherlands
(20) 627 68 20; fax (20) 623 71 46

IFI membership consists of representatives of national interior design
organizations from 25 countries, such as the American Society of Interior
Designers from the United States. It provides an international overview
of the profession. The secretariat in Amsterdam responds quickly and
knowledgeably to questions. Though individuals may not be members,
they may become "Friends of IFI," a benefit of which is receipt of the
newsletter, published four to six times per year. The fee is approximately
$75. The following is a paraphrase from the "Friends" brochure which
states the group's goals:

1. to raise the standards of interior design

2. to improve and expand the contribution of interior design in all countries

3. to initiate programs to benefit public health, safety,and welfare

4. to promote recognition of the profession

International Furnishings and Design Association (IFDA)
107 World Trade Center
P.O. Box 580045
Dallas, TX 75258
(214) 747-2406; (800) 727-5202; fax (214) 747-2407

Membership, approximately 2,000, is open to executives in all phases of the furnishings industry, including designers, manufacturers, and writers. No certification is required for membership. Services include awards, a membership directory, annual conference, speakers bureau, a quarterly newsletter, and local chapter programs. Formerly the National Home Fashions League.

*International Interior Design Association (IIDA)
341 Merchandise Mart
Chicago, IL 60654-1104
(312) 467-1950; fax (312) 467-0779; Internet, http://www.iida.com

On July 1, 1994, the International Society of Interior Designers (3,000 professional and supporting members), the Institute of Business Designers (5,300 professional and supporting members), and the Council of Federal Interior Designers (160 members) merged their organizations to form IIDA, approximately 9,500 members. The group's mission is to "enhance the quality of life through excellence in interior design and to advance interior design through knowledge." There are nine international geographic regions and eight "forums," or areas of specialization. The forums are the following: commercial, education/research, government, healthcare, hospitality, residential, facility planning and design, and retail. Each forum will have its own newsletter and bulletin. IIDA also publishes *Perspective*, as noted in **Chapter 11, Magazines,** and the quarterly newsletter *Vantage*. IIDA sponsors competitions and accredited continuing education seminars. Applicants must qualify for membership, by, among other things, providing either NCIDQ or NCARB certification. In addition, members must maintain Continuing Education Unit (CEU) credits, representative of IIDA's desire to build a body of knowledge for the field.

International Society of Interior Designers (ISID)

See International Interior Design Association above.

National Association of Schools of Art and Design (NASAD)
11250 Roger Bacon Dr., Ste. 21
Reston, VA 22090
(703) 437-0700; fax (703) 437-6312

> NASAD accredits schools of art and design and studio art programs. Many schools of interior design are accredited not only by FIDER, but also by NASAD.

*National Council for Interior Design Qualification (NCIDQ)
50 Main St.
White Plains, NY 10606-1920
(914) 948-9100; fax (914) 948-9198

> NCIDQ was incorporated in 1974 to create a standardized, accepted test to certify interior designers. Only professional design organizations and licensing boards may be members. Passage of the exam is essential for membership in most national design organizations such as ASID or the newly established IIDA or to be licensed in most U.S. states or Canadian provinces which have statutes governing interior design professionals. The council is studying qualifications for granting advanced standing in specialty fields. Now a part of the NCIDQ, the Governing Board for Contract Interior Design Standards recognizes designers who specialize in contract interior design and who meet its requirements. Certification for advanced standing in residential design is being developed.

National Council of Acoustical Consultants
66 Morris Ave., Ste. 1A
Springfield, NJ 07081-1409
(201) 564-5859; fax (201) 564-7480

> All members are professional acoustical engineers who do consulting in the field. The council publishes a listing of members which is arranged geographically and indexed by both firm and individual names.

National Fire Protection Association (NFPA)
Batterymarch Park
Quincy, MA 02269-9101
(617) 770-3000

> NFPA is an organization that influences fire safety internationally through its codes and standards publications. *The Life Safety Code*, NFPA 101, and the *National Electrical Code*, NFPA 70, are most

familiar to designers. The *NFPA Buyers' Guide* is an annual directory of
fire protection products.

National Kitchen & Bath Association (NKBA)
687 Willow Grove St.
Hackettstown, NJ 07840
(908) 852-0333; fax (908) 852-1695

> NKBA certifies individuals who are qualified to design kitchens and
> baths with the designation "CKD," Certified Kitchen Designer, and
> "CBD," Certified Bath Designer. As of January 1996, NKBA requires
> NCIDQ certification and its own examinations for membership. NKBA
> sponsors the annual National Kitchen and Bath Show. See **Chapter 15,
> National Product Expositions and Conferences.**

Organization of Black Designers (OBD)
300 M St., SW, Ste. N110
Washington, DC 20024-4019
(202) 659-3918; fax (202) 488-3838; Web address http://
www.core77.com:80/OBD

> African-American professional designers in the fields of interior, graphic,
> industrial, and fashion design may join this organization. Scholarships,
> recognition awards, and a resource library are among the services offered.

Society for Environmental Graphic Design (SEGD)
One Story St.
Cambridge, MA 02138
(617) 868-3381; fax (617) 868-3591

> Membership is open to international design professionals, artisans,
> suppliers, and educators. The society publishes a newsletter, *Messages*,
> and a journal; sponsors professional competitions and student grants; has
> a lending library; develops educational programs; and publishes a
> membership list.

Southern Building Code Congress International (SBCCI)
900 Montclair Rd.
Birmingham, AL 35213-1206
(205) 591-1853; (800) 877-2224

> SBCCI publishes the *Standard Building Code*, one of the three model
> codes. It also publishes its own mechanical and plumbing codes.

Trade Associations

Allied Board of Trade, Inc. (ABT)
200 Business Park Dr.
Armonk, NY 10504-1712
(914) 273-2333; fax (914) 273-3036

Founded in 1925, the ABT has approximately 30,000 members. The organization supports both residential and contract designers, though the focus is weighted toward residential design. It offers a broad range of support to its members, including being a credit reference to suppliers for immediate credit approval (*Green Book*), a source and general information library, a collection service, an insurance program, publication of the *National Directory of Professional Interior Decorators & Designers*, and discounts in book and magazine purchases and travel arrangements.

*American Hotel & Motel Association (AH&MA)
1201 New York Ave., NW, Ste. 600
Washington, DC 20005-3931
(202) 289-3100; fax (202) 289-3158

AH&MA's 10,000 members represent nearly 82 percent of the annual revenue in this industry. Interior design firms may become allied members with dues based on the firm's gross revenue. For example, a firm which grosses between $0 and $999,999 per year pays $550 in dues. There are several assets to membership, foremost of which is the monthly *Construction & Modernization Report*, which provides contact names, phone numbers, and locations of new construction and renovation projects in the United States and Canada. Its mailing list is for sale, there is a large information center accessible to members, and it publishes *The Directory of Hotel & Motel Companies*. The group holds an annual spring convention and show.

American Society of Furniture Designers (ASFD)
P.O. Box 2688
High Point, NC 27261
(910) 884-4074; fax (910) 884-1737

ASFD focuses on education for professional furniture designers, teachers, students, and corporations that supply products and services related to furniture design. It offers a placement service, sponsors seminars, publishes an illustrated directory, and publishes a newsletter and bulletin.

American Textile Manufacturers Institute, Inc. (ATMI)
1801 K St., NW, Ste. 900
Washington, DC 20006-1301
(202) 862-0502; fax (202) 862-0570

> ATMI members produce 80 percent of the textiles manufactured in the
> United States. The interior design industry is one of many industries
> which purchases threads, yarns, and fabrics from the member companies.
> The group represents the U.S. textile industry with the federal govern-
> ment, and provides economic information and education. It publishes a
> *Member Product Directory.*

APA - The Engineered Wood Association
(formerly the American Plywood Association)
7011 S. 19th St., P.O. Box 11700
Tacoma, WA 98411-0700
(206) 565-6600; fax (206) 565-7265

> The organization is devoted primarily to structural wood, though there is
> some mention of surface treatments for interiors. It is a certified agency
> for inspecting and testing laminated wood products in reference to North
> American quality standards and is recognized by the Council of Ameri-
> can Building Officials (CABO). Mills with its approval meet ANSI
> standards.

Architectural Woodwork Institute (AWI)
1952 Isaac Newton Square
Reston, VA 20190
(703) 733-0600; fax (703) 733-0584

> Members include suppliers and manufacturers of casework, fixtures, and
> paneling. The institute promotes architectural woodwork, establishes
> standards, sponsors seminars and a quality certification program, follows
> governmental and environmental issues, and provides valuable publica-
> tions on its specialty. See the **Codes and Standards** section of **Chapter
> 1, Reference.** Affiliate memberships are available to members of
> professional design organizations such as ASID and IIDA. Members
> receive the annual *Source Book,* and may receive free consultations on
> technical matters. *Design Solutions* magazine is reviewed in **Chapter 11,
> Magazines.**

Association for Contract Textiles (ACT)
c/o DesignTex Fabrics, Inc.
P.O. Box 557
Rockville Centre, NY 11571-0557
(718) 335-9000; fax (718) 335-1280

> The group was founded in 1985 and has written Performance Guidelines
> for specifying fabrics. It has established five symbols which represent
> accepted performance levels regarding fire retardance, colorfastness to
> crocking and light, abrasion, the physical properties of drapery, uphol-
> stery, and vertical surfaces. These symbols appear on textile labels and
> may be used only by ACT members. However, those members sell more
> than 90 percent of the textiles sold to the contract market (Marilyn
> Zelinski, "A Symbol of the Times," *Interiors*, August 1993, p. 54).
> Members include, for example, Brunschwig & Fils, DesignTex Fabrics,
> and Scalamandre.

*Business and Institutional Furniture Manufacturers Association (BIFMA)
2680 Horizon Dr., Ste. A-1
Grand Rapids, MI 49546
(616) 285-3963; fax (616) 285-3765

> BIFMA publishes a newsletter, research reports, and a membership
> directory; holds educational seminars; tracks industry performance; and
> accredits facility managers. In conjunction with ANSI (see above under
> **Professional Organizations** section), it has established essential
> standards for contract furniture safety and performance and flammability
> of upholstered furniture. The standard for computer workstation furniture
> has been a particularly valuable contribution to the industry. BIFMA
> cooperates with the Canadian General Standards Board to write compat-
> ible standards for office furniture designed in the two countries.

Carpet and Rug Institute (CRI)
Box 2048
Dalton, GA 30722
(706) 278-3176; (800) 882-8846 for designer and specifier inquiries; (706)
278-0232 for publication orders; fax (706) 278-8835

> CRI is a national trade organization to which 95 percent of U.S. carpet
> manufacturers belong. Useful publications such as a membership
> directory, a specifier's handbook, and IAQ (indoor air quality) informa-
> tion as it relates to carpet, commercial, and residential installation
> standards are available. CRI's voluntary indoor air quality testing

program uses an independent lab to test carpet samples according to an EPA Dialogue consensus. Those products falling within an accepted range of VOC emissions are allowed to so label the specific product type that was tested.

Ceilings and Interior Systems Construction Association (CISCA)
1500 Lincoln Hwy., Ste. 202
St. Charles, IL 60174
(630) 584-1919; fax (630) 584-2003

CISCA publishes a handbook of environmental acoustics, *Ceiling Systems Handbook, Recommended Spec Level of Gypsum Board Finish, Standard Specifications: Ceiling Sound Transmission Test by Two-Room Method*, and other titles geared towards subcontractors.

Center for Health Design
4550 Alhambra Way
Martinez, CA 94553
(510) 370-0345; fax (510) 228-4018

This nonprofit group promotes the benefits of good health care design through publications, conferences, and competitions. They are represented in **Chapters 10, 11, and 15.**

Ceramic Tile Council
700 N. Virgil Ave.
Los Angeles, CA 90029
(213) 660-1911

The group publishes numerous "Field Reports," which are well-written advisories on specific installation situations.

Color Association of the United States (CAUS)
409 W. 44th St.
New York, NY 10036
(212) 582-6884; fax (212) 757-4557

CAUS publishes color forecasts for interiors, textiles, home furnishings, and clothing. The organization also publishes books and a newsletter, offers consultations, and supports a reference library with archival information which dates to 1915. The library consists of palette forecasts and may be accessed by members only unless the associate director's permission is given for a special project.

Color Marketing Group (CMG)
5904 Richmond Hwy., #408
Alexandria, VA 22303
(703) 329-8500; fax (703) 329-0155

> CMG was founded in 1962 as a nonprofit organization of 1,500 color designers who work together to "forecast" color "directions" for consumer and commercial products and services. According to the CMG the factors involved in color trends may include "social issues..., politics, the environment, the economy, and cultural diversity..." Color forecasts are developed at semiannual meetings. Members receive "Consumer and Contract Color Directions Forecast" and "Colors Current" palettes and *Color Chips*, a quarterly newsletter.

Cotton Incorporated
1370 Avenue of the Americas
New York, NY 10019
(212) 586-1070; fax (212) 265-5386

> This is a promotional organization for the cotton industry, which may be an asset if specific information regarding this material is required.

Door and Hardware Institute (DHI)
7711 Old Springhouse Rd.
McLean, VA 22102
(703) 556-3990

Green Seal
1730 Rhode Island Ave., NW, Ste. 1050
Washington, DC 20036-3101
(202) 331-7337

> Green Seal is an independent, nonprofit group oriented primarily toward consumer products, such as paper, appliances, and cleaners. Of interest to designers are its analyses of adhesives, lighting products, paints and coatings, water fixtures, and doors and windows. Criteria for approval are "environmental impact, product performance and packaging." It publishes a catalog of certified products. UL is the primary testing lab for Green Seal.

Gypsum Association
810 First St., NE, #510
Washington, DC 20002
(202) 289-5440; fax (202) 289-3707

> The group sponsors research and publications concerning application techniques, structural assemblies, and fire resistance of drywall.

Hardwood Plywood & Veneer Association (HPVA)
P.O. Box 2789
Reston, VA 20195-0789 or 22090-0789
(703) 435-2900; fax (703) 435-2537

> HPVA develops voluntary product standards for the industry, issuing several joint standards with ANSI. It maintains a laboratory to ascertain performance properties, promote research and development, and evaluate product compliance with national codes and standards. The group also sells copies of its membership directory, which lists dealers of species and specialty products.

International Linen Promotion Commission
290 Lexington Ave., Rm. 225
New York, NY 10016
(212) 685-0424; fax (212) 725-0483

Marble Institute of America
30 Eden Alley, Ste. 201
Columbus, OH 43215
(614) 228-6194

National Association of Home Builders, Remodelers' Council
15th and M St., NW
Washington, DC 20006
(202) 822-0200

> This organization may be of use to interior designers by putting them in touch with large residential projects that need interior designers. It also certifies contractors for kitchen and bath remodeling and general remodeling. This certification may be valuable to designers in hiring contractors for remodeling jobs.

National Association of the Remodeling Industry (NARI)
4900 Seminary Rd., Ste. 320
Alexandria, VA 22311
(703) 575-1100; (800) 966-7601; fax (703) 575-1121

> NARI provides certification of remodelers, which can lend validity and safety when a designer hires a remodeler.

National Cotton Council of America (NCCA)
1030 15th St., NW, Ste. 700
Washington, DC 20036
(202) 745-7805

National Institute of Building Sciences (NIBS)
1201 L Street, NW, Ste. 400
Washington, DC 20005-4024
(202) 289-7800; fax (202) 289-1092; Internet www.nibs.org

> Though established by Congress, this is a nongovernmental agency whose goal, as stated in its brochure, is to develop and disseminate "...technical and practical information for the building community." NIBS reaches its goals through "...research, consensus-building, the development of authoritative guidance documents, and the publication of printed and electronic tools for building professionals..." One of the group's projects is the CADD Council, whose goals include developing a national CADD standard to integrate CADD throughout the life cycle of a facility. NIBS produces *SPECTEXT*; see entry in **Chapter 1, Reference,** under **General References** section.

National Lighting Bureau (NLB)
2101 L St., NW, Ste. 300
Washington, DC 20037
(202) 457-8437

> NLB, which is affiliated with the National Electrical Manufacturing Association, is an "...information source to create more awareness of and appreciation for the benefits of good lighting..." Its publications are heavily illustrated and written in nontechnical language. Its pamphlet *The...Guide to Retail Lighting Management*, and the book *Lighting and Human Performance: A Review*, may be of interest to designers. Members are usually manufacturers of lighting.

National Oak Flooring Manufacturers' Association
P.O. Box 3009
Memphis, TN 38173
(901) 526-5016

> Its standards hold true for all hardwood flooring.

National Paint and Coatings Association
1500 Rhode Island Ave., NW
Washington, DC 20005
(202) 462-6272

National Terrazzo and Mosaic Association
3166 Des Plaines Ave., Ste. 132
Des Plaines, IL 60018
(800) 323-9736

National Wood Flooring Association
233 Old Meramac Station Road
Manchester, MO 63021-5310
(314) 391-5161

Resilient Floor Covering Institute
966 Hungerford Dr., Ste. 12B
Rockville, MD 20805
(301) 340-8580; fax (301) 340-7283

> The institute offers free publications which are of interest to designers, including methods of removing asbestos materials.

Tile Council of America
P.O. Box 1787
Clemson, SC 29633-1787
(803) 646-tile; fax (803) 646-2821

> Membership is restricted to U.S. manufacturers of ceramic tile. The council publishes two documents of interest to designers, *Handbook for the Installation of Ceramic Tile* and *ANSI A108—Specifications for the Installation of Ceramic Tile*. Its independent laboratory conducts tests of tiles and tile installation methods according to ANSI and ASTM standards.

Underwriters Laboratory, Inc.
333 Pfingsten Rd.
Northbrook, IL 60062
(312) 272-8800

> ULI which has been in existence since 1894, promotes public safety throughout the world. It tests electrical related products and materials in its independent laboratories. Of particular interest to designers are publications *Fire Resistance Index* and *Building Materials Directory*.

Upholstered Furniture Action Council (UFAC)
223 S. Wrenn St.
High Point, NC 27261
(910) 884-5000

> UFAC represents the residential furniture industry and establishes voluntary guidelines with industry for safety and performance for flammability of residential furniture.

U.S. Green Building Council
7900 Wisconsin Ave., Ste. 405
Bethesda, MD 20814
(301) 657-3469

> The council is a nonprofit consensus coalition of building-product manufacturers, environmental groups, building owners and operators, architects, engineers, utilities, state and local governments, and universities. Its mission is to improve the energy efficiency and environmental quality of the interior built environment.

Wallcovering Information Bureau
355 Lexington Ave., 17th Fl.
New York, NY 10017
(212) 661-4261

United States Government Agencies

Architectural and Transportation Barriers Compliance Board (ATBCB) or
(Access Board)
1111 18th St., NW, Ste. 501
Washington, DC 20036
(800) 872-2253 (voice), (800) 993-2822 (TDD), for ADA information and
documents; (202) 272-5448, electronic bulletin board

> ATBCB was originally created to supervise compliance of the *Architectural Barriers Act* (ABA) which was enacted in 1968. The ABA governs accessibility to federally owned or financially assisted facilities. Since the ADA (*Americans with Disabilities Act*) went into effect in 1992, the ATBCB has been required to issue guidelines for it. The various offices of the ATBCB are sources for technical information, publications, and enforcement.

Indoor Air Quality Information Clearinghouse (IAQ INFO)
U.S. Environmental Protection Agency, Indoor Air Division
P.O. Box 37133
Washington, DC 20013-7133
(800) 438-4318; (202) 484-1307; fax (202) 484-1510

> The clearinghouse provides current information on sources of pollution, testing procedures, means of control of pollutants, and pertinent standards and guidelines. It is a source for government publications, references to other organizations, and topical bibliographies. It has published *Building Air Quality: A Guide for Building Owners and Facility Managers* (1991) and several study programs for the same market.

National Institute on Disability and Rehabilitation Research
600 Independence Ave., SW
Washington, DC 20202
(202) 205-8146; (800) 949-4232 (voice and TDD)

> NIDRR funds 10 research centers around the country to provide information, materials, and technical assistance for Titles I, II, and III of the *Americans with Disabilities Act* (ADA).

Occupational Safety and Health Administration (OSHA)
200 Constitution Ave.
Washington, DC 20210
(202) 219-8148; (202) 586-5575

> OSHA, a branch of the Dept. of Labor, writhes and enforces workplace
> safety regulations. Designers are affected by rules governing construction
> and installation.

U.S. Department of Energy, Office of Conservation and Renewable Energy
1000 Independence Ave., S.W.
Washington, DC 20585
(202)586-9220

> The office provides both technical and consumer information. As with
> most government departments, publications are usually either inexpen-
> sive or free.

U.S. Department of Justice
10th and Constitution Ave., N.W.
Washington, DC 20530
(800) 514-0301 (voice); (800) 514-0383 (TDD); (202) 514-6193 (electronic bulletin board); Internet http://www.usdoj.gov/crt/ada/ada

> The Department of Justice provides technical assistance to those who
> have rights and responsibilities under Title II, Title III, and *Standards for
> Accessible Design* of the ADA (*Americans with Disabilities Act*).

U.S. Department of the Interior (DOI)
Preservation Assistance Division, National Park Service
P.O. Box 37127, Ste. 200
Washington, DC 20585
(202) 343-9573

> The purpose of the Preservation Assistance Division is to provide
> stewardship of cultural resources for the benefit and education of the
> populace. This is accomplished through physical preservation of sites and
> interpretation of their cultural significance. Research, preservation,
> restoration, and access to sites are carried out by the division and through
> its cooperative and teaching associations with independent local and state
> interest groups.

Boston Public Library. Main staircase. McKim, Mead, and White, 1887–1895. Renovation, Phase 1, Shepley Bulfinch Richardson and Abbot, 1984–1994. Photograph by Richard Cheek.

Chapter 14

Research Centers

The following sources of information are for-profit companies, nonprofit organizations, and educational institutions. They are sources which were located in the course of research for this book and represent a mixture of topics and levels of quality. During the time that *Interior Design Sourcebook* was in progress, at least six of the sites have closed and others have reduced their support. As alternate sources of information, professional and trade organizations, found in **Chapter 13**, are some of the most reliable. Design schools with specialties in the subject you are researching offer additional opportunities. The only positive aspect to the unreliable nature of these resources is that a new source that just suits your needs may be developed!

American Hotel & Motel Association
1201 New York Ave., NW, Ste. 600
Washington, DC 20005-3931
(202) 289-3193; fax (202) 289-3186; e-mail infoctr@ahma.com;
homepage http://www.ahma.com

> This trade association maintains a professionally staffed information center, including a large clipping file taken from the trade press over the previous five years and a file outlining design trends. Various pertinent bibliographic databases are available, including publisher John Wiley & Sons' *Hospitality Index*. Nonmembers may use research services for a fee.

American Institute of Architects Library
1735 New York Ave., NW
Washington, DC 20006
(202) 626-7300

> The AIA Library is a tremendous resource for members. Books will be
> mailed to patrons and subject bibliographies compiled. Some service is
> available through AIA*Online*, which is reviewed in the **General Refer-
> ences** section of **Chapter 1.** Research conducted by committees of the
> AIA provides up-to-date information and committee members make
> excellent contacts for specific questions.

American Society of Interior Designers Library
608 Massachusetts Ave., NE
Washington, DC 20002
(202) 546-3480; fax (202) 546-3240; e-mail network@asid.noli.com

The Center for Architectural Research
Rensselaer Polytechnic Institute
110 8th St.
Troy, NY 12180-3590
(518)276-6000

> Research publications.

Cooper Hewitt, National Museum of Design/Smithsonian Institution
2 E. 91st St.
New York NY 10128
(212) 860-6868; fax (212) 860-6909

> The Cooper Hewitt has wonderful collections, with both breadth and
> depth, of books, journals, and objects pertinent to the decorative arts.

The Furniture Library
1009 N. Main St.
High Point, NC 27262
(919) 833-4011

> This 7,000-volume collection is comprehensive in the areas of style and
> design of furniture and includes works that date to 1640. Materials must
> be used on site. A bookstore offers current titles for sale.

Herman Miller Research Institute
855 E. Main Ave., P.O. Box 302
Zeeland, MI 49464
(616) 654-3000; web address http://www.hermanmiller.com/

>Herman Miller has a history of supporting research. Its "Research Summaries" are very popular with interior designers.

IDEC Bibliography for Interior Design
Tom C. Peterson, IDEC Bibliography Chair
Utah State University
Logan, UT 84322-2910
(801) 750-1556; fax (801) 750-3845

>Searches of the IDEC computer database will be conducted for a fee.

International Facility Management Association (IFMA)
Research Library
1 E. Greenway Plaza, 11ᵗʰ Fl.
Houston, TX 77046-0194
(713) 4362; (800) 359-4362; fax (713) 623-6124

>The IFMA library provides customized library services on a fee basis. The library draws information from its own collection, IFMA research, and the 350 databases which are available online through the DIALOG commercial database service.

Lighting Research Center
Rensselaer Polytechnic Institute
115 Greene Bldg.
Troy, NY 12180-3590
(518) 276-6000; fax (518) 276-2999

>The center's publications include *Guide to Performance Evaluation of Efficient Lighting Products* and *Specifier Reports* for energy efficient technology. It also publishes the newsletter *Lighting Answers,* which analyzes lighting subjects such as specific lamps, ballasts, or dimming controls in detail, all of which relate to energy and resource conservation in lighting.

National Trust Library
c/o McKeldin Library
University of Maryland
College Park, MD 20742
(301) 405-6320

> 12,000 books, 300 periodical titles, ephemera, National Park Service reports, trade catalogs. Materials do not circulate. Staff will prepare bibliographies and research specific requests. The collection covers all aspects of the preservation of the historic built environment, including interiors.

North Carolina State University
College of Textiles
Burlington Textile Library
Centennial Campus, Box 8301
Raleigh, NC 27695
(919) 515-3043; e-mail tx-lib@tx.ncsu.edu

> The Burlington Library has an excellent technical textile collection. Fabric samples, journals, indexes, and books make up the collection.

Philadelphia College of Textiles and Science
Paul J. Gutman Library
School House Land and Henry Ave.
Philadelphia, PA 19144
(215) 951-2840

> The school has a famous textile program, and, among others, a color science program. Standard library resources are enhanced by the Paley Design Center, which houses thousands of fabric swatches.

Steelcase, Inc.
P.O. Box 1967
Grand Rapids, MI 49501
(616) 698-4489; web address http://www.steelcase.com/

> Steelcase publishes many valuable research reports and supports an on-line magazine called, "the Knowledge Report."

Trace Research and Development Center
University of Wisconsin
S-151 Waisman Center
1500 Highland Ave.
Madison, WI 53705-2280
(608) 262-6966; fax (608) 262-8848; TT/TDD (608) 263-5408

The Trace Center was founded to assist people who are nonspeaking, but
has since expanded to include research for ways to make computers
accessible to people with disabilities. It is "...funded as a *Rehabilitation
Engineering Research Center on Adapted Computers and Information
Systems*, through the National Institute on Disability and Rehabilitation
Research, U.S. Department of Education" (*Progress Update*, Madison,
Wisc.: Trace Center, University of Wisconsin-Madison, n.d.). Designers
may want to use the center's referral and reference services, its CD-ROM
(*ABLEDATA*) of assistive devices, or its list of publications.

Yale University
Art and Architecture Library
180 York St., Box 208242
New Haven, CT 06250
(203) 432-2645

The library holds the Birren Collection on Color, called by Hope and
Walch the "largest and most authoritative color library in America."
(Hope, Augustine and Margaret Walch. *The Color Compendium.* New
York: Van Nostrand Reinhold, 1990. p. 41.)Faber Birren donated his
private collection of approximately 2,000 volumes to Yale, where he
taught color.

Hynes Convention Center, Boston. Kallmann, McKinnell, and Wood, 1988. Photograph by Peter Vanderwarker.

Chapter 15

National Product Expositions and Conferences

National product expositions and conferences are an excellent one-stop source for designers to examine new and current products. They also provide an opportunity for professionals to establish relationships with new manufacturers. Most shows specialize in specific fields, such as contract or residential furniture, lighting fixtures, or textiles. Often these trade expositions are held in conjunction with conferences on the same topic. Only major shows held in the United States are listed below, but international, national, and local shows are included in the "dates" or "calendar" columns of the interior design, architecture, and trade journals. Educational opportunities and professional interaction in a stimulating setting make expositions and conferences a pleasant way to grow professionally.

American Institute of Architects National Convention and Expo
American Institute of Architects
1735 New York Ave., NW
Washington, DC 20006
(202) 626-7300

> Programs and exhibitions address architecture in its broadest sense.
> Many programs and vendors will be of interest to interior designers.

Construction, Renovation and Maintenance, Materials, Modernization (CRAMMM)
Retail Store Image Magazine
Intertec Publishing Corp.
151 Powers Ferry Rd., NW
Atlanta, GA 30339-2941
(770)-955-2500

> This conference has been meeting for 11 years and is cosponsored by *Retail Store Image* magazine. Exhibits and programs are designed for both retailers and designers.

Coverings
Trade Show International, Inc. (TSI, Inc.)
900 E. Indiantown Rd., Ste. 207
Jupiter, FL 33477
(800) 881-9400; fax (561) 747-9466; web address www.coverings.com

> Coverings combines the International Flooring Exposition, the International Wall Covering Exposition, and the International Tile & Stone Exposition. It is held in the spring.

HEALTHFocus
341 Merchandise Mart
Chicago, IL 60665
(312) 467-1950; (800) 677-6278; fax (312) 467-0779

> This annual conference for healthcare designers features doctors and medical facility directors as speakers. The AIA Academy on Architecture for Health, the American Hospital Association Society of Hospital Engineering, ASID, and the American Academy of Medical Administrators support the conference. One of the sponsors is *Interior Design* magazine. CEU credit courses given during this conference.

Illuminating Engineering Society of North America National Conference (IESNA)
121 Wall St., 17th Fl.
New York, NY 10005
(212) 248-5000

> This group of 10,000 members has a technical approach to lighting, though many designers and architects are members. IES offers courses on lighting design and publishes valuable journals and books.

International Hotel/Motel & Restaurant Show
George Little Management Inc.
Ten Bank St., Ste. 1200
White Plains, NH 10606-1954
(914) 421-3315

> This show is sponsored by *Hospitality Design* magazine and *Lodging* magazine, which is published by the American Hotel and Motel Association. The Gold Key and Platinum Circle Awards are announced at this conference.

International Contemporary Furniture Fair (ICFF)
George Little Management Inc.
Ten Bank St., Ste. 1200
White Plains, NH 10606-1954
(914) 421-3315

> This trade show, sponsored by *Metropolis* magazine, features both mass-produced and one-off modern furniture.

International Home Furnishings Market
International Furnishings and Design Association (IFDA)
300 S. Main St., P.O. Box 5687
High Point, NC 27262-5687
(910) 889-0203; fax (910) 889-7460

> The market is held in April and October and attracts approximately 2,200 manufacturers and 70,000 attendees. Furniture, upholstery, lighting, and rugs are shown.

IIDEX
Association of Registered Interior Designers of Ontario (ARIDO)
417 Church St.
Toronto, Canada M4W 2M5
(416) 921-2127; fax (416) 921-3660

> Exposition and convention for Ontario interior designers.

InterPlan, the Interior Planning & Design Exposition
c/o Miller Freeman, Inc.
P.O. Box 2549
New York, NY 10116-2549
(800) 950-1314; or, in New York, (212) 714-1300; fax (212) 279-3969

> InterPlan is cosponsored by Designer's Saturday, Inc., the trade associa-
> tion that formerly conducted the event, for interior designers, interior
> architects, facilities managers, contract dealers, and others in the contract
> field. *The* annual contract and residential market for New York and the
> East Coast. Accredited continuing education courses are given during the
> show. It is held in early November.

Lightfair International
1133 Broadway, Ste. 520
New York, NY 10010-7903
(212) 206-1281; fax (212) 206-1327; e-mail IALD@iald.org

> Sponsored by International Association of Lighting Designers.

National Kitchen and Bath Association Show
687 Willow Grove St.
Hackettstown, NJ 07840
(800) 843-6522

> The NKBA annual show is *the* exhibition of kitchen and bath products in
> the United States. In addition to U.S. manufacturers, high profile
> Canadian and European dealers attend each year and smaller, more
> exclusive foreign companies attend at regular intervals. The show is very
> large and is held in a different city each year.

NeoCon and the Buildings Show
470 Merchandise Mart
Chicago, IL 60654-1104
(312)527-7600; fax (312) 527-7782

> (IIDA) will make NeoCon its annual national conference and exposition
> event. Included are continuing education courses, speakers, awards, and
> banquets.

Symposium on Healthcare Design
The National Symposium on Healthcare Design, Inc.
4550 Alhambra Way
Martinez, CA 94553
(510) 370-0345; fax (510) 228-4018

>   Lectures, workshops, continuing education classes, technology and trade show.

Westweek
Pacific Design Center
8687 Melrose Ave., Ste. M60
Los Angeles, CA 90069
(310) 657-0800; fax (310) 659-5214

>   West Coast conference/residential and contract furniture mart, which includes continuing education units accredited by the Interior Design Continuing Education Council.

World Workplace
World Workplace Consortium, IFMA
1 E. Greenway Plaza, Ste. 1100
Houston, TX 77046-0194
(713) 629-6753; fax (713) 623-6124

>   WW is the primary conference and exposition of the International Facilities Management Association. IFMA, as host, invites other organizations, such as AIA, ASID, CSI, IALD, and the U.S. Green Building Council, to participate. Exhibitors, speakers, and accredited continuing education programs are part of the exposition, which is designed to be held in different cities. Courses offering the various organizations' equivalents of continuing education units are available.

Names/Organizations Index

G

H

I

Madden, Chris Casson, 130
Maggi Edition, 200
Maggs, Carol V., 94
Mahnke, Frank H., 112
Mahnke, Rudolf H., 112
The Making of Interiors: An Introduction, 64
Malkin, Jain, 121
Malnar, Joy Monice, 63
Managing AutoCAD in the Design Firm, 169
Managing CADD, 168
Mannington Builder Products, 188, 203, 212
Manual of Graphic Techniques, 142, 171
Manual of Practice, 38, 246
Marberry, Sara, 112–13
Marble Institute of America, 259
Marcus, George H., 29
Margulis, Stephen T., 124–25
Marketing and Selling Design Services, 175
Marketing for the Small Design Firm, 175–76
Massey, Anne, 70
MASTERSPEC, 20, 33, 246
Materials and Components of Interior Design, 96
The Materials of Interior Design, 94
Mayhew, Edgar deN., 70
McCorquodale, Charles, 70
McGowan, Maryrose, 33
McGraw-Hill Dictionary of Art, 33–34
Means, R. S. Company, 234
Means Interior Cost Data, 77
Means Legal Reference for Design & Construction, 175
The Measure of Man and Woman: Human Factors in Design, 45–46
Mechanical and Electrical Equipment for Buildings, 102, 108
Medical and Dental Space Planning for the 1990s, 121
Member Product Directory, 255
Messages, 253
Metropolis, 226
Metropolitan Home Awards, 189
Metropolitan Home Magazine, 189
Metropolitan Museum of Art, 86, 90
Miller, Herman, 124, 173, 195
Miller, Herman Research Institute, 267
Miller, J. Abbott, 129–30
Miller, Judith, 58
Miller, Martin, 58

Miller, Peter Bookstore, 238
Miller, William E., 141
Modelbuilder's Notebook, 171
Modern Furniture Classics Since 1945, 84
Modern Healthcare, 226
Moebel Interior Design, 226
Moholy-Nagy, Laszlo, 61
Molesworth, H. D., 86
Monacelli Press, 234
Monsanto Contract Fibers, 204
Montgomery, Charles F., 86
Moore, Charles, 130
Moore, Fuller, 107, 171
Morgan, Jim, 175–76
Morris, William, 15
Mortimer,Raymond, 89
Moss, Roger W., 97
Mount, Charles Morris, 130
Mundy, Michael, 130
Munsell, Albert H., 113
Murphy, Dennis Grant, 94, 176
Murphy, Leo, 143
Musee du Louvre, 89
Museum of Fine Arts, 90
Myers, Bernard S., 33–34
Myers, Minor Jr., 70

N

Naeve, Milo M., 34
Nagoya International Design Competition, 184
National Association of Home Builders, Remodelers' Council, 259
National Association of Schools of Art and Design (NASAD), 252
National Association of the Remodeling Industry (NARI), 260
National Audubon Society, 117
National Building Code of Canada, 49
National Cotton Council of America (NCCA), 260
National Council for Interior Design Qualification (NCIDQ), 26, 36, 37, 44, 45, 54, 62, 63, 64, 65, 76, 77, 78, 80, 81, 93, 96, 100, 101, 102, 103, 105, 108, 109, 117, 131, 132, 133, 174, 175, 176, 235, 236, 241, 249, 252, 253

O

Y

Z

Subject Index